ROME

APA PUBLICATIONS
Part of the Langenscheidt Publishing Group

INSIGHT GUIDE
ROME

ABOUT THIS BOOK

Editorial
Managing Editor
Dorothy Stannard
Editorial Director
Brian Bell

Distribution

UK & Ireland
GeoCenter International Ltd
The Viables Centre, Harrow Way
Basingstoke, Hants RG22 4BJ
Fax: (44) 1256 817988

United States
Langenscheidt Publishers, Inc.
46–35 54th Road, Maspeth, NY 11378
Fax: 1 (718) 784 0640

Canada
Thomas Allen & Son Ltd
390 Steelcase Road East
Markham, Ontario L3R 1G2
Fax: (1) 905 475 6747

Australia
Universal Press
1 Waterloo Road
Macquarie Park, NSW 2113
Fax: (61) 2 9888 9074

New Zealand
Hema Maps New Zealand Ltd (HNZ)
Unit D, 24 Ra ORA Drive
East Tamaki, Auckland
Fax: (64) 9 273 6479

Worldwide
Apa Publications GmbH & Co.
Verlag KG (Singapore branch)
38 Joo Koon Road, Singapore 628990
Tel: (65) 6865 1600. Fax: (65) 6861 6438

Printing
Insight Print Services (Pte) Ltd
38 Joo Koon Road, Singapore 628990
Tel: (65) 6865 1600. Fax: (65) 6861 6438

©2003 Apa Publications GmbH & Co.
Verlag KG (Singapore branch)
All Rights Reserved
First Edition 1988
Third Edition 1999
Updated 2003

CONTACTING THE EDITORS
We would appreciate it if readers
would alert us to errors or out-
dated information by writing to:
Insight Guides, P.O. Box 7910,
London SE1 1WE, England.
Fax: (44) 20 7403 0290.
insight@apaguide.demon.co.uk
NO part of this book may be reproduced,
stored in a retrieval system or transmitted
in any form or means electronic, mechanical, photocopying, recording or otherwise, without prior written permission of
Apa Publications. Brief text quotations
with use of photographs are exempted
for book review purposes only. Information has been obtained from sources
believed to be reliable, but its accuracy
and completeness, and the opinions
based thereon, are not guaranteed.

www.insightguides.com

This guidebook combines the interests and enthusiasms of two of the world's best-known information providers: Insight Guides, whose titles have set the standard for visual travel guides since 1970, and Discovery Channel, the world's premier source of nonfiction television programming.

The editors of Insight Guides provide both practical advice and general understanding about a destination's history, culture, institutions and people. Discovery Channel and its Web site, www.discovery.com, help millions of viewers explore their world from the comfort of their own home and also encourage them to explore it firsthand.

How to use this book

The book is structured both to convey an understanding of the city and its culture and to guide readers through its sights:

◆ To understand Rome today, you need to know about its past. The first section covers the city's **History** and then its culture in lively, authoritative **Features** written by specialists.

◆ The main **Places** section gives a full run-down of all the

EXPLORE YOUR WORLD

attractions worth seeing. The principal places of interest are coordinated by number with full-colour maps.

◆ The **Travel Tips** section provides all the practical information you are likely to need. This may be located quickly by using the index printed on the back cover flap.

The contributors

This edition of *Insight Guide: Rome* builds on the work of **Udo Gümpel**, editor of the first edition. Gümpel, a correspondent in Rome for German newspapers and television, recruited fellow foreign correspondents to work on the book, including **Dr**

Werner Raith, **Henning Klüver**, **Peter Kammerer**, **Ulrich Friedhoff**, **Horst Schlitter** and **Maria Morhart**.

It also draws on the strengths of the last edition, masterminded by managing editor **Dorothy Stannard**. She enlisted the help of Rome-based **Jane Shaw** to revise the chapters on the City's Changing Face, Trastevere, archaeological sites, the Appian Way, and the northern section of the Centro Storico. Shaw also wrote the chapter on Renaissance and baroque architecture.

Liaising on the project with Jane Shaw was **Sam Cole**, who first went to Rome as part of his degree course on the History of Art and now makes his living there as a writer. For this book Cole worked on the chapters on Via del Corso, Aventine and Testaccio, Quirinale, Termini and San Lorenzo, Rome's environs and the southern section of the Centro Storico chapter.

Rowlinson Carter tackled the history chapters, finding plenty to fire his imagination in Rome's awesome history. Introducing modern Romans is **Lisa Gerard-Sharp**, who has a long-standing interest in Italy and is a contributor to Insight Guides to Florence, Tuscany, Naples, Venice, Sicily and Northern Italy. She also contributed features on the Colosseum, catacombs, Vatican Museums and Bernini.

Jon Eldan wrote a new chapter on Food and Drink, plus new material for the Travel Tips. Everything was brought together by editors **Martin Rosser**, **Sue Heady**, **Jane Ladle** and **Jane Hutchings**. For the latest update, **Giovanna Dunmall** checked every fact and provided new information on a changing city. **Jeff Evans** proofread and indexed the guide.

Map Legend

– • –	National Park/Nature Reserve
Ⓜ	Metro
✈	Airport
🚌	Bus Station
Ⓟ	Parking
ⓘ	Tourist Information
✉	Post Office
⛪	Church/Ruins
	Castle/Ruins
∴	Archaeological Site
∩	Cave
⚊	Statue/Monument
★	Place of Interest

The main places of interest in the *Places* section are coordinated by number (e.g. ❶) with a full-colour map, and a symbol at the top of every right-hand page tells you where to find the map.

INSIGHT GUIDE
ROME

CONTENTS

Maps

A map of Rome is also on the inside front cover.

A map of the Vatican and plans of the Forum and Palatine are on the inside back cover.

Fountain from 1575 by Jacopo della Porta, opposite the Pantheon

THE ETERNAL CITY

Once the heart of an empire, Rome has attracted poets,
artists, writers and travellers for thousands of years

Dubbed the Eternal City by poets and artists, Rome is one of the most exhilarating and romantic travel destinations in the world. With its soft, ochre-coloured *palazzi*, classical colonnades and dramatic centrepieces such as the Colosseum and the Pantheon, it is a city that inspires the mind, appeals to the senses and captures the heart. As is frequently pointed out on souvenirs and T-shirts, Roma is *amor* spelt backwards.

Home to the Vatican and once hub of a great empire, it has been at the centre of European civilisation for well over 2,000 years. It has attracted travellers for a millennium. Pilgrims came in the Middle Ages – in the "Holy Year" of 1300 alone, some 2 million pilgrims visited the city – and by the 17th century it was seen as a finishing school for European courtiers and gentlemen, the source "of policy, learning, music, architecture and limning [painting], with other perfections which she disperteth to the rest of Europe."

In the 19th century Rome attracted a stream of poets, writers and painters of all nationalities, including Goethe, Stendhal and Henry James. But the English Romantics – notably Byron, Keats and Shelley – were especially drawn to the city, relishing the pathetic charm of greatness brought to its knees. Rome also offered them a retreat from the repressive morality of England, and they saw in Rome's ruins a reflection of themselves: Romantic exiles misunderstood and despised by their own country. At one point there were so many British and American expatriates living around Piazza di Spagna that it was dubbed "Grosvenor Square".

In Italy itself, Rome is something of a loner, which is both indulged and resented by the rest of the country. It is neither northern nor southern, and, although the capital, it is not considered as sophisticated as fast-paced Milan. It has all the problems of a major metropolis and a few more besides. It has a fantastic archaeological and architectural legacy to maintain, which is both a burden and a source of pride. While traffic pollution erodes the monuments – turning marble into limestone – the civil authorities fight to protect them. As the British journalist George Armstrong remarked: "Rome is the only European capital which each year must spend millions of pounds restoring ruins – restoring them at least to their state of ruin of 100 years ago." ❑

PRECEDING PAGES: baroque ceiling fresco, by Il Baciccia in the Gesù church; Fontana delle Naiadi, Piazza della Repubblica; Bernini's Fontana dei Quattro Fiumi on Piazza Navona; Mussolini's EUR district. **LEFT:** a red-carpet welcome on the Spanish Steps.

Decisive Dates

THE RISE OF THE ROMAN EMPIRE: 27 BC–AD 211

31 BC–AD 14 Augustus founds the Empire and establishes peace. The arts flourish, especially in Rome. Roads are built to the extremities of the Empire.

AD 64 After setting fire to Rome, Nero builds his famous Domus Aurea, the "Golden House".

69–79 Vespasian has the Flavian Amphitheatre built (later renamed the Colosseum). The Arch of Titus is erected in the Forum to commemorate the destruction of Jerusalem in AD 70 by Vespasian and his son, Titus.

98–117 The Roman Empire achieves its greatest territorial expansion under Emperor Trajan. It extends as far north as the East Friesian islands, east to Mesopotamia, south to North Africa and west to Spain and Britain. The arts flourish across the Empire.

117–38 Hadrian builds walls to secure the Empire's borders. He is buried at Castel Sant'Angelo.

161–80 Marcus Aurelius. The column of Marcus Aurelius, with reliefs showing his victories over Danubian tribes, still stands today in Rome's Piazza Colonna.

193–211 Septimius Severus. A grand arch in the Forum commemorates his victories over the Parthians.

DECLINE AND DEFEAT: 250–1100

250 Persecution of Christians under Emperor Decius.

284–305 Diocletian. During his reign the empire begins its decline; he introduces the tetrarchy, whereby four persons share power simultaneously. Renewed persecution of the Christians.

312 Constantine defeats Maxentius near the Milvian Bridge across the Tiber. Christianity officially recognised. In 330 Byzantium, now Constantinople, becomes the official capital of the Empire.

395 The Roman Empire is divided. In 404, Ravenna becomes the capital of the Western part.

410 Rome taken by invading Visigoths under King Alaric.

455 Rome plundered by the Vandals.

476 Fall of the Western Roman Empire. Power is now assumed by the Germans: first by Odoacer, then by Theodoric, king of the Ostrogoths.

536 Rome captured by Byzantium. East Roman rule in Italy re-established.

590–604 Pope Gregory the Great protects Rome from further pillaging by making peace with the Lombards.

750s Pepin the Short, king of the Franks, comes to the aid of Pope Stephen III, returns to the church the lands taken from it by the Lombards, and lays the foundation of the temporal sovereignty of the popes (Papal States) by giving the pope the exarchate of Ravenna.

800 Pope Leo III crowns Charlemagne emperor in St Peter's. The Roman Empire is restored in name.

12th century An insurrection, which is led by the churchman Arnold of Brescia, takes place during the papacy of Adrian IV (Nicholas Breakspear, the only English pope). Arnold of Brescia is executed in 1155.

PAPAL ROME: 1309–1801

1309 Clement V removes the seat of the papacy to Avignon in the south of France. The so-called 'second Babylonian captivity' of the popes begins.

1377 Gregory XI returns to Rome. The resulting 'western schism' within the church is finally extinguished only in 1417 with the election of Pope Martin V.

15th century Rome undergoes a new phase of prosperity during the Renaissance and again becomes the capital of the known world. The Popes attract famous artists to Rome to have their city, and especially the Vatican, decorated. They include Bellini, Botticelli, Bramante, Donatello, Leonardo da Vinci, Michelangelo, Palladio, Raphael and Titian.

1527 Charles V's army sacks Rome (Sacco di Roma).

1585–90 Rome receives a new series of fine buildings under Pope Sixtus V. He commissions architects Fontana, Bernini, Borromini and Maderno to build churches, palaces, squares and fountains. This brief period of prosperity is followed by a steady decline in Rome's political, cultural and economic importance. The Italian peninsula splits into smaller states, among them the Papal States, with Rome as their capital. Only

Italian unification, which starts in Turin in 1859, leads to a new period of prosperity for Rome.

1798–9 Rome becomes a French-style republic. Pope Pius VI dies in French captivity in 1799.

1801 Pope Pius VII concludes a concordat with Napoleon to preserve the independence of Rome and of the Papal States. Rome becomes part of the French Empire under Napoleon's son.

1814 Papal States are restored to Pius VII at the Congress of Vienna.

NEW KINGDOM OF ITALY: 1848–1945

1848 Pope Pius IX gives the Papal States a constitution but refuses to intercede for Italian unification. He is forced to flee and is not able to return to Rome until 1850.

1870 Rome and the Papal States are conquered.

1871 Rome becomes the capital of the new kingdom of Italy. The popes live as prisoners in the Vatican.

1922 Benito Mussolini assumes power in Italy, naming his party the Fascisti after the *fasces* (rods), the symbol of a magistrate's authority in Ancient Rome. Broad streets are built alongside many monumental new buildings. Suburbs are built around the city.

1929 The Lateran Treaty is signed between the Italian state and the Vatican, making the latter an independent sovereign state with the Pope as its head.

1943 The king has Mussolini placed under arrest. The Allies land in southern Italy. The king and the government leave Rome.

1944 The Allies liberate Rome on 4 June.

1945 Mussolini is hanged in Milan.

THE REPUBLIC: 1946–PRESENT DAY

1946 After a referendum, Italy decides to become a republic. Rome remains the capital; King Umberto II is exiled to Portugal.

1957 The European Economic Community (now the European Union) is established by the Treaty of Rome signed by six European nations.

1962 Pope John XXIII opens the Second Vatican Council, which lasts until 1965.

1978 Aldo Moro, Italy's prime minister and head of the Christian Democrat Party, is kidnapped by the Red Brigade terrorist organisation and killed. Cardinal Karol Wojtyla from Krakow becomes the first Polish pope and assumes the name John Paul II.

1981 The Turk Ali Agca makes an assassination attempt on the pontiff in St Peter's Square.

PRECEDING PAGES: a 19th-century depiction of life in the Forum. **LEFT:** sculpture in EUR's Museo della Civiltà Romana. **RIGHT:** Silvio Berlusconi, media mogul and prime minister in 1994.

1992 Pope John Paul II officially withdraws the church's 1633 condemnation of Galileo Galilei.

1993 Italy gains a government of national unity, headed by President Scalfaro and Premier Ciampi. Giulio Andreotti, Roman power-broker and seven-times Italian premier, is investigated for Mafia association.

1994 Elections usher in a new Italian republic, with a system modelled along British "first past the post" lines. Media magnate Silvio Berlusconi is the new premier. By late 1994 he is forced to resign.

1995 Andreotti goes on trial.

1996 First left-wing government elected in Italian postwar history, a coalition including former communists.

1997 Berlusconi receives a suspended prison sentence for fraud. Andreotti trial continues.

1998 The centre-left coalition that led Italy through the economic boom of the late 1990s and to the first tier of fiscal stability in Europe gives way. Former communist leader Massimo D'Alema is named prime minister, extending the tenure of Italy's first left-wing government.

1999 Projects to prepare Rome for the year 2000 culminate in a frenzy of restoration work.

2000 Millions flock to Rome for the Holy Year celebrations. After right-wing candidates make important gains in regional elections, the centre-left coalition falls and Giuliano Amato is named prime minister of a technocratic government.

2001 Berlusconi becomes prime minister for the second time as leader of a right-wing alliance.

2002 Marco Biagi, a government labour adviser, is assassinated by presumed left-wing terrorists. ❏

ANCIENT ROME

Monarchy, republic, dictatorship, empire: over a thousand years Rome
grew mighty and then declined into a city of ruins

Although the souvenir industry has ordained Romulus and Remus, the twins famously suckled by a wolf, as the founders of Rome, they are not the only candidates. The most prosaic claim is that an Etruscan king, a keen equestrian sportsman, simply noted that the dimensions of a valley between two of Rome's seven fabled hills ("650 yards long by 162 yards wide") would make a wonderful race course.

Pliny the Elder (AD 23–79) offered a more complicated story also involving the Etruscan royals. It seems that a noblewoman at court was surprised, while her back was turned, by a male organ soaring from the ashes in a fireplace. She fell pregnant, and the child of this remarkable union survived an even more remarkable mishap – while peacefully asleep, his head exploded in a ball of fire – to become King Servius Tullius, builder of the eponymous wall around Rome.

Implausible pregnancy is a feature of many of the legendary accounts, and this is no accident. Archaeology has unearthed evidence of scattered settlements in the Roman hills in 1200 BC, but these early Latins were culturally overshadowed by Etruscans, who took over most of the Italian peninsula from the 9th century BC onwards, and by Greek colonies established in the south a century later. Roman historians acknowledged that one or the other, if not both, made a significant contribution to the gene pool of the Roman nation, but in the interest of chauvinism they preferred a neat break with the past so that Roman history could start afresh. Miraculous conception was just the ticket.

History according to Livy

A large part of Livy's *History of Rome*, written in the 1st century BC and running to 140 books, is devoted to weighing up various theories about the origins of Rome, including a theory by the contemporary poet Virgil, who was an excep-

tion to the general rule in that he relished the idea of classical Greece as Rome's cultural and spiritual cradle. Aeneas, the hero of Virgil's *Aeneid*, is a Greek survivor of the sack of Troy who drifted to the coast of North Africa and was engrossed in a cave with the voluptuous Queen Dido of Carthage when the gods intervened

GIBBON'S *DECLINE AND FALL*

Edward Gibbon, the English historian, was "musing amid the ruins of the Capitol" in 1764 when he conceived his great work, *The History of the Decline and Fall of the Roman Empire*. The six-volume set is now a popular stereotype, the archetypal dusty old academic tome.

In truth, Gibbon's work is still a monument to historical literature. It covers an incredible 13 centuries, starting with the age of Trajan and the Antonines, and it shows how Ancient Rome created the forge in which modern Europe was hammered out.

The rise of the teutonic tribes, Charlemagne, the crusades, the Turks taking Constantinople – Gibbon's volumes show that, vast though the Roman Empire may have been, the shadow it cast down the centuries was greater by far.

with a timely reminder that he was cut out for rather bigger things, namely transporting himself to Italy and founding Rome.

While Livy was prepared to tolerate the idea of Aeneas settling in Italy, marrying a local princess and thereby starting a line of Graeco-Latin kings, he resorted to miraculous conception to cleanse royal Roman blood of this Greek strain. King Numitor of Alba Longa, the ancient Latin capital founded by Aeneas's son Ascanius, was usurped, Livy explains, by his brother Amulius, who took the normal precaution of murdering Numitor's sons to reduce the danger of a counter-coup and restoration.

In the case of Numitor's daughter, Princess Rhea Silvia, Amulius rashly believed that

LEFT: Gaius Julius Caesar Octavianus (63 BC – AD 14), known as Augustus, the first Roman emperor.

committing her to the Vestal Virgins would keep her chaste for at least 30 years. Her pregnancy and delivery of the twins Romulus and Remus raised all sorts of awkward questions.

Livy said "it seemed less wrong if a god were the author of her fault", so paternity was pinned on Mars, who apparently consoled Silvia while she had taken refuge in a cave, hiding from a wolf. The murderous Amulius did not believe a word of it. Silvia was manacled and thrown into a river; the twins were placed in a basket and cast adrift to meet their fate. However, a drop in the water level left the basket stranded in the mud, and the cries of the babes then attracted

edly virtuous Etruscan noblewoman needed an unexpected phallus in a fireplace.

Livy tries to tie up these suspicious loose ends by suggesting that Mars appeared before the twins in later life and clarified any doubts they may have had about their origins before pointing them towards their glorious destiny. The twins founded Rome, declares Livy, in 753 BC.

According to popular belief, fraternal relations between the twins later soured over the location of Rome and its name. Remus proposed a site on the Aventine Hill and the name Rema; Romulus demanded the Palatine Hill and Roma. The latter was seemingly endorsed by

the interest of a she-wolf. By suckling the wolf, the twins survived to later be rescued by the shepherd Faustulus.

At this juncture, Livy goes on the defensive. Faustulus's wife, Larentia, was a notoriously playful woman, he concedes, and probably not as true to her somewhat lacklustre husband as she should have been. The sudden appearance of twins in their household (they already had 12 other children) begged more awkward questions, and Livy could not entirely rule out the possibility that Larentia needed a story about abandoned babes in a basket and a considerate she-wolf as urgently as Silvia needed an encounter with the god Mars and the suppos-

the gods when 12 vultures flew over the Palatine compared with only six over the Aventine.

An unrepentant Remus ridiculed the walls his brother was busy constructing on the Palatine by jumping over them. This was an unbearable affront, and Romulus's honour was not restored until Remus was stretched out dead and the new city walls were ritually anointed with his blood.

Livy's *History of Rome* is not yet over. The population of Rome grew rapidly, he adds, but with a grave imbalance of males over females. Romulus decided to lay on a festival of games so magnificent that all the surrounding tribes were bound to attend. What the excited visitors did not know was that the women would not be going home. This ruse has been immortalised as the "Rape of the Sabine Women".

Laws of the land

Royal Rome extended over the reign of six kings after Romulus. Codified laws laid down the contractual obligations between patricians and plebeians, the behaviour required of women, and a father's authority over his sons. The patrician class provided priests, magistrates and judges while plebeians were responsible for agriculture, cattle-breeding and trade. A patrician helped plebeians to realise "the tranquillity of which they particularly stood in need", and

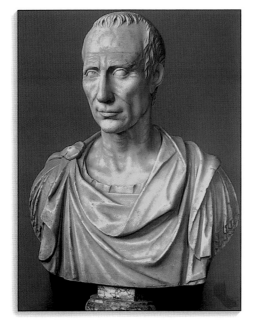

by way of return plebeians made sure that the patrician had enough money to settle his debts and provide dowries for his daughters. These financial contributions were not redeemable; the plebeian donors were supposed to regard them as their privilege. If the nature of this relationship seems somewhat loaded in favour of patricians, the plebeian had some consolation in being able to choose his own patrician and, if dissatisfied, to switch his allegiance to another.

Marriage was for life and wives had an equal share of the conjugal property. In other respects,

LEFT: Etruscan sarcophagus recovered from the Villa Giulia. ABOVE: marble bust of Julius Caesar.

though, the husband was the senior partner. He could, if his wife fell short of "virtue in all things", administer appropriate corrective measures, up to and including death. Legal guidelines recommended that "merciless severity" be reserved for wives who poisoned the children or made unauthorised copies of their husbands' keys. A wife who drank wine was presumed to be an adulteress, as the first weakness was certain to lead to the second.

Roman historians boasted that these marriage customs worked so well that there was not a single divorce in Rome between 751 and 231 BC. The fine print of history, however, has revealed a certain Lucius Annius and his wife splitting up in either 307 or 306 BC.

At this time a father exercised absolute authority over his son. At his discretion, he could have him put to work in the fields, imprisoned, flogged, chained or executed. No-one was to think the worse of him if he sold his son into slavery, and if the son somehow managed to earn his freedom, there was nothing to prevent the father from selling him a second or third time. Thereafter the son was safe, and the law was later amended so that fathers could not sell their sons once they were married.

Although husbands and fathers clearly enjoyed significant privileges in royal Rome, the most irksome disparity was between Etruscans and Romans, the former being almost synonymous with the patrician class and the latter with the plebeians. Their differences came to a head over another celebrated rape in early Roman history, that of Lucretia, the Roman wife of the Etruscan King Tarquinius Superbus. Although the king was personally blameless in this lamentable affair, the Roman populace could no longer tolerate the licentiousness of the Etruscan court.

Marcus Junius, a Roman who had once foiled the king's assassins by pretending to be an idiot, led the revolt which drove the last of the seven Etruscan kings into exile. In 509 BC, Marcus Junius was elected one of the two consuls who ruled Rome under a republican constitution.

Republican Rome prospered against the backdrop of an Etruscan attempt to retake the city and restore the monarchy, seen off by Horatius's sterling defence of the bridge leading into the city; the Gallic invasion of 390, when cackling geese sounded the alarm; the Punic Wars with Carthage, with Hannibal leading his elephants across the Alps; the invasions of Gaul and Britain, and the expansion of the Roman Empire to the banks of the Danube. Although the Republic abolished the former Etruscan oligarchy, it was far from

AKA BRUTUS

Marcus Junius was better known by his nickname, Brutus, given to him for his habit of feigning idiocy.

like a contagious disease… The senators were seized by a panic of fear, both for the public safety, lest these secret conspiracies and nocturnal gatherings contain some hidden harm or danger, and for themselves individually, lest some relatives be involved in this vice."

The acceptable form of religion was a mixture of Etruscan traditions and animist spirit worship. Business between humans and gods was governed by a college of pontiffs or "bridges", who pronounced on the significance

democratic. A Roman elite inherited the old patrician privileges, and it was only after intense agitation that the plebeians exacted from them in 450 the famous Twelve Tables, a code of laws displayed on bronze tablets in the Forum so that all sections of society knew where they stood. As things turned out, foreigners, freedmen and slaves stood very low in the pecking order and had few civic rights.

Intellectually, the Romans distanced themselves from the philosophical bent of the Greeks by concentrating on the practical sciences, astrology and Eastern mysticism. The spread of Bacchic rites, however, caused alarm. "This pestilential evil spread from Etruria to Rome

of birds in flight, bolts of lightning, the behaviour of sacred chickens and the meaning contained in the livers of sacrificial victims. An ox throwing itself off the top of a three-storey building was the kind of omen that could cause panic. Flamens, or priests, had to live according to a strict regimen which meant, for example, that they never removed their hats, had no contact with she-goats, raw meat, ivy or beans and slept in special beds with clay smeared on the legs.

Flamens were assisted by Vestal Virgins who were recruited when they were between six and 10 years of age for 30 years of chastity, after which they could discharge themselves and marry. The penalty for premature violation of the vow of chastity was burial alive in a special plot near the Colline Gate.

The rules of marriage were relaxed. A system known as *usus* presumed a *de facto* marriage if a couple lived together for a year; the woman could escape the obligations of *usus*, however, by merely staying away from her husband for three nights in a year. Married couples were expected to show no affection in public and very little in private. "Never kiss your wife unless it thunders," said Cato who, according to Plutarch, expelled from the Senate a man who kissed his wife in front of their daughter. Plutarch thought caught red-handed in the actual preparation of the brew. When they protested that the stuff was harmless, they were invited to prove the point by swallowing a mouthful. All fell over dead.

Pyrrhic victories

Rome made no attempt to develop an industrial or economic base: it simply lived on the proceeds of military booty. The Etruscans, whose power lay mainly north of Rome, eventually fulfilled their own prophecy by disappearing off the face of the earth. In the south, the ineffectiveness of Greek campaigns led to the expression "Pyrrhic victory" – their military

this was going a little too far, personally, although he agreed that embracing and kissing in public were unacceptable.

Militant feminism made its mark in the year 331 BC when difficult husbands began dropping like flies. The symptoms indicated poisoning, but suspected wives had a standard explanation, which was to blame one or other of the plagues that were almost endemic. Eventually a number approaching 200 wives were arrested for possession of lethal substances, 20 of them commander, Pyrrhus of Epirus, was a cunning tactician but, even when he appeared to have won the day, seemed always to lose more men than the Roman enemy. With the final defeat of the great city of Carthage in 146 BC Rome controlled the whole of Italy and most of the Mediterranean basin.

A mighty military machine was needed to run the conquered provinces. Gaius Marius, an officer of relatively humble origins, exploited discontent in the army to advance up the military ladder, and he repeated his success by presenting himself to the civilian population as a man of personal integrity willing to engage the corrupt and incompetent ruling clique in Rome. If

LEFT: Cicero appeals to the unity of Rome against the "public enemy" Catiline. **ABOVE:** Emperor Gaius Octavianus Augustus was deified after his death.

anything, he preached too eloquently, because the whole of Italy rose in revolt in the Social Wars of 92–89 BC.

A less scrupulous general, Sulla, used the unrest as a pretence for seizing power in 82 BC and installing a ruthless military dictatorship. The Roman Republic was dead.

Caesar and Cleopatra

After Sulla died an agonising death, power passed to Pompey, a bully who always yearned for popular approval. From 59 BC he shared power in the First Triumvirate, his partners being Crassus, an unscrupulous property developer, and Julius Caesar, who hoped to make enough money out of politics to settle a mountain of personal debt. He found wealth instead as a brilliant commander who conquered Gaul and led his legions across the English Channel.

Lest he be forgotten in Rome during his absence, Caesar made sure that a generous share of his booty went back to the capital to buy political support. The Senate guessed what he was up to, and they forbade his return to Italy. However, in 50 BC Caesar crossed the Rubicon with the intention of taking power from Pompey. Caesar's pursuit of Pompey led to Egypt, a land of incomparable splendour.

Pompey's supposed friends in Egypt finished him off, but Caesar was in no hurry to return to Rome, having become besotted by Cleopatra, Egypt's young queen. A leisurely Nile cruise culminated in Cleopatra presenting him with a son, and when at last he returned to Rome for a belated triumph, she accompanied him.

Caesar endeared himself to the Roman populace with efficient government and a spectacular building programme, but anti-monarchy instincts were stirred by the thought that, by marrying Cleopatra, Caesar would, technically, become a king. Jealous senators welcomed any detraction from his growing personality cult, and it was they who, on the Ides of March, 44 BC, cut him down.

Mark Antony's passion for Cleopatra provides the romantic interest through the 13 years of civil war that followed Caesar's murder. Octavian, who later took the name Augustus, emerged as the victor and first Roman emperor, and it seems that the incorrigible Cleopatra may have had designs on him, too. Instead, her expropriated treasure funded Augustus's transformation of Rome from "a city of brick into a city of marble". His conquests abroad vastly enlarged the Empire. The Augustan Age was Rome's cultural apex, producing among others Virgil, Ovid and Livy, who tried so diligently to explain how it had all come about.

The civil service which Augustus gave Rome kept the Empire and its capital going through

the fantastic malfeasance of some of his successors. While emperors such as Tiberius, Caligula, Nero and Egabalus acted like monsters at the pinnacle of society – Suetonius's *Twelve Caesars* is a classic study of wretched Roman excess – anyone in need of guidance on points of morality and etiquette turned to the scholarly Plutarch, who produced more than 60 treatises on the subject. It was vulgar, he said, to strain wine or use snow to cool drinks. Gentlemen were punctual for dinner, and turned the conversation towards thoughtful subjects like which came first, the chicken or the egg.

Plutarch meticulously practised what he preached, as he demonstrated while watching one of his slaves being flogged. The slave enquired between blows how Plutarch reconciled the punishment meted out for a trivial offence with his popular treatise on self-control and the evil of anger, which the slave said he had read and admired. "You think I am angry?" Plutarch replied in measured tones. "From my face and voice and colour and words would you assume that I am angry? My eyes do not blaze, my speech is not confused, I am not shouting, I do not foam at the mouth or grow purple in the face, I am saying nothing to be ashamed of or to regret. I am not trembling with rage or throwing myself about in a paroxysm. In case you do

the purpose of the book on which he was embarking, he said, to describe the prosperity and happiness and then, from the death of Mark Antony onwards, to detail the decline and fall, "a revolution which will ever be remembered and is still felt by the nations of the earth".

By the 4th century, the decline was so far advanced that the Emperor Constantine moved the imperial capital to the shores of the Black Sea, to the city which took his name, Constantinople. Many theories have been advanced to explain the move of the capital. It has been suggested that Constantinople was much nearer the threatened imperial frontiers, especially where

not know it, those are the symptoms of fits of temper." He had a few things to add, but he interrupted his flow to turn to the man doing the whipping. "While he and I are discussing things," he remarked, "you just carry on."

Honour was restored to the imperial throne by a succession of worthy emperors, notably Trajan, Hadrian and the two Antonines. "In the second century of the Christian era," wrote the author Edward Gibbon, "the empire of Rome comprehended that fairest part of the earth and the most civilised portion of mankind." It was

the Goths gathered beyond the Danube. It has also been said that, entertaining the idea of legalising Christianity, Constantine wished to make a fresh start in a neutral location unhampered by pagan traditions.

The explanation that would most please Virgil, however, is that Constantine's intention was to complete the circle begun by Aeneas when he embarked on the *Aeneid*, and to that end he built "The Second Rome" as close as was practical to the ancient site of Troy. Two centuries later, the population of the original Rome had shrunk from more than a million to fewer than 20,000 people inhabiting an almost derelict ruin on a dirty river. ❑

LEFT: Nero with his tigress, Phoebe.
ABOVE: gladiators in combat before Nero and Agrippina.

CHRISTIANITY AND THE POPES

Ancient Rome died and Christianity grew stronger. For 11 centuries the popes
were secular as well as religious authorities, until they too declined and fell

As the emperor who put Christianity on an official footing in the Roman Empire, Constantine the Great (*circa* 274–337) wears an honorary halo that tends to obscure less worthy traits, like a homicidal streak that disposed of his mother (drowned in a hot bath), his eldest son and, according to the historian

Eutropius, "a great many of his friends". He may or may not have seen in the sky a flaming cross and the inscription "In this sign thou shalt conquer", but that shouldn't detract from Bernini's superb equestrian statue in the Portico of St Peter's.

Nevertheless, in 324 Constantine undoubtedly recognised Christianity as a state religion in tandem with paganism, although he did not personally convert until he was virtually on his deathbed 13 years later, probably because Christianity alone offered forgiveness for sins as appalling as the ones he had committed in his lifetime. Official recognition of Christianity was a huge step forward from the bad old days of

Nero's reign (54–68), when Christians were rolled in wax and used as human candles. This was, Nero quipped, the first known instance of Christianity shedding light on anything. But, although Christianity made swift inroads in the Eastern Empire, Rome remained predominantly pagan for some time after Constantine's death.

Eventually, Christianity and paganism fused, the Roman church aping the structure of the pagan priesthood, which was headed by a kind of pope and made up of priests who were tonsured and wore white vestments. Colourful images of the goddess Isis metamorphosed smoothly into the Christian Madonna. Religion provided the leadership which filled the vacuum left by the imperial government's departure for Constantinople and, as the historian H.A.L. Fisher observes, "It was not perhaps difficult to foresee that one day the place of the absent emperor would be taken by a Roman priest."

The sacking of Rome

Although the imperial administration had been transferred to Constantinople, Rome was still the seat of the so-called Western emperors who increasingly clung to office on the strength of foreign mercenary armies. At the turn of the 5th century, Emperor Honorius engaged the services of Alaric, a Visigoth king, but Honorius then found himself in the awkward position of not being able to pay him.

Alaric broke into the city in 410 and helped himself to what was left of the imperial treasure. As a gentleman and a Christian (albeit of the Aryan persuasion), Alaric spared women and religious buildings. None of this was of much comfort to Honorius. Rome was clearly not safe, so he moved the seat of the Western Empire to Ravenna, "an inaccessible fortress… where he might securely remain, while the open country was covered by a deluge of barbarians".

A quarter of a century later, Rome's worst fears materialised in the person of Attila, the "Scourge of God". Pope Leo I bought him off with a wealthy bride, Princess Honoria of Burgundy. She went along with the marriage, but only so far.

Attila was soon found dead in the conjugal bed lying in a pool of blood. Officially, the cause of death was said to have been a haemorrhage.

After Rome's narrow escape from Attila, Eudoxia, the young widow of Emperor Valentinian III (the feeble nephew of Honorius who "haemorrhaged" or perhaps was stabbed to death by his bodyguards) took the extraordinary step of issuing an invitation to Genseric, whose Vandal hordes had been terrorising the Mediterranean basin for a quarter of a century. The destruction of Rome

PAPAL POWER

While the emperor sat in Constantinople, the popes moved into Rome and assumed secular power.

who spoke Latin, respected the Roman Senate and restored the city's ancient monuments.

German rule over Rome flew in the face of the Eastern Emperor Justinian's dream of restoring the empire of old. The Byzantine armies were ultimately successful, but Rome was destroyed in the process. Moreover, it proved impractical to administer Rome from distant Constantinople, and this opened the way for the local religious authorities to take over the secular reins. To that end, the pope left Ravenna and installed himself in the Castel

that followed in 452 apparently satisfied some grievance Eudoxia was nursing. In any case, Genseric married her.

By 467, German tribes were the commanding presence in Italy, and the last of the Western emperors was a German puppet known mockingly as Romulus Augustulus. When the joke wore thin, the German Odoacer himself took over as "Patrician", only to be usurped by Theodoric the Ostrogoth, the "Dietrich von Bern" of the *Nibelungenlied*. Theodoric ruled for 36 years, a "New Barbarian" and Aryan Christian

Sant'Angelo, named in honour of St Michael after he rid Rome of a virulent plague. As kings of the castle, the popes were poised to become the highest temporal power in the land.

Under Gregory the Great (540–604), papal horizons expanded. Gregory was so seized by the beauty of some Anglo-Saxon youths on sale in the Rome slave-market that he was inspired to convert their country to Christianity. The conversion of Ireland and England led in due course to rewarding missionary work among the Franks and Germans, and it was the eventual alliance between the papacy and the newly converted Frankish kings, especially against Germanic Lombards who sought to control Italy at

LEFT: Pope Leo I (440–461). **ABOVE:** the siege of Rome by the Ostrogoth King Vitiges, 6th century AD.

Rome's expense, that pushed the papacy yet higher on the ladder of secular authority.

Charlemagne is crowned

The partnership between the papacy and the Frankish kings was sealed by Pope Leo III's coronation of Charlemagne as Holy Roman Emperor on Christmas Eve 800. By placing the crown on Charlemagne's head, Leo wanted everyone to understand that popes preceded emperors. Practically speaking, however, the papacy needed the buttress of Frankish power, and when that disintegrated after Charlemagne's death, Rome's vulnerability was exposed. The

Kaifer Juftinian. (482—565.)   Kaiferin Theodora. (? 548.)

Saracens invaded Italy in 846, looted St Peter's and settled in places like the village of Saracinesco above Rome, where some of their descendants are still to be found.

There was in any case turbulence enough without interlopers like the Saracens. Romans fought Romans, either as Guelfs, who were more or less loyal to the pope, or as Ghibellines, who preferred the Holy Roman Emperor. Popes fought popes, even when one of them was dead. In 897, Stephen VII exhumed Formosus, his predecessor, for a formal trial. The corpse was dressed up in papal regalia for the proceedings and then, on conviction, stripped. The three fingers on the right hand used for benediction were

chopped off and the remains dumped in the Tiber. When the body was later retrieved by fishermen, it was miraculously intact, a miracle that warranted its reburial with full honours.

A measure of stability was introduced into the papacy in the 11th century under the influence of the Cluny monastery in Burgundy, which insisted on clerical chastity, piety and discipline. Cardinal Hildebrand, elected Pope Gregory VII in 1073, attempted to claw back papal supremacy over the Holy Roman Empire at the expense of Henry IV, the ruling emperor. The contest boiled down to an imperial army versus papal bulls of excommunication. Military might carried Henry to the walls of Rome, whereupon Gregory misguidedly appealed to Robert Guiscard, the Norman warrior ruler of southern Italy. Guiscard's army included a large number of Saracen levies completely indifferent to a squabble between Christians. Their sacking of Rome in 1084 surpassed the worst excesses of the Goths and Vandals.

Confusion reigned once again in the 12th century. In Anacletus II, Rome had of all things a Jewish pope, and to make matters worse he contrived to lose a ridiculous war with tiny Tivoli. Desperation led to an attempt in 1145 to bring back the Roman Republic complete with Consuls and a Senate. The author of this scheme, Arnold of Brescia, was unseated by Pope Adrian IV who, being English, was as unique in his own way as had been Anacletus II. Arnold was tortured and then hanged.

The rot was eventually stopped by Innocent III, who wielded sufficient authority to appoint his own emperor. He disciplined unruly European monarchs, launched a crusade against the Moors in Spain and chased the Germans out of central Italy and Sicily. He was tarnished by the Fourth Crusade, which ransacked Christian Constantinople instead of marching on the infidel in the Holy Land. Under Pope Innocent, Rome had a foretaste of Renaissance prosperity and artistic brilliance, and there was probably genuine regret over his undignified death. He was found naked on the floor of Perugia cathedral, supposedly the result of poison impregnated in his bedroom slippers although his feet were bare when the body was found.

Pope Boniface VIII could not maintain Innocent's fast pace. The English and French kings sneered at his bulls of excommunication and, to compound the humiliation, he was kidnapped by the French and eventually replaced by a French pope, Clement V. In 1309, France moved the papacy to Avignon on the French border, where seven successive French popes lived through the years of the so-called "Babylonian captivity".

Pilgrims had long been Rome's principal source of revenue. Although Gregory the Great had once considered destroying all antiquities to concentrate the minds of visitors on spiritual matters, ordinary Romans welcomed any excuse to line their pockets. Deprived of one of its main

14TH-CENTURY ROME

Pilgrims complained about the derelict state of Rome in 1350: a "shapeless heap of ruins", said Petrarch.

Rome's former glories and had the oratorical gifts of a born demagogue, which he used to rally popular support. The warring nobility laid down their arms and watched incredulously as Rienzo proclaimed a new Roman Republic – a united Italian nation that was ruled from Rome but was independent of the papacy. He was five centuries ahead of his time.

While the warlords were ready to kill Rienzo to protect their interests, he was overthrown by those who had been his most fervent supporters, the masses. They rose in

attractions by the papacy's removal to Avignon, Rome hit on the idea of "Jubilee Years" to drum up the pilgrim business. The idea proved profitable. The 1350 Jubilee attracted 5,000 arrivals a day – and complaints of fleecing by Romans who turned every available shack into a "hotel".

Pilgrims complained about the derelict condition of the city, and Petrarch even referred to Rome as "a shapeless heap of ruins". The cause of the pilgrims was taken up by Cola di Rienzo, the enterprising son of a local tavernkeeper and a washerwoman. Rienzo dreamt of restoring

---

LEFT: Emperor Justinian with his wife, Theodora.
ABOVE: *Meeting with the Pope*, by Vittore Carpaccio.

revolt when Cola proposed the unthinkable – that Roman people should pay taxes. He was lynched, and his Roman republic died with him.

Return of the popes

The papacy returned to Rome in 1377 when France was confident that future popes could be made to toe the French line, but it was at once engulfed in the Great Schism, fundamentally a clash between very different French and Italian ideas about the papacy's proper role. The row polarised the whole of Europe, setting off early tremors of the Reformation that lay ahead. Two competing popes were joined by a third before the whole lot were swept aside and replaced by

Martin V, a Colonna man who "placed the papacy before the Church, Italy before Europe, his Colonna kinsmen before everybody". Predictably, the other nobles rose in revolt.

While posterity is indebted to the Renaissance popes for their munificent patronage of the arts, it was viewed with some suspicion at the time, with northern Europeans wondering aloud whether the popes were not merely Italian princes extending their temporal dominions at the expense of their Italian neighbours. These fears were confirmed by Machiavelli with the publication of *The Prince* in 1513, a case study of contemporary political intrigue based on

Sack of Rome in 1527. The Swiss Guard were killed to a man while friars and priests were beheaded, "old nuns beaten with sticks, and young nuns raped and taken prisoner". St Peter's and the Holy Palace were turned into stables and two-thirds of the city reduced to ruins. Contemporary commentators decided that the sack could only be divine retribution.

Pope Clement VII, extremely fortunate still to be alive in Castel Sant'Angelo, decided that resistance was futile and he became the first of a succession of popes who lamely threw in their lot with the Spanish Empire. They borrowed the concept of the Inquisition from Spain and

MACHIAVELLIAN PRINCIPLES

Niccolò Machiavelli (1469-1527) was the first to realise the rules of Realpolitik: "the end justifies the means provided the end be good." The Florentine patriot, political theorist and statesman came from an impoverished family. Native cunning and political guile, later dubbed "Machiavellian", secured his rise through diplomatic ranks. Cesare Borgia, the ruthless and amoral prince, helped to model his early political thinking. Machiavelli counselled prudence and brilliant strategems: "to be able to defend oneself with Italian *virtù* against foreigners". His guiding principle was "virtue", implying military might, and colonialisation not conqest. Yet as a ruler he believed it was better to be feared than loved. He describes *The Prince*, his seminal work of statecraft, as "debating what a princedom is, how they are gained and kept, why they are lost". He loathed moral decay, but was torn between the search for truth and a fear of upsetting his vainglorious patrons.

Cesare Borgia, the "nephew" (actually son) of Alexander VI, a Spaniard who had bribed the Sacred College to make him pope and then proceeded to develop a form of statecraft "unweakened by pity and uninfluenced by ethics or religious faith". This model was widely emulated, most conscientiously by the son, who advanced his career with lashings of poison.

The enormous wealth generated by dubious means made Italy a prize over which the European powers, especially France and Spain, fought for 60 years. Eventually, French, Spaniards, and landless German Lutherans made common cause under the colours of Charles V's imperial army for the infamous

applied it in Rome with a rigour that made even Spaniards bite their lips. Artists who had fled from Rome in 1527 drifted back, among them Michelangelo, but the spirit had deserted them. Michelangelo's *Last Judgment* in the Sistine Chapel (1536) is said to reflect the sombre mood of the time.

The Reformation

To make matters worse, the shockwaves of the Reformation in France, Germany and England were felt in Rome. A worried Pope Paul III responded by importing the Jesuits from Spain. Pius IV (reigned 1559–65) was receptive to Reformation critics, and he reconvened the

Council of Trent to see what could be done: "The Council shall reform what wants to be reformed, even in our own person and even our own affairs." One of the decrees issued by the Council was the obituary of High Renaissance art.

Some observers subsequently saw an "improvement" in the political and religious climate. "Several popes in succession have been men of irreproachable lives," wrote Paolo Tiepolo in 1576, "hence all others are become better, or have at least assumed the appearance of being so. Cardinals and prelates attend mass punctually; their households are studious to avoid anything that can give scandal; the whole

the League of Nations and the United Nations. The papacy was thus deprived of its cherished role as the foremost international mediator.

With its sails trimmed, the papacy slipped back into one or two meretricious habits of old but these improved, if anything, Rome's tourist appeal. Edward Gibbon was a visitor in 1764, recounting "the strong emotions which agitated my mind as I first approached and entered the eternal city… Several days of intoxication were lost or enjoyed before I could descend to a cool and minute investigation." The cool and minute investigation produced *The History of the Decline and Fall of the Roman Empire*. "I am

city has put off its old recklessness and is become much more Christian-like in life and manners than formerly."

In the meantime, Protestant-Catholic enmity flared – and proceeded to blow itself out – in the course of the Thirty Years' War (1618–48), practically a dress rehearsal for World War I. The Peace of Westphalia afterwards was a turning point in European diplomatic history and had implications for Rome. It established the principle of states settling their differences around an international conference table, the genesis of

convinced," he told his father as work on the mighty tome commenced, "that there never before existed such a nation, and I hope for the happiness of mankind there never will again."

The ribaldry of what looked suspiciously like pagan festivities ended in 1796 on receipt of what was supposed to be good news from Napoleon: "Peoples of Italy, the French army comes to break your chains; the French people is the friend of all peoples; meet us with confidence. Your property, your religion, and your usages will be respected. We make war as generous enemies, and we have no quarrel save with the tyrants who enslave you." Napoleon was declaring that the papacy was no obstacle

LEFT: Machiavelli, author of *The Prince*. **ABOVE:** view of Rome in the 18th century by Gaspare Vanvitelli.

to his imperial ambitions. After defeating the papal army at Ancona, Napoleon demanded money from the Vatican, its art treasures, and sovereignty over some Papal States. Romans were not sorry to see the French drive the Austrians out of Italy, but they were horrified by the looting of art galleries and punitive French taxes. Pope Pius VII was bundled across the French border to Valence.

Napoleon incorporated the papal territories into the French Empire. He installed his mother in the Palazzo Bonaparte in the Piazza Venezia and gave his sister Maria Pauline to Prince Camillo Borghese. The prince reciprocated by

giving his new brother-in-law the Borghese art collection for 13 million francs. Pauline's wedding present to her husband was a statue by Canova of her as a semi-nude Venus.

After Napoleon's downfall, papal rule was restored at the Congress of Vienna in 1815, but the same peace arrangements also restored Austrian control over large parts of Italy, and that kindled the Risorgimento, the rise of modern Italian nationalism. The first flames were part of the nationalist conflagration that swept through most of Europe in 1848, and most Italians pinned their hopes on Pope Pius IX ("Pio Nono") who was perceived as a liberal reformer. The *sine qua non* of Italian independence, how-

ever, was to throw off the Austrian yoke, and the pope could not bring himself to war on the Roman Catholic Habsburgs.

The pope's military inhibitions played into the hands of the anti-clerical Giuseppe Mazzini, and it was not difficult to persuade Italians howling for Austrian blood that an Italian republic was the answer. The pope was deposed from his temporal power and a republic proclaimed with Mazzini as head of a governing triumvirate. In France, however, Louis Napoleon needed Catholic support, and the restoration of the pope seemed a certain way to win it. Giuseppe Garibaldi's 4,000 red-shirted irregulars were no defence against the French army, but rather than surrender he marched his band out of Rome and across Italy to achieve immortality in the history of the Risorgimento.

The reinstated Pio Nono sat on his throne behind a cordon of Louis Napoleon's troops while the patchwork of Italian states (but not Rome) threw off their princes and united, not behind the republic mooted by Mazzini but, thanks to Count Cavour, a nascent Kingdom of Italy under Victor Emmanuel II of Sardinia. The pope passed his time devising the doctrine of the Immaculate Conception and, in 1864, laid down as error that "the Roman Pontiff can or ought to come to terms with progress, liberalism, or modern civilisation".

The end of Papal rule

He had just worked out the doctrine of Papal Infallibility when, in 1870, an explosion rocked the Old Aurelian Wall. With the French garrison mulling over reports of Prussian guns encircling Paris, the Italian army poured through the breach. The pope barricaded himself in the Vatican and, from the dungeon, the three remaining prisoners of the Inquisition were led blinking into unfamiliar sunshine, for all the world, like Rome itself, adjusting to the prospect of life after 11 centuries of papal rule. ❑

LEFT: Italians pour into Rome, 1870. **RIGHT:** Giuseppe Garibaldi (1807–82), commander of the Risorgimento.

MODERN TIMES

The united Kingdom of Italy was short lived, and Mussolini brought Fascism to Rome. After the war, Italy as we know it today was born

When Rome was proclaimed the capital of the united Kingdom of Italy in 1871, a third of the city's population, then about 200,000, were beggars. While the clerical elite had left no stone unturned over the previous century or so to live in great personal comfort, no attention had been paid to mundane matters like drainage, at which the ancient Etruscan kings had excelled. Every flood on the Tiber cascaded through the Old City, and the record of high-water marks was left for posterity by dozens of plaques on walls. The surrounding countryside was a malarial wasteland infested with bandits.

The spectre of bedlam in the Paris Commune in 1871 persuaded the city fathers that the new Rome would be better off without a resident working class. The wretches could commute – and that they did, but only from shanty-towns that sprang up everywhere on the periphery. Assessing the results of this policy, Alberto Moravia unsurprisingly concluded that Rome did not represent the whole Italian nation.

Mussolini and a world at war

Despite Rome's experiment in social cleansing, Italian politics developed along mostly liberal lines into the early 20th century. World War I was for Italians virtually a private fight against the pro-German Austrian forces in the north, and Rome itself was not directly implicated. The repercussions came later in the person of Benito Mussolini, the former editor of a Socialist paper who came out of the war "burning with patriotism and bursting with ambition, a *condottiere* of fortune, prompt, fiery, clear-headed, shrinking from no violence or brutality, a born master of conspiracy".

Mussolini named his party the Fascisti after the *fasces,* the rods that were the symbol of a magistrate's authority in Ancient Rome. The party evolved in Milan, dressing its storm-troopers in black shirts and silencing critics by

literally forcing castor oil down their throats. On 30 October 1922, Mussolini marched on Rome ostensibly to save the country from the peril of Bolshevism.

With the king nominally left on his throne, Mussolini made the trains run on time and much more, pushing through sweeping changes in the

look and order of Italian society. He bulldozed wide roads through the historic city centre to speed up other traffic. "All merely picturesque things are to be swept away," he declared, "and must make room for the dignity, the hygiene and the beauty of the capital. It is necessary to reconcile the demands of ancient and modern Rome." Mussolini was not alone in this belief. The Fascist intelligentsia embraced technology and modernity to the exclusion of any vestiges of the past – except those that might associate the new regime with the glory of Ancient Rome.

Pope Pius XI, a semi-recluse in the Vatican, warmed to the dictator as he restored the crucifix to schools and worked towards a treaty

LEFT: Mussolini greets supporters from a balcony of Palazzo Venezia. **RIGHT:** King Victor Emmanuel III.

between the Vatican and the Italian State. This was formalized in the concordat of 1929, when the Vatican and the Italian state agreed sovereignty and relations.

The pope caught the spirit of Mussolini's dream of a reborn Roman Empire, to which end Mussolini annexed Abyssinia and Albania. "Rome is the new Zion and all peoples that live in the Roman faith are Romans," the pope cried. "The cross," replied Mussolini, rather changing the priorities, "follows the eagle's flight." Mussolini took Italy into World

HITLER'S APPROVAL

In *Mein Kampf*, Hitler expressed his admiration for Mussolini, "this great man south of the Alps".

Sicily. King Victor Emmanuel III had Mussolini arrested and appointed Marshal Badoglio as head of the Italian government. Guessing that Italy would soon sue for peace with the Allies, Hitler ordered a German occupation of Italy, and once again a Fascist government controlled Rome. "For reasons of principle," Hitler signalled to the German ambassador in Rome, "we shall be interested in receiving the names of about 30 important personalities in the army, politics, and the royal family known to be notorious opponents of

War II on 9 June 1940 when he felt confident that Germany would win the war. On being woken with the news, Winston Churchill in England growled: "People who go to Italy to look at ruins won't have to go as far as Naples and Pompeii in future."

One military disaster followed another, and Mussolini was only deterred from the desperate measure of bombing Athens and Cairo when Churchill threatened to retaliate by bombing Rome. "It is in fact quite obvious," Hitler observed, "that our Italian alliance has been of more service to our enemies than to ourselves."

By July 1943 the Allies were mopping up in North Africa and preparing to invade Italy via

ours." The ambassador bravely declined to supply names.

The armistice was duly declared, Mussolini was rescued by the SS and made the puppet ruler of a Fascist republic in northern and central Italy, and the German army occupied Rome.

Romans suddenly displayed martial qualities that had been absent in the Italian North African armies. Italian gallantry at this turn of events was conspicuously demonstrated by the shelter given to Jews, well-known anti-Fascists and escaped Allied prisoners-of-war. An escape organisation was set up in Rome by Major S.I. Derry of the British Army, who entered the city hidden in a pile of cabbages in order to make contact with Monsignor Hugh O'Flaherty, an Irish priest attached to the Vatican.

They met in St Peter's Square. The major slipped into a cassock and together they passed through German lines into the neutrality of the Vatican City proper, ironically to the German College staffed by anti-Nazi German nuns. Luckily, Derry and other escapees happened to have their chequebooks on them, and the funds needed to run the organisation were provided by locals who were prepared to cash cheques – on London banks – "and trust to time, honour and the course of the war for repayment".

About 4,000 escapees were shepherded to

for symbolic reasons it was the greatest prize of the Italian campaign. The battle for Rome, said Hitler, "must be fought in holy wrath against an enemy who is waging a pitiless war of extermination against the German people".

When at last the city's capture by the Allies seemed inevitable, Field Marshal Kesselring, the German commander, wanted to destroy the bridges across the Tiber. Hitler suddenly changed his tune, declaring that his enemies could go down in history as the destroyers of the Monte Cassino monastery, but he was not going to join them as the destroyer of Rome.

Historians have since questioned Hitler's

safety by the Rome organisation, but these and other resistance activities provoked the Germans into harsh reprisals. When 10 German soldiers were killed by partisans in an ambush, the German commanders took 335 men from Rome's Regina Coeli prison to the Ardeatine caves just outside the city and shot them.

The Allies launched a bombing offensive against Rome, but the targets were generally pinpointed, the church of San Lorenzo being one of the rare accidental victims. Compared with Cassino, Rome had no strategic value, but

LEFT: Mussolini at the Vatican. **ABOVE:** Enrico Berlinguer, head of the Italian Communist Party (PCI), 1972–84.

apparent devotion to antiquity by pointing out that, as he spoke, the battle for Rome had been downgraded by the impending Allied landings in Normandy. Rome fell on 4 June 1944, yet it was not until 28 April the following year that Mussolini was captured, shot and left hanging from a lamppost in Milan.

The onset of corruption

Conditions in Rome immediately after World War II have been grippingly portrayed by contemporary neorealist films by, among others, Vittorio de Sica *(Bicycle Thieves)* and Roberto Rossellini *(Rome, Open City)*. The most familiar location backdrop to these films was no longer the Colosseum, but the high-rise blocks that proliferated under Salvatore Rebecchini, Rome's mayor from 1947 to 1956. Property developers presented the city with a token patch of land in an undeveloped suburban area. The value rocketed as soon as the city laid on roads, power and water, and the profits paid for bribes to bureaucrats. Rome's empty spaces filled with illegal buildings: at one point, over 500,000 Romans lived in housing lacking planning permission. This system passed effortlessly from the

REFUGEE CRISIS

In the 1990s, the break-up of Eastern Europe brought an influx of Albanians and former Yugoslavians to Italy.

minority parties, says Barzini, "pursued the public interest only incidentally; most of the time they exerted themselves to build up their own financial and political power, and their electoral following, often by dubious means, in order to cope with the Communist menace." No Italian party was large enough to form a government; the result was a run of coalitions.

New popes and clean hands

The election of a new pope in 1978 also proved fraught. A puff of white smoke from the Sistine

Christian Democrats to the Communists in 1976.

Politically there was nothing edifying about post-war Rome. While the Treaty of Rome in 1957 spelt out a grandiose vision of a European Common Market, life on the ground over the next two decades was blighted by frequent strikes and left-wing terrorist attacks.

According to the Italian author Luigi Barzini, at the heart of the political problem was the Italian Communist Party, which emerged from the war as the largest communist party in Europe outside the Soviet Union, albeit a minority party. All other Italian parties agreed that the communists had to be restrained by any means. They agreed on nothing else. The non-communist

Chapel chimney signals a successful conclusion to the conclave's deliberations; this time it backfired and the influx of smoke almost suffocated the 122 cardinals assembled within. The cardinals recovered their composure, but no sooner had they dispersed than the successful candidate, Pope John Paul I, died suddenly. In the same year, the political mayhem reached a peak with the kidnapping and murder of Aldo Moro, the Christian Democrat prime minister.

Karol Jozef Wojtyla of Poland, who as Pope John Paul II became the first non-Italian pope in 450 years, brought international prestige to the Vatican only to see it compromised by disclosures of huge irregularities in the Vatican's finances, including Mafia dealings and the laundering of drug money. Suspicions about the death of John Paul I were given an edge when "God's banker", Roberto Calvi, was found hanging from a bridge in London. The government fought back by taxing the Vatican's business activities and revoking Constantine the Great's edict of AD 324 – Roman Catholicism is no longer the state religion of Italy.

Over the next decade the dominance of the Christian Democrats faded when coalition partners took important government posts and the judicial system began cracking down on organised crime. A group of judges became national

system of corruption and kickbacks that had ruled postwar Italy began to crumble.

In the wake of all the upheaval, multi-millionaire industrialist and media-mogul Silvio Berlusconi and his right-wing party Forza Italia briefly held power, until the Northern League, a secessionist minority, decided not to participate. In 1996, the centre-left Olive Tree coalition under Romano Prodi brought together a parliament of reformed communists and hardliners, as well as liberal elements.

After his centre-left coalition fell apart, Prodi moved on to the European Commission. In his place, former communist Massimo D'Alema

heroes when they persistently pursued the Mafia. Out of the woodwork crawled *pentiti* – mob insiders who gave evidence in return for leniency, breaking the *omerta* (code of silence) which had until then made the Mafia impregnable to mass prosecutions. The Mafia struck back, and two Sicilian judges were murdered in 1992.

The greatest changes came from an anti-corruption campaign, begun in 1992 under the name *mani pulite* (clean hands). Hundreds of businessmen and politicians were tried or gave testimony in exchange for leniency, and the old

FAR LEFT: Roberto Calvi, "God's banker". **LEFT:** Giulio Andreotti, seven-times premier. **ABOVE:** Parliament.

served for two years as prime minister. D'Alema continued many of the sound fiscal policies of the Prodi government. In early 2000, the ruling coalition fragmented yet again, and former Prime Minister Giuliano Amato was called in to lead a technocratic government.

After a lengthy and generously self-financed electoral campaign, May 2001 saw media magnate Silvio Berlusconi become Italy's prime minister for the second time, as leader of a right-wing alliance called the *Casa delle Libertà* (the House of Liberties). Amid much protest from the centre-left and the trade unions, the government soon embarked on a set of reforms of taxes, pensions and the labour market. ❑

THE ROMANS

The citizens of Rome share a glorious history which the city reminds them of every day – unfortunately, this has engendered some terrible modern attitudes

The Romans are not loved by their fellow-countrymen. SPQR, the city motto, stands for *Senatus Populusque Romanus* (the Senate and the Roman People). However, modern critics prefer to read it as: *sono porchi questi romani* (what pigs these Romans are).

The travel writer, Jan Morris, confirms this bloody-minded view: "Recession, pollution, crime and triple-parking seem to pass them by; if the city were suddenly Scandinavianised, all its buildings spick and span, all its traffic ordered, all corruptions cleansed, the Romans would hardly notice."

As denizens of the Eternal City, the Romans are exhausted by their ancient wisdom and self-evident superiority. According to Alberto Moravia, the greatest Roman novelist: "The Roman tag of eternal should be understood in the sense of *ennui*, of eternal boredom." Romans have seen everything before (and bought the T-shirt). It is a mood epitomised by the city slogan *"pazienza"*, both a shrug of resignation and a gesture of indifference to their glorious heritage.

Myth makers

Rome is *the* place for contemplating the passage of time and the vanity of human wishes. "Within a short time you forget everything; and everything forgets you," said Marcus Aurelius. The world-weary populace has little inclination to relive the glory, decline and fall. Nonetheless, there is a residual melancholy and romantic nostalgia for the grandeur of Imperial Rome.

This nostalgia is tinged with a feeling of living in the ruins. Yet, unlike the Athenians, the Romans are not inhibited by their heritage. They have domesticated it. Roman cats command the ruins; housewives hang washing over sacred shrines; and youths scrawl graffiti on noble statues. All Romans have been brought up with the

PRECEDING PAGES: taking advantage of the Vatican's postal system; young men pose. LEFT: time out from the tourists. RIGHT: customised transport.

demigods of Romulus and Remus and a memory of imperial megalomania. The Roman complicity with their own myths knows no bounds: for instance, the city is built over 12 hills rather than the mythical seven. The Romans do not wish to be roused from their somnolence, and yet the film director Federico Fellini dared to

stir them in *Roma*, a fable about modern Rome. In one symbolic scene, underground frescoes crumble before one's eyes when they are exposed to the air and the light. In real life, however, it is difficult to see the Romans behind their legendary icons.

Mamma Roma

The mythical founders of Rome were saved by a she-wolf, at whose breast they suckled. This female symbolism has since shifted to the city itself, transforming Rome into the "mother of civilisation". However, the maternal image is more a foreign romanticisation of Rome than a reality. Fellini turned the nurturing image on its head by praising the city as a mother who is ideal because she is indifferent: "Rome is a mother with too many children who asks for nothing and expects nothing." Extending the metaphor, he denounced Romans as "a city of lazy, sceptical and badly brought up children".

Roman society

In the popular imagination, Ancient Rome was peopled by emperors and orators, poets and politicians, patricians and plebeians, valiant gladiators and avaricious tax collectors. Republican Rome boasted a degree of upward

All roads lead to Rome

In the 19th century Rome had the smallest middle class of any major European city. But by 1900 a population boom saw the number of inhabitants double; the city was further swollen by the exodus from southern Italy that followed World War II. In the 1960s, the population reached 2 million, but by the 1990s it had topped 3 million. The new arrivals were quickly assimilated by a city that prides itself on its tolerance. Nonetheless, the influx of outsiders has shaped the composition of Roman society. Yesterday's emblematic types have been replaced by civil servants and clergy, business

mobility, or at least cultivated popular aspirations. However, in practice, society separated quite distinctly into the proletarian masses and a patrician elite.

The Colonna dynasty traces its lineage back to the Etruscans, but most of Rome's aristocratic families rose to prominence during the Renaissance. This elite band provided popes and cardinals as well as the noble Corsini, Farnese and Orsini dynasties. The patrician elite survives, often ridiculed these days as concierges to a decadent heritage. Fellini portrayed the Roman aristocracy as inbred, uncultured, grasping landowners whose "ignorance is seen as their god-given right".

administrators and boutique owners, not to mention *tifosi*, football fans and the cocky youths Fellini dubbed *vitelloni* (fat calves).

Diverse though they are, Romans share a sense of urban design. The Romans were arguably the greatest builders of antiquity, combining monumentality and utility with Greek grace and a sense of creation for eternity. The Colosseum, what Fellini called "the skull of antiquity", is matched by the purity of the Pantheon or the baroque monumentality of St Peter's. However, real Roman artists are rare, restricted to Pietro Cavallini, the medieval artist who created the mosaics in Santa Maria in Trastevere, or Giulio Sartorio, whose modern frescoes adorn the parliamentary chamber at Palazzo di Montecitorio.

Romans harbour attachments to certain quarters in the *Centro Storico*, from the Ghetto, still home to several thousand Jews, to Campo de' Fiori, a lively *popolare* quarter peopled by fruit sellers and furniture restorers. Trastevere, the ancient immigrant quarter, until recently formed the backbone of the Roman proletariat. Although sailors and small craftsmen still live there, its cheeky proletarian character is submerged under a Bohemian gloss. Testaccio, the hilly 19th-century working-class quarter curled around the former slaughter-house, is newly

intra muros, based on the "Seven Hills", is periodically closed to cars. To avoid the traffic chaos, many Romans resort to *motorini* (mopeds). En route, Romans are fortified by strong coffee and several *cornetti* (sweet croissants) in a bar.

In the past, mealtimes in Rome were sacred, with offices and shops all over town literally closing down between 1 and 4pm and the majority of workers going home for a cooked meal. Times have changed however, and in what many consider to be a regrettable but necessary drive for greater efficiency, extended mealtimes and siestas have largely become a

fashionable and considered preferable to the *borgate*, the faceless modern suburbs many Romans are forced to live in. By contrast, Parioli, the leafy suburb north of Villa Borghese, is dotted with chic villas and finds favour with the *nouveaux riches*.

Roman rhythms

According to Moravia, "Foreigners find a certain serenity in Rome," but this is not a sentiment shared by most Romans. The day begins and ends in traffic jams because *Roma*

LEFT: two of a kind times two.
ABOVE: a sunny outlook by the Spanish Steps.

thing of the past. Office-workers now get an hour off for lunch and many shops stay open throughout the day. The only exception are family-owned or small boutiques which still make the most of their three-hour lunch-breaks.

Political parasites

As a city of two capitals, the meeting place of temporal and spiritual powers, Rome seems a harmonious spot. Yet, as the political capital, Rome enjoys a reputation as the flea on the back of long-suffering northern Italy. The anti-Rome prejudice is kept fresh with constant tales of bloated bureaucracy and crippling inefficiency in the city. In the eyes of other Italians, the Romans are greedy parasites and power-brokers bent on keeping the administrative spoils within the family. The city is smothered by a web of political mismanagement and the culture of corruption, embracing the stranglehold of clientalistic contracts and the misappropriation of public funds.

Italians resent the cushy lifestyles enjoyed by the *Palazzo*, Rome's political establishment. The city is also envied for its monopoly of international institutions such as FAO, the United Nations food organisation. The capital tends to turn everything into institutions. As a diplomatic crossroads, Rome conveys the illusion of impe-

City of religious sceptics

As a sovereign state and the capital of Catholicism, the Vatican celebrates its triumph over paganism. However, these sentiments are not shared by sceptical Romans. In keeping with their eclectic past, Romans are ritualistic rather than religious, formalistic rather than faithful. Ancient Romans were conditioned by superstitions, ranging from an irrational terror of lightning to the compulsive offering of human sacrifices on the Ides of May.

In Roman eyes, the Church soon symbolised temporal power. Today, the Vatican is seen as a political institution, the corporate arm of the

rial power. The city hosts two diplomatic corps, with 109 embassies accredited to the Italian government and 59 to the Vatican.

According to Moravia, "Rome is an administrative city dominated by two institutions: the State and the Church. That aside, there is no communication, no flow of ideas." In Ancient Republican Rome, citizens regarded the state as the highest good, a Roman sentiment which has been transmuted into an expectation that the state will provide. As Italy's capital, Rome lives and breathes politics. Civic virtue has long been the lofty but rarely realised ideal – it crumbles on contact with more robust Roman values.

papacy, albeit one with a good cashmere gift-shop attached. Anticlerical attitudes have been confirmed by the Vatican financial and political scandals of the early 1980s and the conservatism of Pope John Paul II.

Today, Rome is a secular, sophisticated city, if one coloured by a religious caste of mind. *"Roma venuta, fede perduta"* (once in Rome, faith is forsaken) runs a cynical local saying. The city may have more than 900 churches, but only 3 percent of Romans regularly attend Mass. If the papacy intrudes on daily Roman life, it is only as a source of sexual proscription or a cause of traffic congestion. To the world-weary Romans, the Wednesday papal audience simply serves to clog the city streets with yet more traffic.

When Pope John Paul II was almost assassinated in 1981, the news barely impinged on the city's preparations for a major football match. The typical response from Roma fans was: "*Il papa è morto? Se ne fa un altro*" (The Pope is dead? Well, they'll just have to find another one). The Vatican state across the Tiber from central Rome is held in low esteem. As local Roman wisdom has it: "Faith is made here but believed elsewhere."

WHO IS "ROMAN"?

Moravia said: "There are no Romans, only people from all parts of Italy who adopt Roman characteristics."

"civic", "plebeian" and "pontificate" – terms that define public life to this day. Yet compared with the people of other cities, the Romans have not clung to a strong regional dialect. Romanesco, which was once the local parlance, survives only in the Roman clipped speech, rolling accent and certain vernacular expressions: "born in a shirt" means rich. The *cadenza romana* is a raucous guttural accent in which *questo* (this) is reduced to *'sto*; *va bene* (fine) becomes a clipped *vabbé* while *andiamo a dormire* (time for bed) is

In search of real Romans

Modern-day Romans claim that the real Romans are consigned to the history books. Since the population of the city multiplied in the 19th century, "real Romans" are scarce and treasured for their authenticity. However, most modern Romans are of mixed ancestry, with roots going back fewer than five generations.

Classical Roman writers have enriched the Western world through the language that every educated person once spoke: Latin. The political legacy of Latin is heard in such concepts as

---

LEFT: flocking to St Peter's.
ABOVE: body language is also part of local parlance.

abbreviated to *'namo a dormi*. Religious and political graffiti represent a Roman art form. Many squares are adorned with plaques containing papal pronouncements or pompous tributes to former emperors. However, the Romans are equally at ease with high-flown prose or the populist slogans daubed by Roma football fans.

Populists and elitists

The stratified society of Ancient Rome has bequeathed two contrasting traditions: the populist and the elitist. While the former is full-blooded, earthy, exuberant and rebellious, the latter is cerebral and refined, albeit eviscerated. The two traditions meet in a common passion for politics, religion, the family, food and Roman heritage.

The Trastevere poets, commemorated by statues in the riverside quarter, represent the populist strand of Roman society. Gioacchino Belli, the 19th-century dialect poet, was foremost among the satirical poets who railed against the acquisitiveness of Roman rulers, whether cardinals or aristocrats. Trilussa, his best-loved modern successor, satirised the overweening ambitions of Mussolini as well as Roman foibles and a fondness for Castelli Romani white wine. "*Dentro 'sta boccia trovi er bonumore che canta l'inni e t'imbandiera er core*" (every mouthful bursts with spirit enough to sing hymns and bedeck your heart with banners). Still today, Trasteverini, the inhabitants "over the Tiber", pride themselves on their vigour and passion for life.

Pier Paolo Pasolini, the controversial writer and film-maker, followed in the boisterous steps of the Trastevere popular poets. Murdered in murky circumstances in 1975, Pasolini was a Marxist, Catholic and homosexual whose disturbing films challenged conventional ideas and sexual mores. As an anti-establishment figure, Pasolini immortalised rough Roman youth in his tales of a dying way of life in the city slums. Nor are Pasolini's driftless, rabble-rousing *ragazzi* so very different from the *plebs*, the common people of ancient Rome. Although only a Roman by adoption, Pasolini embodied the populist spirit.

Caravaggio's painterly sense of light and shade, and his decadence and Bohemian lifestyle, made him worthy of becoming an adopted Roman. His flight from the city after murdering a man in a drunken brawl followed a roistering Roman tradition.

A WORD OF WARNING

"Power wears out those who don't have it," was one of seven-times premier Giulio Andreotti's sayings.

Elitist values

At the elitist end of the scale lies the intelligentsia, a medley of politicians, professionals, artists and academics. Eugenio Scalfari, editor-in-chief of *La Repubblica*, Rome's best-selling newspaper, is a Roman by adoption and one of Italy's foremost opinion-leaders. Turning his back on the bulwarks of Communism and Catholicism, Scalfari stands for pluralism, modernism and public probity, the professed values of the liberal, agnostic Roman intelligentsia.

Alberto Moravia, the archetypal Roman intellectual, denied the existence of the species, yet he was the mainstay of sophisticated Roman society until he died in 1990. His novels reveal a remorseless observer of Roman society. But, like a true Roman, he affected disdain and indifference towards the city of his birth. He only cared for it nostalgically, "like a woman one had once loved". He considered himself a European not a Roman writer, someone who merely used the city as a scenic backdrop to his work.

High-profile Romans by adoption include the virtuoso novelist Italo Calvino and the idiosyncratic Dacia Maraini, the erstwhile companion of Moravia and a literary lioness of Rome.

Giulio Andreotti, seven-times Italian premier, was for a long time a symbol of longevity in power, and he typified the Roman politician for ingly Roman: "*a pensar male si fa peccato ma ci si indovina*" (Thinking the worst of others is sinful yet often turns out to be for the best). His enemies called him a string-pulling cardinal, "more Catholic than Christian", but this too is Roman, as was his scepticism, pragmatism, and love of family and football. "Sooner or later, old foxes end up as fur coats," warned Craxi, a vanquished political enemy, but the wily fox survived longer than most.

Cultural raiders

The Romans are essentially artistic connoisseurs and cultural raiders who see no need to

all seasons. Known as "the divine Giulio", he was born a stone's throw from Julius Caesar's birthplace and had much in common with his namesake. Also nicknamed *il volpe* (the fox), the Machiavellian Christian Democrat politician was famed for his patrician disdain as well as his love of power.

Andreotti's Roman hauteur and professed piety helped to save him from numerous investigations into alleged Mafia links, until the justice system caught up with him in 1995. Nonetheless, his best-known epigram is chill-

---

LEFT: Romans believe in conspicuous consumption.
ABOVE: the city has long been a home to immigrants.

stoop to creativity themselves. In classical times, Greek art, philosophy and poetry shaped Roman culture while naturalistic Etruscan statuary inspired Roman busts. During the Renaissance, papal patrons lured the greatest painters and sculptors from Florence, Milan or Urbino to Rome. Pope Julius II transformed St Peter's with the help of Tuscans such as Michelangelo.

According to Alberto Moravia, "Rome receives everything yet gives nothing back." This talent for theft, also known as cultural assimilation, can be traced back to Ancient Roman practices and a propensity for hedging bets with all manner of alien gods. In particular, the *exoratio* was a favoured imperial battle ritual in which the enemy's gods were invoked and invited over to the Roman camp. In return for victory, the Romans transported their vanquished foe's idols to a dusty yet cosmopolitan collection on the Capitoline Hill. There, they were worshipped as assimilated Roman gods.

Romans at play

The 1950s *dolce vita* playground of Hollywood starlets has disappeared, leaving behind a less sophisticated scene. However, Romans are more at home in a provincial, populist culture. It is more authentic to watch Romans at play in low-brow settings like the sentimental Christ-

Romans believe in conspicuous consumption. Versace-swathed Romans cluster around the *alta moda* shops in Via Condotti while wealthy matrons take every opportunity to drape themselves in Roman-designed Fendi furs or Valentino gowns.

Roman enjoyment is less evident in glamorous settings such as the opera or a Via Veneto piano bar. Instead, night owls can be found downing a *digestivo* such as Sambuca, Strega or Fernet-Branca near the Pantheon or simply looking cool with a speciality ice-cream on Piazza Navona. Romantic couples may haunt the fish restaurants on the lakes outside Rome.

mas market on Piazza Navona or Mercato di Porta Portese, a glorified flea market. The browsers munch fritters, *suppli* (deep-fried croquettes) or *porchetta* (sucking pig) and display great gusto. Romans might cultivate a philosophical world-weariness but this is rarely reflected in their social life.

Ordinary Romans enjoy strolling through the gardens of Villa Borghese or admiring the ancient city at sunset from the Gianicolo Hill. On Sundays, lifelong football fans flock to Stadio Olimpico to watch Roma or Lazio play at home. Young families prefer to relax in Villa Borghese, enjoying the view from a rowing-boat or a horse-drawn carriage. Bourgeois

However, the locals are most at home in a packed *trattoria* in Trastevere, tucking into a hearty *saltimbocca alla romana, carciofi alla giudea* (artichokes fried in oil) and *misticanza*, a salad of wild leaves. As populist Romans say: "In a lovely setting you'll eat like a dog."

Romans are omnivorous but, according to food critic Leo Pescarolo, have "neither the culture nor the patience to invent a refined cuisine". This preference for rusticity colours culinary attitudes: "The more you spend, the worse you eat." If Romans are what they eat, then they should resemble rustics, with a vast array of vegetables and *semifreddi* desserts such as *tiramisù*. This gutsy cuisine represents proletarian Roman tastes: tripe, spicy pasta, salads and *antipasti* are often washed down with Castelli Romani wine, especially straw-coloured Frascati.

More exotic Roman kicks range from racing around the city centre in customised cars to snorting cocaine or indulging in sexual encounters with Brazilian transvestites. At times, society gossip about satanic rites, patrician incest or other deviant sexual practices conjures up the decadence of Pasolini's *Roman Nights*. Yet a lifestyle that in many other cities would be con-

EATING HABITS

Romans prefer a simple *trattoria*: "In a lovely setting you'll eat like a dog."

all right." *Dritto*, the name for Roman cunning, describes the natives' ability to fleece the gullible. Not that the Romans care in the slightest what others think of them: as masters of *nomifregismo*, a couldn't-give-a-damn attitude, Romans ignore criticism.

Indeed, infantile was Fellini's verdict: "The Roman is like a grotesque, overgrown child who has the satisfaction of being continually spanked by the Pope." He thought that Rome lacked neurotics only because the citizens weren't mature enough to develop neuroses. Spoilt, opinionated

sidered outrageous is all part of the eternal Roman stage set. As a *Dolce Vita* for the 1990s, it leaves little to be desired.

Spoilt children

Outsiders see Romans as phlegmatic and philosophical, shrewd and sly, suave and duplicitous, jaded and decadent, vulgar yet vibrant.

Emperor Vespasian personified Roman shrewdness by charging citizens for using public latrines. Contemporary Roman cynics believe that "when the police are on strike, the traffic's

and resilient, the Romans still know how to live. In so doing, they have made Rome, in essence a city of illusion and disillusion, into the most resilient and human of European capitals.

Even today, Rome adopts the civilised veneer of those it conquers. Romans have a welcoming embrace, offering tolerance and a lack of exclusivity that lies at the heart of their great culture. "All contributions welcome", as the signs say in St Peter's.

The promise of Roman citizenship is proffered to all newcomers. Everyone can become Roman in time – even if the official papers fail to materialise – because ultimately, being Roman is a state of mind. ❏

LEFT: Roman nuptials.
ABOVE: a street celebration, part of city life.

THE CINEMA

Rome was a giant on the international film scene even before Mussolini's Cinecittà.
This is the world of Fellini and Rossellini, Quo Vadis and Ben-Hur

Cinema is inextricably linked with Rome. Even before Mussolini created Cinecittà – Rome's own little Hollywood designed to win world fame for the Fascist film industry – Rome was at the forefront of cinema worldwide. When the Alberini-Santoni production company released *La Presa di Roma* (1905), about the 1870 rout of the Pope from Rome by Garibaldi's troops, the Italian feature film was born. Much of *La Presa di Roma* was shot on the streets of Rome, anticipating two dominant currents in Italian film history: realism and historical spectacle.

Historical spectacle was taken up with a passion in the early 20th century, and even Hollywood drew inspiration from Italian epics such as Piero Fosco's *Cabiria*, about the conflict between Ancient Rome and Carthage. And the money poured in from wealthy industrialists and members of the aristocracy.

Under the Fascists

"Due to your foresight, Duce, Italian cinema is now an established and growing reality…But the gates of Italian cinema will be for ever closed to three factors: profiteering, bad taste and bourgeois corruption," the Minister for Popular Culture intoned in 1937 during the opening ceremony for the Centro Sperimentale di Cinematografia. Mussolini had grasped the propaganda value of film, and wanted this powerful tool to promote the glory of Italy.

Under the Fascists, directors with ideological credibility got up to 60 percent state financing. In particular, patriotic endeavours, such as *Scipione l'Africano*, a glorification of Italy's African invasions,were often fully funded by the government, and if the government liked the final film, producers were frequently excused any repayments.

However, in this period Italy's best directors went into hibernation. They emerged after World War II, and stimulated by the ruins and

post-war wretchedness, they gave birth to the genre known as neorealism – a vivid kind of realism which laid the foundations for modern film. Among the most famous directors of the time were Roberto Rossellini, Federico Fellini, Vittorio de Sica and Pier Paolo Pasolini. Their subject matter was the Roman underworld of

small-time thieves, of *malavita*, of desperate love and the endemic black market.

Cinecittà provided exactly the right ambience for their films, for in those years Roman slums, high-rise blocks and flimsy buildings were pushing out into the Campagna, getting closer and closer to Cinecittà. Films about the transition from Fascism to post-war Italy, such as *Campo dei Fiori* and *Roma, Città Aperta* (*Rome, Open City*), were followed by the most famous of the neorealist films – Vittorio de Sica's *Bicycle Thieves*, about a bill-poster on a quest for the stolen bicycle essential to his job.

Federico Fellini, who helped Rossellini write *Roma, Città Aperta*, summarised the unique

LEFT: Marcello Mastroianni, Fellini's favourite actor.
RIGHT: Mussolini lays the Cinecittà foundation stone.

atmosphere in Rome that had produced neorealism. "We discovered our own country... we could look freely around us now, and the reality appeared so extraordinary that we couldn't resist watching it and photographing it with astonished and virgin eyes."

Unflinching truth

Roma, Città Aperta was one of the most influential films of the time, and its unflinching confrontation with truth still unnerves audiences. The film follows several resistance workers. Every scene, except for those set in the Gestapo headquarters, was shot on location. It has a

archs to plunder exploitative bakeries. She is utterly convincing on a personal level, and yet she also symbolises the desperate plight of Italian housewives during the war.

After watching *Roma, Città Aperta* in New York, Ingrid Bergman wrote to Rossellini: "If you happen to need a Swedish actress who can speak good English, has forgotten all her German, can express herself in barely comprehensible French and can only manage '*ti amo*' in Italian, I would be prepared to come."

Conveniently enough, Rossellini was at the time being yelled at in Anna Magnani's flat in Rome. "My dear Robertino does so like his

rough visceral throb that was revolutionary for the time. Some sequences seem to be documentary footage; the camera jerks and twists; shots break off suddenly without conventional aesthetic purpose.

Despite the unprecedented and relentless immediacy, *Roma, Città Aperta* has a complex symbolic structure. Each character represents a larger element of contemporary Italian society as well as an individual. The film elevates squalid drug addicts, priests, German lesbians and Austrian deserters until they carry symbolic import without sacrificing unique personalities.

Pina (played by Anna Magnani), for example, is an agonised mother leading a mob of matri-

spaghetti, with lots of sauce... here, take it, I'll give you some cheese, here, take the spaghetti..." Magnani hurled the spaghetti at Rossellini's head, in an echo of a Cinecittà comedy. Magnani left, Bergman arrived, and so began one of the most dramatic love stories in Roman cinematic history.

Federico Fellini's collaboration with Cinecittà made him the uncrowned king of the studios. His films *La Dolce Vita*, *Roma* and *Intervista* were homages to his adopted city. *Roma* satirised the Catholic Church while *La Dolce Vita*, filmed on the once glamorous Via Veneto, satirised the idle Roman rich. Fellini was the culmination of neorealist philosophy.

His characters are constantly torn between the desire to realise their true selves and the urge to conform to society. His heroes swing wildly between the desire to be like no one and the need to be like everyone else.

These characters were painted large on the screen by actors such as Marcello Mastroianni. Fresh directorial talent was growing up close by Cinecittà. The graduates of the nearby Directors' School who later worked at Cinecittà included Liliana Cavani, Marco Bellocchio, Nanni Loy and Carlo Verdone.

THE BIG BREAK

In the early years, directors, actors and young hopefuls took the tram to Cinecittà.

ton Heston and the memorable chariot racing sequence in 1959, and *Cleopatra* with Elizabeth Taylor and Richard Burton (1963).

In these glorious years, more than a million actors, extras, technicians and directors made more than 1,000 films. Cinecittà had 16 theatres, an artificial pond and three restaurants. But the shift towards American cinema led to meagre times when Hollywood went into crisis. Cinecittà fell into decline and television – arch enemy of the cinema – moved in.

These days, most films showing in Rome are

Hollywood comes to town

It is ironic that Mussolini's film city only achieved real recognition through bourgeois, commercial American epics laden with schmaltz. However, they made the name of Cinecittà a household word for millions around the world. The unmistakable atmosphere of Cinecittà that created the 1951 production of *Quo Vadis*, a spectacular epic with a cast of thousands, including Robert Taylor and Deborah Kerr. It also produced *Roman Holiday* with Audrey Hepburn (1953), *Ben-Hur* with Charl-

foreign, mostly American, and dubbed. The Italians, historically great connoisseurs of film, have no patience for subtitles – perhaps because the Italians dub better than anyone else.

The supposed dearth of home-grown films is often decried, but in reality Italy's film industry is doing quite well. Foreign productions have returned to Rome to take advantage of a streamlined bureaucracy and the technical talent, and domestic returns are setting new records. Recently, a lighthearted Italian comedy became the most successful film of the year in Italy. Unfortunately, these successes go unnoticed abroad, and runaway successes like *Cinema Paradiso* and *Il Postino* are rare. ❑

LEFT: neorealist director Federico Fellini. **ABOVE:** actors Gregory Peck and Audrey Hepburn in *Roman Holiday*.

RENAISSANCE AND BAROQUE ART AND ARCHITECTURE

A wealthy, secure papacy left a rich legacy of Renaissance and baroque works

Walking through Rome's *Centro Storico*, one is frequently amazed by the sheer size and grandeur of the buildings crammed into its narrow, winding streets. At other times one might be struck by an exquisite fountain or facade which, though obviously the work of a major artist and worthy of being the pride of any other city, is ignored by the traffic and pedestrians rushing past.

There are exceptions, but a high proportion of these architectural gems date from the period between 1454 and 1670, when, thanks mainly to a securely established papacy, Rome was one of the principal cities in Europe and a centre of Renaissance and baroque art and architecture.

A rebirth

The Renaissance was a rediscovery and development of ancient art and culture that had been abandoned after the Roman Empire fell in the 5th century. It began in Italy in the late 14th century and over the following 150 years swept across Europe, influencing culture and teaching and leading to fundamental changes in the way people thought and lived.

Christopher Columbus, Marco Polo and Vasco da Gama discovered new countries and trade routes; Galileo made discoveries about the universe; and philosophers such as Erasmus and Thomas More studied and reapplied the humanist philosophies of the ancients. While not yet questioning the supremacy of God, they proposed that man was capable of achieving and creating great things without reference to God and the Bible at every turn. This basic change in emphasis led ultimately to a questioning of the dogma of the Catholic Church and to the birth of Protestantism.

It was in art and architecture, however, that the new movement was most visible – in the development of perspective, the more naturalistic presentation of subject matter (especially compared to the Byzantine-inspired style that preceded it) and in the use of classical proportions and styles in building.

Most of the great artists of the time came to Rome at some point in their careers, either to study the classical proportions of the Forum and

other ancient remains, or to complete commissions for the Pope. However, it was really in northern Italy, and particularly in Florence, that the Renaissance developed.

Two events in the middle of the 15th century marked the re-emergence of Rome as a cultural centre. Firstly, the papacy of Nicholas V (1447–55) established a line of popes with time, money and the desire to improve Rome's appearance. Secondly, the Italian League of 1455 ushered in a degree of peace across Italy, leaving the popes free to more peacefully occupy themselves with art and architecture.

Many of the changes made over the next 70 years can be seen in Rome today. Nicholas V

PRECEDING PAGES: Michelangelo's ceiling fresco in the Sistine Chapel. **LEFT:** the baroque Fontana del Moro, designed by Bernini, in Piazza Navona.
RIGHT: Fontana delle Tartarughe in Piazza Mattei.

ordered the demolition of the old St Peter's and the present building was worked on by some of the greatest artists of the 175-year period that it took to complete. Many of the details and interior decorations were executed later, in the baroque period, but Renaissance masters who left their mark include Bramante, whose *Tempietto* on the Gianicolo is regarded as the first truly Renaissance building in Rome, Raphael (as director of works), whose frescoes can be seen in the Vatican and at Villa Farnesina, and Michelangelo, who designed the

PAPAL BACKLASH

Papal patronage turned to censorship in 1563 with a decree on artistic style.

great works of art, to be found in all the main collections but especially in the Vatican, Palazzo Barberini and Palazzo Doria Pamphilj.

During the latter part of the 16th century, creativity was curbed by a papal decree responding to the threat of Protestantism. The 1563 Council of Trent laid down guidelines for church commissions. Realism was allowed to stay but there was to be no prettification and emphasis had to be put on the worldly suffering of martyrs to remind people of the infernal torments awaiting them if they

Campidoglio as well as painting the Sistine Chapel and sculpting the St Peter's *Pietà*.

Artists in residence

Until the 1527 Sack of Rome, artists flocked to the city, working either for the Pope or for the leading families who competed for the papal throne – the Barberini, Borghese, Medici and Pamphilj families are among the most famous.

Dating from this time are churches such as Santa Maria del Popolo and Santa Maria della Pace (both with Bramante additions), palaces such as those on Via Giulia (for example, Palazzo Clarelli designed and lived in by Antonio da Sangallo the Younger), and, of course,

offended the Church, thus terrifying people into remaining loyal to it. Niccolò Pomarancio's gruesome frescoes of martyred saints in the churches of Santo Stefano Rotondo and Santi Nereo e Achilleo date from this period. The Accademia di San Luca was founded in 1577 with the purpose of promulgating the church-approved style of painting.

Another fruit of this period was Caravaggio, although his life-like figures and details, such as saints with dirty finger nails, did not meet with undiluted approval from a public used to the daintier figures of Raphael and Michelangelo, or from factions of the Church who found such naturalism blasphemous.

Baroque begins in Rome

While the Renaissance was imported from Florence, the baroque style started in Rome. Although it may seem strange that the purism of the end of the 16th century should lead to the ornate baroque style of the 17th, both were provoked by the fear that Protestantism would weaken the power of the Catholic Church.

By the 1620s, extravagantly decorated churches with *trompe l'oeil* ceiling paintings and gold-encrusted altars were thought more likely to entice people back into the Catholic fold than portrayals of suffering. The basic shapes of these buildings still owed much to

some impression in spite of its small size. Other highlights of the era include Sant'Ignazio Loyola, which belonged to the Jesuits, and the less ornate Chiesa Nuova. The latter was built for Filippo Neri, who is said to have set his richer followers to work as labourers on the building.

With Rome established as a political and social centre, leading families wanted to demonstrate their wealth and prestige by building massive palaces in the city centre and villas in pleasure grounds outside. The Villa Borghese dates from this period, as do parts of the Palazzo Doria Pamphilj, the Villa Doria Pamphilj and Palazzi di Montecitorio and Barberini. Once again artists

classical models but now everything was highly decorated with statuary and reliefs. Size and impact were the main themes explored in baroque architecture.

This was the age of Bernini and Borromini, whose facades grace most main streets and piazzas in central Rome. Bernini's fountains decorate Piazza Barberini and Piazza Navona, and his sculptures are on Ponte Sant'Angelo, in the Villa Borghese and in churches across Rome. The church of Sant'Andrea al Quirinale was one of Bernini's masterpieces. It creates an awe-

LEFT: Villa Farnesina. **ABOVE:** the flamboyant baroque nave of Sant'Andrea della Valle.

flocked to Rome to cash in on the patronage of its great families. Velasquez, Rubens and Poussin all have major works in Rome.

In the second half of the 17th century, however, the funding dried up. The turmoil of the Reformation was replaced by political squabbles in which art and architecture had little part to play. There have been plenty of smaller improvement and building programmes since the baroque period, but none has marked the city quite so deeply.

The buildings and monuments of Bernini, Borromini and their contemporaries remain, creating a cityscape that is as Roman as the Colosseum and the Forum. ❑

BERNINI AND THE BAROQUE

The Roman Baroque style, perfected by Bernini, was the model for European baroque, celebrating an "age of display, make-believe and emotions"

Gianlorenzo Bernini (1598–1680) was at the forefront of Roman baroque, pioneering sublime and spectacular effects. Although more restrained than elsewhere in Europe, Roman Baroque is theatrical, bold, at times bombastic. Bernini's Rome is an open-air gallery of fountains and facades. Palaces and churches boast sweeping curves, majestic facades and theatrical vistas flanked by flights of steps. As a virtuoso architect and sculptor, Bernini worked in broad brush-strokes, with illusionistic verve. At ease with interiors and exteriors, he was a showman renowned for his theatricality and technical brilliance.

Bernini's style found favour with a succession of popes. Even St Peter's is, in part, a Bernini creation, graced by enfolding, keyhole-shaped colonnades. Other masterpieces include the witty design for an elephant to bear the obelisk of Santa Maria sopra Minerva *(above)* and the graceful angels on Ponte Sant'Angelo. As for palaces, Palazzo Barberini (1629–33) heralded the Baroque style and was completed by Bernini, assisted by Borromini. Their great rivalry has enriched the cityscape and is enshrined in popular legend: on Bernini's Four Rivers fountain in Piazza Navona, the allegorical statue of the River Nile supposedly shields its face, recoiling in horror from the Borromini facade beyond. In fact, the fountain was unveiled in 1651, a year before Borromini's Sant'Agnese was even started.

◁ **APOLLO AND DAPHNE**
Displayed with other Bernini masterpieces in the Galleria Borghese, this is Bernini's most famous sculpture. The magnificent, if youthful, work shows the nymph fleeing from the sun god.

▷ **PIAZZA NAVONA**
Rome's loveliest Baroque square is home to three fountains and other works by the arch-rival architects, Bernini and Borromini. In the foreground is Bernini's Fontana del Moro. Bernini's sumptuous fountains vie for attention with Borromini's church of Sant'Agnese, with its striking interplay of towers, dome and facade.

△ **TRITON**
The Fontana del Moro ("Moor Fountain"), on the southern end of Piazza Navona, is based on Bernini's designs.

▽ **BAROQUE BALDACHIN**
The baldacchino, Bernini's stupendous canopy in the nave of St Peter's, crowns the Papal Altar.

FRANCESCO BORROMINI

Borromini (1599–1667), Bernini's lifelong rival, made use of revolutionary, gravity-defying architectural forms. While Borromini lacked the confidence and all-round virtuosity of Bernini, his churches abound in visual tricks. His work is character-ised by a sculptural quality, the alternation of convex and concave forms, and a fondness for geometric designs as well as for games of light and shade. San Carlo alle Quattro Fontane was Borromini's first solo commission. Based on an oval design, the ingenious church is notable for its illusionistic dome *(above)*. The sinuous, seemingly swaying walls inspired countless baroque artists.

◁ **FOUNTAIN OF THE FOUR RIVERS**
The allegorical figures of Bernini's Fontana dei Quattro Fiumi (1651) represent the Danube, Ganges, Nile and Plate (the rivers of Paradise) and allude to the four corners of the world and the pervasive power of the papacy. Dominating the Piazza Navona, the popular fountain makes use of such sculptural details as seashells, foliage and rocks to complement the shimmering, watery setting.

▷ **BAROQUE PEARL**
Bernini's Sant'Andrea al Quirinale (1658–70) is a subtle *tour de force* inspired by Michelangelo's architectural feats. Reminiscent of an aristocratic ball-room, the oval Jesuit church uses its elliptical interior, illusionistic decoration and multi-coloured marble to great effect.

ANNO · DOM · MDCCCLVIII

PONT · MAX · ANNO

PIVS · NONVS · ANON

MATER·PVRISS

VIRGO·POTENS

FIDES

THE VATICAN STATE

This country has only 200 passport holders, and the pope always holds passport No. 1. But it is a country that has wealth and influence far beyond its size

Size cannot be the only measure of a nation's power or importance, otherwise the Vatican would warrant hardly any attention at all. The Vatican stands as the prime exception to the rule that postage-stamp-sized nations are famous for little more than their postage stamps.

Covering a total area of slightly more than 40 hectares (100 acres), Vatican City is by far the world's smallest independent sovereign entity. What other nation is as small as New York's Central Park? What other nation can lock its gates at midnight, as the Vatican's doorkeepers do each night, opening them only at the ring of a bell? What other nation can be crossed at a leisurely pace in well under an hour?

For centuries the Vatican was the unchallenged centre of the Western world. Its symbolic significance, both past and present, and its enduring international role as both a religious and a diplomatic force, have put this tiny city-state on a par with nations many million times larger. No matter how secular the world has become, divine authority seems still to count, and this serves to keep the Vatican much more than a geographic oddity, much more than an academic footnote.

Ancient origins

The Lateran Treaty of 1929, concluded between Pope Pius XI and Benito Mussolini, established the present territorial limits of the Vatican. The city is roughly trapezoidal in shape, bounded by medieval walls on all sides except on the corner, where the opening of St Peter's Piazza marks the border with Rome and the rest of Italy. Only St Peter's and the Vatican Museum complex are open to the public, although tours of the Vatican Gardens and St Peter's Necropolis (beneath the church) can be arranged through the Vatican Information Office, and the Vatican grounds can be admired from the observation deck on the dome of the church. The

LEFT: ceiling art in the Hall of the Immaculate Conception, the Vatican. **RIGHT:** Swiss Guards on duty.

impressive array of palaces and office buildings behind the walls includes a Vatican prison, a supermarket, and the printing press, which churns out the daily missive *L'Osservatore Romano* and scripts in a wide range of languages, from Coptic to Ecclesiastical Georgian to Tamil. In short, the Vatican is much more than

an oversized museum. It has everything a small state needs.

Subjects of the Holy See

Like other states, the Vatican protects its citizens – though there are just over 400 of them (including 46 curial cardinals, about 90 Swiss Guards, and some 200 bearers of diplomatic passports). To hold a Vatican passport is to belong to one of the world's most exclusive clubs. Vatican citizens either live or work permanently in the city or are abroad on diplomatic missions for the Catholic Church. The privilege of citizenship hinges on a direct and continuous relationship with the Holy See. When ties are severed, the privilege is lost. There is one person for whom severance ordinarily comes only with death: the Pope himself. He carries passport No. 1. He also rules absolutely over Vatican City and holds ultimate authority within the Catholic Church.

Within the Vatican and Catholic hierarchies, the Pope's power is unchallenged. A glance at his official titles, as listed in the *Annuario Pontificio*, the official Vatican directory, dispels any doubt of this supremacy: Bishop of Rome, Vicar of Christ, Successor of the Prince of the Apostles, Supreme Pontiff of the Universal Church, Patriarch of the West, Primate of Italy, Arch-

1993 encyclical (a letter sent to all Roman Catholic bishops), which was six years in the making and part of a concerted plan to purge dissident theologians, denounced contraception, homosexuality and other infringements of the Catholic faith as "intrinsically evil".

Picking the Pontiff

The process of electing a pope is unique, and it makes the papacy the world's only elective monarchy. The Sacred College of Cardinals, a largely titular body of 120 bishops and archbishops appointed by the Pope, assumes responsibility for the selection, convening soon after

bishop and Metropolitan of the Roman Province, Sovereign of the State of Vatican City, Servant of the Servants of God.

The Pope's role is shown by the root of the word "pope". In Greek, *pappas* meant "father" – in this case the spiritual father of mankind. Although the papacy's claim to universality has been eroded since St Peter became Heaven's representative on earth, the Pope's image remains paternal, ordinarily demonstrated by a benevolent concern for the advancement of humanity, occasionally by stern warnings against theological or spiritual deviation. John Paul II, elected in 1978, the year of three popes, has asserted his moral authority vigorously. His

the death knell tolls in the Vatican Palace.

The electors are sealed into the Sistine Chapel – no cameras or tape recorders are allowed – and cannot leave until a new successor has been chosen. Voting can proceed by any one of three methods: by acclamation, whereby divine inspiration provokes the cardinals all to shout the same name at the same time; by scrutiny, in which four ballots are cast daily until one candidate has captured a two-thirds majority plus one; or, as a last resort, by compromise, entrusting a small group to hammer out a resolution.

All modern popes have been selected by the second method. The process is quite speedy. John Paul II was elected in two days, his predecessor, the short-lived John Paul I, in one. But outside authorities have occasionally hurried the cardinals along. After the death of Innocent III in 1216, local magnate Matteo Rosso Orsini forced the electors to enjoy the company of the pope's corpse. Gregory X (1271–76) ordained that after five days the cardinals should be put on a diet of bread and water.

Paper ballots are burned after each tally, and onlookers eagerly await the tell-tale smoke from the chapel's chimney: dark smoke indicates an inconclusive

PETER'S PENCE

The Vatican has two major sources of income: interest from its investments and donations made in every Catholic church on the feast day of St Peter and Paul.

Vatican City and the Church as a whole (they were declared infallible in matters relating to faith by the First Vatican Council in 1870), the immensity of their responsibilities obviously necessitates substantial assistance.

Governance of the Vatican itself is handled by the Pontifical Commission for the state of Vatican City, which consists of seven cardinals, and a lay official, who directs the city-state's administrative affairs. But it is the task of shepherding the spiritual deportment of more than

vote while white plumes denote a winner (electors are provided with special chemicals labelled *bianco* and *nero* so that there can be no mistake). The cardinal dean announces, "*Habemus Papam*," and the chosen cardinal appears in one of three robes (sized small, medium and large) kept on hand for the occasion. The coronation takes place on the following day.

Governing the Vatican

Although popes have absolute legislative, executive, judicial and doctrinal authority over both

Left: a papal audience with Pope John Paul II.
Above: conferring en route through St Peter's Square.

800 million Catholics worldwide, and of managing a global religious bureaucracy composed of 4,000 bishops, 400,000 priests, and at least 1 million nuns, that occupies the time of the great majority of those who work within the Vatican walls. This highly organised body of institutional supervisors (effectively the Vatican's civil service) is known as the Roman Curia. It directs everything from the Church's diplomatic and missionary affairs to the interpretation of Catholic marriage law. It handles all correspondence, organises papal trips, oversees budgets and advises on international diplomacy.

The Curia comprises nine congregations, 12 pontifical councils, five offices, 25 commissions and committees and three tribunals. The most important of the congregations is the Congregation for the Doctrine of the Faith, at one time known by the more notorious name of the Sacred Inquisition. This polices the interpretation of the Catholic faith and denounces anyone who offends it. It was the Sacred Inquisition that condemned Galileo to life imprisonment for supporting the Copernican theory that the earth revolves around the sun.

Of the 4,000 or so people employed in Vati-

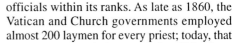

UNIFORM COLOURS

The Swiss Guards' uniform is said to have been designed by Michelangelo.

officials within its ranks. As late as 1860, the Vatican and Church governments employed almost 200 laymen for every priest; today, that ratio is reversed to 200 priests for every layman.

The Second Vatican Council, which was opened by John XXIII in 1962 and lasted into the reign of Paul VI, was responsible for many of the recent changes within the Catholic Church. As well as giving bishops more authority and encouraging the use of "the vernacular" (ie, languages other than Latin) for the celebration of

can City, most operate within the Curia. Once plump with sinecures, this organisation has been markedly pared down in recent times. However, the tightening up could easily go further still. The position of Secretary of Briefs to Princes and of Italian Letters, for instance, is responsible primarily for adapting the dead language of Rome for such new words as "telephone" and "airport". A standard joke about the Vatican's extravagance is that the city's "SCV" licence plates stand not for *Stato della Città del Vaticano* but rather for *Se Cristo Vedesse* – "If Christ could see …".

As well as criticising wasteful practices, the Curia has reformed its policy of elevating lay

Mass, it revised the circumstances under which canonisation could take place.

Most prominent among the non-initiate members of the Vatican are the Swiss Guards, who are exclusively charged with protecting the Holy See. This corps of men – all Catholic, all Swiss, all brightly dressed in blue, red and yellow uniforms – may seem no more than an ornamental regiment. In fact, the Guards have a history of military prowess dating back to the early 16th century. Pope Julius II, impressed by the calibre of Swiss soldiers, introduced the Guards in 1506.

Today their function is not unlike that performed by the Secret Service in America. Rules state that they must be between 19 and 30 years of age and unmarried when they are engaged for their two-year contract. However, they are allowed to marry within these two years if they can secure a married couple's apartment within the Vatican.

Vatican treasures

The Swiss Guards also watch over one of the greatest art collections in the world. The Sistine Chapel is among the most visited sights in Rome, attracting as many as 20,000 people each day, and the Vatican Library, founded by Pope Nicholas V in the 15th century, contains the

However, this fabulous heritage of art and architecture raises income only from admission charges to the museums and from the sales of postcards, books and souvenirs in the museum shops. In 1987 the Vatican opened its ledgers to the public for the first time, and the US magazine *Fortune* was prompted to state that "With investments of some $500 million, the Vatican commands fewer financial resources than many US universities."

The Vatican's financial affairs have not been helped by the scandals surrounding Vatican involvement in Italy's ill-fated Banco Ambrosiano in the early 1980s. The Vatican was forced

S·PETRVS·DE·MVRANO·ANACORETA·IN·PONTIFICEM·ELIGITVR

world's greatest collection of medieval and Renaissance manuscripts. And apart from the many great masterpieces that are fixtures and fittings of the Vatican – including works by Michelangelo, Raphael, Rosselli, Botticelli, Raphael – there are the art collections. These are wide-ranging in their tastes, running from Egyptian and Greek sculpture to 20th-century works by self-confessed communists, such as Diego Rivera and Picasso.

FAR LEFT: Pinturicchio's painting of Alexander VI, a Renaissance pope. **LEFT:** *Miracle of the Mass at Bolsena*, one of the Vatican's many works by Raphael. **ABOVE:** rich tapestries form part of the collection.

to pay out millions of dollars when Ambrosiano collapsed in 1982.

Secure outlook

The Vatican is distinguished by much more than artistic masterpieces. The powers of the Pope and the Church would survive without Vatican City, but its existence helps ensure the continued respect and deference of the world's other leaders. Supported by centuries of tradition and history, the Vatican is unlikely to be incorporated into Italy. Some would argue it is best that a body of the spirit maintains this small perch against the onslaught of governments answering to less thoughtful authorities. ❑

THE CITY'S CHANGING FACE

Every city needs to stay modern, but when you have an architectural legacy like
Rome's, how can you improve without destroying vital parts of the past?

Rome has been a centre of great political power throughout its 2,700-year history. It was home to ancient emperors, then popes; became capital of the new Italian nation in 1870; was the heart of the stillborn empire Mussolini imagined. Each of these periods of greatness has left its mark on today's city.

Rightly or wrongly, the Romans have been blamed for mistreating their archaeological and architectural legacy since ancient times. Emperor Maxentius (AD 306–312) accused his contemporaries of tearing down "magnificent old buildings" to get material for new houses. Pope Pius II (1458–64) shuddered at people burning marble monuments to obtain lime. Popular slogans derided Urban VIII's impact on the city thus: "What the barbarians didn't do, the Barberini did," it was claimed.

The German writer Goethe (1749–1832) made a similar complaint when he said, "What the barbarians left standing, modern architects have destroyed", and in the 19th century the German historian Ferdinand Gregorius (1821–91) raised his voice in thunderous outcry over the Piedmontese remodelling of the papal city. In the 20th century Alberto Moravia classified four-fifths of the city as "a disaster area of civic architecture". Yet these sharp-tongued critics stayed in Rome for months or years. What draws people to this city, and what keeps them here?

Firstly, Rome has the sort of beauty that provokes passionate response. Every corner seems to have something worth stopping to look at; a green shady courtyard with a dribbling fountain; an extravagant baroque facade; a colourful market that's been there for centuries; or an ancient obelisk that blocks the traffic in a way no modern city planner would allow.

A visible past

Rome is a city standing on the shoulders of its predecessors where layers of history run into each other. Not only were materials taken from

older buildings to make new ones, but buildings themselves were adapted to suit the city's changing needs. Medieval church towers rise above the remains of ancient houses; a Renaissance palace balances on top of the Theatre of Marcellus next to a 20th-century restoration of the theatre as luxury apartments; ancient aque-

ducts run along the railway lines leading into Stazione Termini. Even when the buildings have disappeared their shapes remain. One of the key features of Italian city life – the piazza – is a direct descendant of the ancient forum.

Caesar's improvements

Julius Caesar (101–44 BC) was the first to introduce a programme for improving the city. It was highly necessary, for Rome was nowhere near as splendid as its imperial role demanded. "How strange that everywhere we were invited in Rome, we ate off the same silver plates," the Carthaginian ambassador had remarked a hundred years previously. But soon Rome was

LEFT: exhibition scaffolding in the Mussolini-inspired EUR district on the outskirts. **RIGHT:** St Peter's dome.

flaunting its wealth. Under Caesar, 640 gladiators wore silver armour at the city's games.

The Theatre of Pompey, Rome's first permanent theatre, dates from this time. It was intended to offer more sophisticated Greek-style theatre than the bloodthirsty spectacles Ancient Romans usually enjoyed. In fact, this civilising gesture met with only limited success, and the theatre was soon showing as much gore as any of its rivals. The shape of the round building can still be seen behind Campo de' Fiori;

DEVELOPMENT PLAN

The city was intended to develop in the shape of a six-pointed star, supposedly suggested by a comet that Emperor Augustus had seen as a young man.

Under Emperor Augustus the urbanisation of the Campus Martius began in the area now covered by the *Centro Storico*, and was divided into *rioni* – the zones of central Rome that still exist today. The first of the Imperial Fora also date from Augustus's time. By now Rome was the biggest city in the world and its population was too large to be supported by the original Forum.

Ancient Rome was heavily built up. The *insulae* or apartment blocks rose so high that after the fire of AD 64 destroyed

Via di Grotta Pinta follows its curve. The Julian Basilica was also built under Caesar. The new piazza, surrounded by a double row of buildings, had little shops along one side. They were divided into mezzanine floors and had embossed rounded arches (which later became models for Renaissance architecture). It was both a fitting tribute to Caesar and a useful addition to the city for the one million inhabitants who by then lived in Rome.

The Emperor Augustus (27 BC–AD 14) liked to boast that he had found Rome made of brick and left it made of marble. The marble remnants of ancient times that we find in today's buildings mostly date from this period.

the city centre, a decree of Nero's limited their height to 20 metres (60 ft).

In the wake of the fire, a vigorous argument began between the lovers of old historic Rome, who wanted the picturesque alleys retained, and Nero, the innovator and self-glorifier, who wanted broad avenues and low buildings against which to display monuments dedicated to himself. (In fact there were rumours that Nero had had the fire started in order to clear land for his Golden House, a massive palace complex and private pleasure ground covering 140 hectares/ 346 acres.) More practically, Nero forbade the use of wooden ceilings and insisted on the provision of water buckets in houses.

Little of this remains because it was destroyed by Nero's successors (Vespasian 69–79, Titus 79–81 and Domitian 81–96). As part of a public relations exercise to win popularity and dissociate themselves from the notorious Nero, they erected more democratic centres of enjoyment on the site. These included the Colosseum, on land originally covered by Nero's lake. Emperor Domitian's legacy to Rome was the stadium over which Piazza Navona was built.

One of Rome's greatest architects was Apollodorus of Damascus. Master builder of the Emperor Trajan (98–117), he was responsible for Trajan's Forum and the well-preserved

factions within the Catholic Church curbed papal authority. However, most of the churches that exist today were founded during the Middle Ages, and, although some of them have been completely rebuilt since then, many incorporate medieval fragments, towers in particular. Indeed, towers of a military nature were also erected during this troubled period. Surviving towers include the Torre delle Milizie (1309) which rises above Trajan's Markets.

Reconstruction of Rome

In 1447, Pope Nicholas V embarked upon a programme of rebuilding that included the remod-

covered market-place behind it. At the time the market-place was a revolutionary idea and, for a while, it was regarded as one of the wonders of the world. Trajan also built a massive bath complex on land previously covered by Nero's Golden House.

Few major buildings have survived from the period between the fall of the Roman Empire and the Renaissance. Rome had lost the money, power and prestige it had enjoyed as the centre of an empire, and constant wars and squabbling

FAR LEFT: excavating the layers. **LEFT:** sitting on the fence. **ABOVE:** shoring up the past during restoration of Ponte Sant'Angelo, parts of which date from AD 136.

elling of many architectural masterpieces, such as St Peter's. He also became the patron of many artists, craftsmen, humanists, and literary scholars, thus triggering a boom in the arts that lasted for well over 200 years. Nicholas transferred the seat of papal power from the Lateran Palace to the Vatican.

Sixtus IV (1471–84) commissioned the Sistine Bridge, the first bridge to be built across the Tiber for more than 1,000 years. Alexander VI (1492–1503), the Borgia pope, fortified the Castel Sant'Angelo and started work on the Palazzo della Cancelleria. A few years later came Julius II, whose personal architect, Bramante, started work on the new St Peter's – although he died long before work was completed, leaving others, including Raphael and Michelangelo, to take over where he left off.

Leo X (1513–21) commissioned Via di Ripetta, to link the family palace of the Medici and Porto di Ripetta. Another Medici, Clement VII (1523–34), had Via del Babuino built and thus created the "trident" of streets flowing away from Piazza del Popolo. In 1536 Michelangelo drew up the first plans for the rebuilt Campidoglio for Pope Paul III.

Sixtus V's (1585–90) main contribution to city planning was to improve communications for pilgrim traffic. His network of streets built

and papal families who wanted to glorify the Catholic Church, themselves or both. Most of Piazza Navona belongs to this period as do many of the churches, particularly the large or ornate ones, such as Sant'Andrea al Quirinale, the Gesù and Chiesa Nuova. After this the speed and scale of the changes made to Rome's cityscape decreased.

Throughout the 18th century works and improvements were carried out on a smaller scale, although two of the city's most famous sights date from this time.

The Spanish Steps, built to link the French church of the Trinità dei Monti with Piazza di

to link all the city gates is still mostly intact. The Via Felice connected the Porta del Popolo in the north with S. Maria Maggiore and S. Croce in Gerusalemme. With the existing streets it formed a system with four nodal points, at which obelisks were erected: Piazza del Popolo, S. Maria Maggiore, S. Giovanni and S. Pietro. Fortunately Sixtus died before he could implement his plan to demolish the Colosseum, which blocked his route from the Lateran Palace to St Peter's.

Many of the main sights in Rome's *Centro Storico* date from the 17th century, when architects such as Bernini and Borromini designed buildings and monuments for a string of popes

Spagna, were completed in 1726, while the Trevi Fountain, designed by Nicola Salvi for Clement XII, was finished in 1762.

During the 19th century there was political unrest – including outbreaks of war – that was caused firstly by French occupation and then by the struggles to unify Italy. This meant that there were few major architectural developments. The main exception is the Piazza del Popolo and the Pincio Gardens, which were designed by Giuseppe Valadier (1762–1839).

The modern city

From then on, most of the changes made to Rome were utilitarian rather than aesthetic. In

1856 the railway line from Rome to Frascati was opened and the first station was built at Termini in 1862 (although the present Fascist-inspired building was started before World War II and finished in 1950).

After Unification in 1870 the popes ceased to control Rome and Garibaldi and King Vittorio Emanuele became the figures most often celebrated in statues, street names and monuments (most notably the unmissable Vittorio Emanuele monument on Piazza Venezia).

More practical developments included the major roads crossing the city, such as Via Nazionale and Via Cavour. New residential

Then Mussolini ushered in a programme of dramatic changes with his plans to build a city that was fit to be the seat of his intended new Italian empire. Vast roads were cut through the medieval quarter around St Peter's, destroying among other buildings the house where Raphael once lived. Parts of the Fori Romani were covered over to create a suitable avenue for Fascist processions.

On the outskirts of the city he started work on the EUR quarter and the Foro Italico, while massive new buildings were erected all over Rome to house important institutions such as the University and the Post Office.

zones in old neighbourhoods such as Testaccio, and new developments on the city's periphery also date from this period.

Further improvements included the river embankment, the Lungotevere, started in 1870, which put a stop to the regular floods that had plagued Rome until then.

The 1920s saw the creation of the Art Nouveau Coppedè Quarter around Piazza Mincio and the building of the Garbatella residential quarter on what were then the city's outskirts.

LEFT: grafitti ancient and modern. **ABOVE:** the King Vittorio Emanuele II monument, known locally as the "typewriter" or "wedding cake".

The city expands

The famous *Agro Romano* was a wide landscape of hills and fields stretching out from the gates of the city. It was crossed by the consuls' ancient roads and inhabited by farmers and herdsmen.

The idea of building self-enclosed estates on the edge of Rome was first mooted in the town development plans of the "Red" people's bloc under Ernesto Nathan in 1907.

Since 1870 Rome had been the goal of a steady stream of immigrants from the south and Abruzzi. In 1922 there were about 800,000 inhabitants. Just before World War II the number had risen to 1.3 million; by the end of the war it was 1.8 million. Mussolini decided Rome needed "living space and greatness". After his first attempts with detached houses he began building the *borgate* of Prenestina, Pietralata and San Basilio. These were so depressing both in form and material that Pietralata, Tiburtina and Quarticciolo soon became symbols of wretchedness. They were inhabited by poor immigrants from the south and from the mountains. Between 1950 and 1976 slums engirdled Rome. Meanwhile, at the other end of the social scale, the wealthy got planning permission to build on the Via Appia.

Rome has expanded so fast since 1961 that

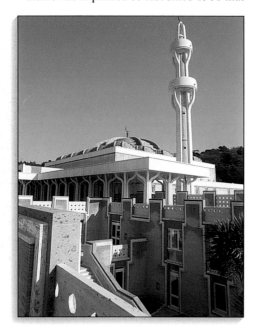

the Agro Romano has disappeared inside the Raccordo Annulare (ring-road). Some 600,000 people moved into developments that had never been planned by any commission, and the number of *borgate*, or *suburbi*, rose to 26.

In 1976, after the election of the communist mayor Carlo Giulio Argan, Rome's great slum clearance started. The *borgate* were given lighting, power, mains water and bus routes. Then came supposedly exemplary new areas such as Tor Bella Mónaca and Tor de' Cenci. But in spite of their architectural modernity and sensible planning, they developed the problems typical of such districts worldwide: poverty, poor services and bad communications. For a while it

seemed there would never be any changes made to central Rome, though better living standards for the city's inhabitants was a key political issue. Most policies included improved public transport, especially the grossly inadequate metro. The much-discussed traffic problem was half-heartedly addressed by introducing pedestrian precincts in some of the most congested areas of the *Centro Storico* and by sporadically banning private cars from entering the centre.

Rome's rejuvenation

Then, after decades of neglect, seemingly endless restoration projects and plans, and a hugely increased environmental toll, the corner was turned. Many of the facades and historical sites that so many come to see are starting to come forth from behind the scaffolding, looking better than ever. Most notably, the city had a facelift for Italy hosting the 1990 World Cup. Some major fountains and facades were treated to delay their decay in the Roman smog. This gives an uncannily new appearance to buildings that had been covered by the grime of centuries.

The most significant new building shows how far the city has come since the popes had the last word on every new building in Rome. Paolo Portoghesi's Mosque, in Villa Ada, was built with major funding from the nearby Egyptian embassy and finished in 1992.

In the early 1990s, Michelangelo's frescoes in the Sistine Chapel were brilliantly restored. But the work has not stopped there. Although the city lost a bid to host the 2004 Summer Olympics, there is ample reason to maintain the momentum of public works that improve the city. Due to the considerable efforts made in anticipation of the celebrations for the year 2000, the city has become far more visitor friendly, with facades restored, zones pedestrianised, tourist services enhanced and museum opening hours extended – improvements that will all be appreciated long after the Holy Year is forgotten. ❑

LEFT: Rome's new mosque, designed by Paolo Portoghesi, 1992. **RIGHT:** the Pyramid of Caio Cestio.

CITY OF THE DEAD

"A desert of decay, sombre and desolate; and with a history in every stone that strews the ground" (Charles Dickens)

The catacombs are the place for spiritual pilgrimage, pleasurable terror, or romantic musings on mortality. For health reasons and habit, the Romans buried their dead outside the city walls; the Appian Way is lined with the tombs of Romans, Christians and Jews – and, for the less wealthy, catacombs, whose labyrinthine galleries are lined with niches (loculi) built into the tufa rock on different levels.

While Christian and Jewish practice was burial of the body, Romans believed in cremation, with the ashes buried in an urn. Christian bodies, embalmed or shrouded in linen, were placed on ledges in the walls, sealed beneath marble slabs on the floor or interred in family vaults (cubicula). The Christianisation of Rome led to the cult of the early martyrs with pilgrimages and renewed interest in the catacombs. The relics of St Peter and St Paul may have been hidden here during the 3rd century. The frescoed interiors are adorned with Christian symbols or graffiti, from the dove, fish or anchor to acanthus leaves and vines.

While some are mossy and mouldering, the weather-worn tombs make an impressive proclamation of faith. It was not Roman practice to desecrate the tombs of any sect but in the course of time some have suffered from relic-mongers. Today, Via Appia is an inspired or desolate scene, depending on one's mood.

▽ **MEMORIAL IN THE CATACOMBS OF SAN CALLISTO**
Callisto was born a slave and became pope before dying as a Christian martyr in 222. These catacombs were only rediscovered in 1850.

▷ **HYPOGEUM**
This chamber is part of an underground tomb or *ipogeo*. These were often frescoed, depicting pagan scenes such as funerary feasts or blood sacrifice. Although Charles Dickens found it "so sad, so quiet, so sullen", Henrik Ibsen enjoyed lying among the tombs – "and I do not think this idling can be called a waste of time".

△ **ST SEBASTIAN**
This fresco, a particularly delicate tomb decoration, is in the catacombs dedicated to the Roman soldier who became a Christian martyr.

△ **JEWISH CATACOMBS**
Many Jews converted to Christianity, but those who kept their faith were buried separately.

SUBTERRANEAN SCENE

"My visit to the Catacombs was not much of a success," confessed Goethe in 1788, who waited "for the return of other visitors who were more daring and less sensitive than I was". More intrepid explorers can sample the city's contemporary subterranean scene, preferably not in the catacombs. The district now draws Romans in search of hallucinatory or erotic experiences.

Elsewhere, celebrities have left the *dolce vita* haunts of Via Veneto for underground cellar bars in the historic centre. However, when the ancient catacombs pall, Rome also offers Disneyfied subterranea, with cavernous clubs adorned as Roman temples. The cellars of Bevitoria, a wine bar on Piazza Navona, incorporate the remains of Domitian's stadium. Grotto-like bars are snugly ensconced in the historic centre.

Subterranean Rome, often synonymous with alternative, is personified by Testaccio clubland. The slopes of Monte Testaccio have long been home to drinking dens carved into the caverns. Ideally, a subterranean Roman night would end in a "troglodyte" hotel: Teatro di Pompeo, for example, displays a dining room built into the remains of a Roman theatre.

◁ TEMPLE OF MITHRAS
Underground Rome has more to offer than catacombs. This first-century temple, dedicated to a polytheistic Persian cult, lies below San Clemente. In a relief, Mithras is depicted slaying a bull, the symbol of fertility; converts were sprinkled with bull's blood.

▷ COLUMN IN THE CATACOMBS OF PRISCILLA
These catacombs are amongst the most ancient and contain the earliest known Madonna (2nd century), as well as a Greek chapel and burial galleries littered with *loculi* (burial niches) carved into the walls.

FOOD AND DRINK

For Romans, the very act of eating is celebrated as much as the food itself. Simple yet delicious dishes are the city's mainstay

Culinary traditions run deep in Rome, reaching back to the ancient peoples who first populated the region. For centuries the Romans have held firm against the influence of many new ingredients, dishes and cooking techniques that have come as a result of Rome's contact with the rest of the world, as well as the fads of the upper classes, emperors and popes.

Though exotically spiced sauces, fancy game dishes and "delicacies" like fried parrots' tongues dressed with honey, have faded into history, something does remain from the high cuisine of the past: the decided pleasure with which Romans go to table. It is probably not the place to hunt down the top restaurants – few consider *la cucina romana* to be the best of Italy's regional cuisines – but Rome may well be one of Italy's most pleasurable cities in which to dine. Often, what might seem to be slow service is merely the Roman way of stretching the meal out into the night. In general, restaurants plan on one seating per evening, so you will not be rushed, or pressured to leave. When in Rome, make a point of having a long, lingering meal (in the open air, if weather allows).

La Cucina Romana

A good portion of the local cuisine involves offal, the so-called *quinto-quarto* (fifth quarter) of the animal. While dishes like *rigatoni con pajata* (pasta with veal intestines) and *trippa alla romana* (tripe with tomato sauce, Roman mint and *pecorino*) are long-time local favourites, you will find that most restaurants in the centre of town tend to avoid such specialities in favour of dishes from other parts of the country which are more familiar to their clientele, such as pasta with pesto sauce, risotto and polenta. But you needn't eat innards to eat Roman, and every restaurant will have at least a few home-grown dishes, all of them sharing

LEFT: a variety of pasta shapes.
ABOVE RIGHT: a tempting array of *antipasti,* including grilled aubergine, roast peppers and *bruschetta* (toasted bread with garlic, olive oil and tomatoes).

the frugality that marks the region's food, perhaps better called cooking than "cuisine". Pricey restaurants offer adventurous dishes with long names, but the menu of a typical Roman eatery tells a different, less complicated story: *spaghetti alla carbonara* (with rendered bacon, egg and *pecorino* cheese), *bucatini alla gricia*

(with *guanciale* – cured pork jowl), *cacio e pepe* (with *pecorino* cheese and black pepper) and *all'amatriciana* (with *guanciale* or rendered bacon and tomato sauce) all share an undeniable simplicity. Pasta even makes its way into Roman soups: *pasta e ceci* (chick pea soup flavoured with rosemary) and *broccoli e arzilla* (clear soup of broccoli and skate fish). *Gnocchi alla romana* (potato dumplings in a meat sauce) are traditionally prepared on Thursdays, while *baccalà* (salt cod) is served on Fridays.

Nor is fish fussed over: clams tossed with spaghetti and olive oil becomes *spaghetti alle vongole* and *pesce azzurro* (fish from the sea) is baked in the oven *(al forno)* or cooked on the grill *(ai ferri or alla griglia)*. Two common meat dishes are *saltimbocca alla romana* (veal slices rolled with prosciutto and sage) and *coda alla vaccinara* (braised oxtail in a tomato and celery sauce), but the meat to try is *abbacchio* (milk-fed lamb), usually roasted with herbs and garlic or *alla scottadito* (grilled chops).

Save room for vegetables, which abound in Rome's produce markets all year long and find their way to the table in basic preparations, often steamed or blanched, then briefly sautéed. Romans are the undisputed masters of the artichoke, in season from November through April and traditionally prepared in several ways,

restaurants. A few common starters are melon or figs with *prosciutto* and *fiori di zucca* (deep fried *zucchini* flowers filled with mozzarella and anchovies). Popular desserts are *torta di ricotta* (ricotta tart), *panna cotta* (eggless firm custard made of cream and served with a fruit sauce) and *tiramisù* (Italian espresso trifle).

The local wines – those from Frascati are the most famous – are often lamented in guidebooks as not being as good as they once were. On the contrary, they are probably better than they have ever been, but pale in comparison with wines produced in other parts of the country, now much better known and readily available.

among them *carciofi alla giudia* (deep fried), and *carciofi alla romana* (stuffed with garlic and Roman mint and stewed). A typical winter salad is *puntarelle*, made from shredding the stalks of a local chicory and serving them with a lemon-anchovy dressing. Summer brings roasted peppers, aubergines and *zucchini* (courgettes) served in a variety of ways, and large tomatoes stuffed with herbs and rice, while in spring you'll see asparagus and *fave con pecorino* (raw broad beans served with *pecorino* cheese).

Many Italians are pleased to start right in on a first course and finish off a good meal with a piece of fruit. Accordingly, appetisers and desserts get little attention in most Roman

Wine bars are very popular in Rome, and offer a great alternative to a restaurant meal. Choose from usually about a dozen wines available by the glass (or from more than a thousand different labels by the bottle) and a great selection of high-quality cheeses, cured meats, and smoked fish, as well as soups and salads, quiches and gratins, and home-made desserts.

Roman pizza

Though it is the Neapolitans who are credited with inventing pizza, the Romans eat their fair share. There are more *pizzerie* than restaurants in town, and they even have their own version. A Roman pizza is plate-sized, rolled very thin and flat and baked in a wood-burning stove (*forno a legna*), while the Neapolitans make a thicker, softer pie with a raised border. A night out at a *pizzeria* (few are open for lunch) is a quintessential Roman experience.

On the go

For Romans, *gelato* (Italian ice-cream) is not as much dessert as it is an afternoon or after-dinner snack to accompany a stroll around town. Accordingly, *gela-terie* are never far away and stay open until late. Other treats to

PASTA MUSEUM

Gourmets should visit the Museo Nazionale delle Paste Alimentari (daily: 9.30am – 5.30pm, tel: 06 6991119), on Piazza Scanderbeg near the Trevi Fountain.

to find. Thicker than *pizzeria* pizza and topped with dozens of imaginative combinations, *pizza al taglio* is always sold by weight; an *etto* (100 grams) makes a small portion. A good number of these shops also sell *supplì* (fried balls of rice and mozzarella), a classic Roman snack.

For the gastronomically curious, a visit to a good *alimentaria* is as rewarding as a trip to any museum. You'll find regional products from all over the country, but the local cheese to try is *pecorino romano*, made from

pick up from street vendors around town are roasted chestnuts in autumn and winter and *grattachecca* (shaved ice with syrup) and water-melon wedges in the summer.

Romans often stop at the local bar a couple of times a day, for a breakfast of espresso or cap-puccino and a *cornetto* (the Italian version of the French *croissant*), followed by another espresso and perhaps a snack, such as a *panino* or *tramezzino* (small sandwiches).

Pizza al taglio (by the slice) is also very easy

ewe's milk into big wheels, which are bathed in brine and aged for 18 months. A by-product of this is *ricotta di pecora*, brought in fresh from the farms and delicious on its own. A memo-rable sandwich can be made from *porchetta* (whole roasted pig, sliced to order), a speciality of the towns in the hills around Rome. If you are not travelling any further, take the opportunity to try *mozzarella di bufala* (hand-made moz-zarella cheese, made from the milk of water buf-faloes), or several kinds of *prosciutto* from central and northern Italy. Two *alimentari* with particularly good quality and selection are Franchi (Via Cola di Rienzo 200), and Emilio Volpetti (Via Marmorata 47). ❑

LEFT: polenta with ragout of beef, garnished with sprigs of rosemary. **ABOVE:** Roman treats – tempting pastries topped with fresh fruit, cream and chocolate.

PLACES

*A detailed guide to the entire city, with principal
sights cross-referenced to the maps*

Rome is crammed with great sights. In no other city are the accumulated layers of history so evident. Every corner and crest seems to lead to a famous monument, church or square.

However, for first-time visitors trying to grapple with the layout of its 12 hills – not the seven usually attributed to it – the city can seem confusing. The best way to orientate oneself is to look upon Via del Corso as a spine, with the leafy Villa Borghese quarter at the top, the archaeological zone at the bottom, the Centro Storico to the west, Piazza di Spagna to the east, and the Vatican and Trastevere on the far bank of the River Tiber.

The order of the Places section in this book reflects both the sightseeing priorities of most visitors and, for the first three chapters, the key episodes in the city's history, tracing what Rose Macaulay in *The Pleasure of Ruins* called "the tale of western historical man". It thus begins with the archaeological zone, the city's foundations – including the Capitol, Forum, Palatine and the Colosseum – and then moves on to the Centro Storico, the dense centre of Rome contained in the great bend of the River Tiber.

From there, it moves across the Tiber for a tour of St Peter's and the Vatican. After this, the book dips into the quarters verging on these key areas – Via del Corso and Piazza di Spagna (Spanish Steps); the Villa Borghese quarter in the north of the city; fashionable Trastevere and the Gianicolo (Janiculum Hill) on the west bank; the university quarter of San Lorenzo near Stazione Termini; the Quirinale, Esquiline and Viminale Hills, and thence to more peripheral areas such as the Lateran, the Appian Way, and Aventine and Testaccio.

The section ends by exploring Mussolini's Rome – EUR to the south, and Foro Italico to the north – and then journeys into Rome's environs with a selection of easy day trips. Advice on getting around the city, and to sights and towns further afield, is contained in the *Travel Tips* section of this guide. ❑

PRECEDING PAGES: San Paolo fuori le Mura; ancient aqueduct on the Tuscolana; St Peter with the keys to the Kingdom of Heaven.
LEFT: finding one's bearings from Piazza San Pietro.

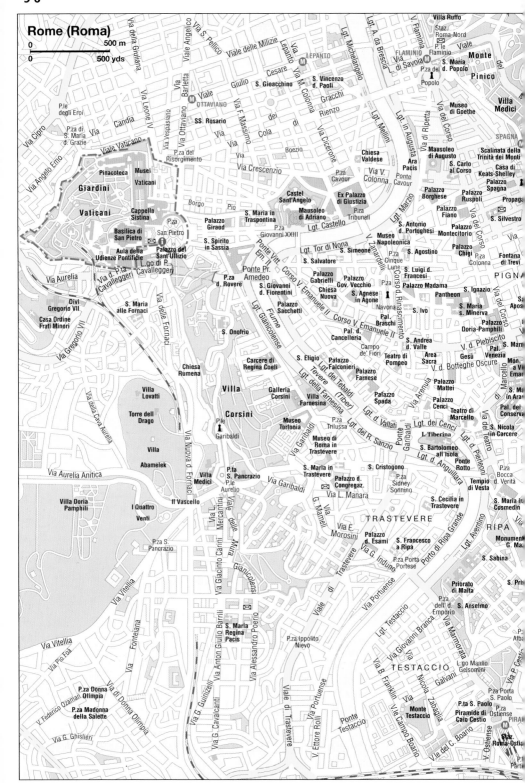

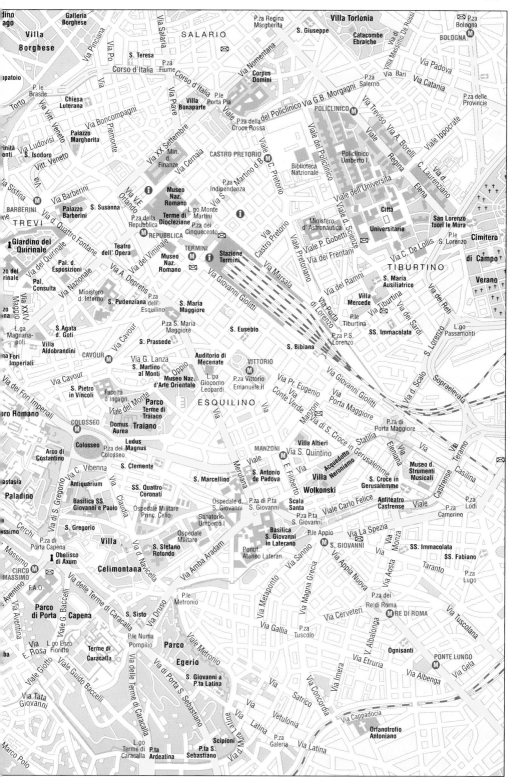

ROME'S FOUNDATIONS

Map, page 100

This chapter shows you some of the places where Ancient Rome thrived, declined and eventually fell. Here lie the remains of the Capitol, Forum, Palatine, the Colosseum and much more

A t 7.30 in the morning, a traffic jam blocks the intersection of Via Labicana and Via dei Fori Imperiali, the boulevard commissioned by Mussolini for the greater glory of the fascist empire. **Via dei Fori Imperiali** slices through the heart of Rome's ancient sites. Here, Nero built an artificial lake to grace his palace and the Flavians – in a bid to return the tyrant's palace to the people – built the Colosseum, the world's most famous amphitheatre. Now thumbs down have given way to feet down – on the accelerator.

Via dei Fori Imperiali – started in 1932 and then called Via dell'Impero – is a relatively recent attempt to use Ancient Rome's monuments to underwrite modern political ambition. Bulldozers flattened one of the city's oldest medieval quarters for the route, destroying approximately 5,500 flats. Some 280,000 cubic metres (366,200 cubic yards) of earth were removed, along with 50,000 cubic metres (65,400 cubic yards) of ancient walls, imperial palaces, temples and arches, some of which dated from the 3rd century BC.

Kowtowing architects ignored the archaeological massacre. When *Il Duce* ordered the removal of a pile of stones near the Colosseum, nobody pointed out that they marked the Meta Sudans, an ancient spring. Ludwig Curtius, then director of the German Archaeological Institute, said: "It would have been easy while building the street to excavate those parts of the Fora of Julius Caesar and of Trajan still lying underground, and to direct the road over them as a bridge, but the dictator, concerned only for his next demonstration of power, was in a hurry…"

Originally, Mussolini had hoped to excavate the Imperial Fora, which would have served as decoration alongside his new processional road, symbolically connecting his regime with the glory of Roman antiquity. If these plans had been followed, an Archaeological Park would have extended from the excavated Forum area to the ruins of the Baths of Caracalla and on to Via Appia Antica. Unfortunately, the project was never realised and the road, renamed Via dei Fori Imperiali, became a major thoroughfare. It is very unlikely that the ruins under the road will ever come to light.

LEFT: view of the Temple of Venus and Rome, with the church of Santa Francesca Romana behind. **BELOW:** two-wheeled carriages.

The Capitoline Hill

A good place to start a tour of Rome's ancient foundations is Capitoline Hill. Only 50 metres (150 ft) high, it is the smallest hill in Rome, but in ancient times it looked quite different: cliffs of tufa fell down steeply on all sides of its twin crowns. On the southern crown of the hill, known as **Campidoglio** (the Capitol), stood the **Tempio di Giove** (Temple of Jupiter), which was the religious hub of the state. Originally as big as a football pitch, it was begun by

The courtyard of Palazzo dei Conservatori has fragments of a colossal statue of the Emperor Constantine. When it was intact it stood nearly 12 metres (40 ft) tall.

the Etruscan kings and dedicated in 509 BC, the first year of the Republic. Behind its six-pillared, south-facing front lay a great anteroom that led to the shrines of Jupiter, Juno and Minerva. Here, the ancient Romans honoured the goddess Juno Moneta, who is supposed to have warned them of an attack by Gauls in 390 BC by making her sacred geese honk. The mint also stood here, hence the word *moneta*, meaning money.

Every New Year's Day, the consuls were inaugurated in a formal ceremony on the Capitol. The triumphal processions followed **Via Sacra**, the holy road, coming up the hill from the Foro Romano. Remnants of the basalt paving of this street can be seen quite clearly from **Via di Monte Tarpeo**. Anyone guilty of treason was thrown from the **Rupe Tarpea** (Tarpeian Rock), the southern precipice of the Capitol.

The other crown was known in ancient times as the **Arx** (the Citadel). Today, it is home to the 6th-century church of **S. Maria in Aracoeli** ❶ (St Mary of the Altar in the Sky). The church hides behind a 13th-century brick facade, but the columns of the church are from ancient buildings. Inside, the church has a coffered ceiling (1572–75) and a striking Cosmatesque floor. In the first chapel on the right are the famous Renaissance frescoes by Pinturicchio that tell the stories of S. Bernardino. Around the church are many examples of Roman art, dating from the 13th to the 18th centuries.

The Piazza del Campidoglio

In between the two peaks, **Piazza del Campidoglio** ❷ (Capitol Square) was once the Asylum, a sacred sanctuary that protected the persecuted and was supposed to date back to the time of the founder of the city, Romulus. The

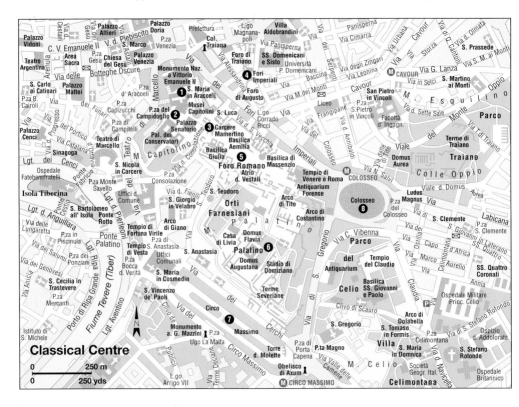

Classical Centre

0 — 250 m

0 — 250 yds

Tabularium was built around the older **Veiovis Temple**. The best view of the Tabularium, which served as a state record office from 78 BC, is from the Foro Romano. Seventy metres (210 ft) long, the building had ten arches opening on to the Forum, though all but three are now bricked up, and rose four storeys high. Even today, the city of Rome keeps some of its archives here.

The piazza today owes much to Michelangelo, who drew up plans for the paving and building facades for Pope Paul III in 1536, even if they were not finished until the 17th century. The two *palazzi* to the right and left – Palazzo Nuovo (New Palace) and Palazzo dei Conservatori (Conservators' Palace) – house the recently renovated and restored **Musei Capitolini** (open Tues–Sun 9am–7pm; entrance fee; tel: 06-6710 2071).

In the centre of the piazza is a first-rate copy of the equestrian statue of Emperor Marcus Aurelius. The original, just inside **Palazzo Nuovo**, is the only one of its kind, so it is kept indoors to protect it from pollution and the elements. In the 16th century, the statue stood in the piazza, where it probably only survived those destructively devout times because people thought it was a statue of Constantine (306–37), who had the good grace to be baptised albeit on his deathbed. The museum houses other Roman sculpture, including the beautifully evocative 3rd-century BC statue of a dying Gaul, the *Venus of Cnidia*, and an interesting collection of busts of emperors and philosophers, as well as more mundane subjects, including a drunken woman and children with various animals.

One of the most famous exhibits of **Palazzo dei Conservatori** is the much-copied wolf wet-nursing Romulus and Remus. The wolf is Etruscan, dating from the 5th century BC, but the twins were added in the 15th century and are

Map, see opposite

TIP

Climb the stairs of Palazzo Senatorio to get an overview of the piazza and its beautiful pavement.

BELOW: Piazza del Campidoglio.

MAMERTINUM
LA PRIGIONE dei SS APOSTOLI
PIETRO e PAOLO
IL PIÙ ANTICO CARCERE di ROMA
XXV SECOLI di STORIA

BELOW: the Etruscan
statue of the she-
wolf in Palazzo dei
Conservatori.

attributed to Pollaiuolo. Other highlights include a 1st-century boy removing a thorn from his foot and an earlier Venus. The walls are covered with frescoes of Roman legends, painted by Cavalier d'Arpino in 1613, and there is a collection of late Renaissance and baroque art, including works by Caravaggio, Guercino and Rubens.

From Piazza del Campidoglio, take the road that leads down to the left of **Palazzo Senatorio** (Senatorial Palace) and continue down the stairs. Below the Church of S. Giuseppe dei Falegnami is the so-called **Carcere Mamertino ❸** (Mamertine Prison; open summer, daily 9am–12.30pm, 2.30–6.30pm; winter, daily 9am–noon, 2–5pm; donation expected; tel: 06-679 2902). It was here that defeated kings and generals, having been paraded through the streets in their victor's triumphal march, were imprisoned before being executed. A small chapel next to a spring commemorates St Peter, who is said to have been incarcerated here, and to have baptised his prison guards using water from a spring that he miraculously created. From the Mamertine Prison, the road leads down past Foro di Cesare (Caesar's Forum) to Via dei Fori Imperiali.

The Imperial Fora

The **Fori Imperiali ❹** (Imperial Fora) are mostly buried under Via dei Fori Imperiali, but there is still plenty to see from the road. The first "imperial" forum, the Foro di Cesare, was built in 51 BC by Julius Caesar when the original became too small for Rome's increasing population. It was dedicated, still unfinished, in 46 BC and completed under Augustus (23 BC–AD 14). Following Hellenistic models, it was square-shaped and enclosed by pillars. On the west side of the forum stood the **Temple of Venus Genetrix**, built because Caesar

believed himself to be a descendant of the goddess. The excavations have uncovered only one-quarter of the site.

Across the street, the **Foro di Augusto** (Forum of Augustus) was built along similar lines. In the centre stood the temple of the war god Mars Ultor and in the great apses of the square stood statues of the mythical ancestors of Augustus's family. To the right is the **Foro della Pace** (Forum of Peace), commissioned by Emperor Vespasian and dedicated to the peace goddess Pax in recognition of Vespasian's victory in the Jewish War (AD 71). It was decorated with spoils from Jerusalem, among them the seven-branched candlestick. The library of the forum, now the **Basilica dei SS. Cosma e Damiano**, contained the marble map of Septimius Severus, which measured 20 by 15 metres (60 by 45 ft) and was a scale record of Roman land ownership.

The **Foro di Traiano** (Forum of Trajan) measures a massive 330 by 180 metres (990 by 540 ft). The biggest of the fora, building it meant removing a small hill between Quirinal and the Capitol. To the northwest, it was bound by the **Basilica Ulpia**, a hall with five naves. In its western apse, the **Atrium Libertatis**, slaves were emancipated. Many market stalls had to be moved to make room for all the building, so the **Mercati di Traiano** (Trajan's Market) was built on the slopes of Quirinal to accommodate them. Its remains stand behind the forum, between two libraries, and they reflect the complex system of streets on various levels, with shops, administrative offices and space reserved for public grain distribution. The forum and market are open to visitors (Apr–Sept, Tues–Sun 9am–6.45pm; Oct–Mar until 4.45pm; last entry 45 mins before closing; entrance fee; tel: 06-679 0048) and can be entered from Via IV Novembre or Salita del Grillo. Visitors can walk through

Map, page 100

By Trajan's Market.

BELOW LEFT: Trajan's Column.
BELOW RIGHT: interior of SS. Cosma e Damiano.

The simplest way to reach the Foro Romano is by Metro, taking line B, or bus numbers 85, 87, 175, or 186, to Colosseo. From Trastevere you can also take tram no. 3.

the structure and market stalls, some of which are filled with marble fragments found on the site. By the end of 2002 a new Museum of the Imperial Fora should also be open on this site.

The magnificent **Colonna Traiana** (Trajan's Column) stands nearby. Built between AD 107 and 113 to celebrate the victory of Trajan (AD 98–117) over the Dacians, it stands 40 metres (120 ft) high and is covered by a 210-metre (630-ft) long spiral of reliefs telling the story of Trajan's Dacian campaigns (AD 101–102 and 105). The reliefs were originally brightly painted and would have been visible from the balconies of the libraries. In AD 177, a golden urn containing the remains of the emperor Trajan was buried under the column.

The Foro Romano: west

The entrance to the **Foro Romano** ❺ (Roman Forum; open Apr–Oct, daily 9am–6.30pm; Nov–Mar, daily 9am–one hour before sunset; free; tel: 06-699 0110) is on Via dei Fori Imperiali, opposite the Forum of Peace. Another entrance to the Forum is opposite the Colosseum, by the Arch of Titus. A path leads down to the ruins of the ancient streets that were the political, commercial and religious centre of republican Rome. When excavations began in the 18th century, most of this forum was buried under 3 metres (10 ft) of rubble, and the place was known as Campo Vaccino, the cow pasture. (A plan of the Forum can be found on the inside back cover of this guide.)

To the right of the Forum lie the remains of the **Basilica Aemilia**. Commissioned in 179 BC by censors M. Aemilius Lepidus and M. Fulvius Nobilitor as shelter for traders, the ruins are of a building restored after a fire in 410, when Alaric the Goth conquered Rome. Stains of coins burned into

BELOW: ongoing restoration.

the floor are still visible. Until 1500, most of the hall was still standing, but Bramante, Rome's chief architect during the High Renaissance, used some of it to build Palazzo Girau-Torlonia in the Borgo quarter. On the steps, you can see the modest remains of a temple to Venus, which was nicknamed *Cloacina* because the small circular building marks the spot where the **Cloaca Maxima** (the city's main sewer) divulges into the valley of the Forum. The sewers, built in the 1st century BC, are still very much in use today. They drain into the Tiber at the **Foro Boario** near Ponte Rotto. *Cloaca* comes from the Latin verb *to rinse*.

Along the western side of the Basilica Aemilia is the **Argilentum**, not immediately recognisable today as the connecting route to the housing areas of **Esquiline Hill** and the **Foro di Nerva** (Forum of Nerva). It is where the Senate sat in Imperial times. Having been the political heart of the Republic, it became much less important when the emperors took over and Julius Caesar decided to move the senators to the Curia.

In the Middle Ages, the Curia was consecrated as a church, but the current building, a replica of Diocletian's, dates from 1937. In the 17th century, the original doors to the Curia were removed to S. Giovanni in Laterano – the present doors are copies. The inner hall is impressive – 30 metres (90 ft) long, 20 metres (60 ft) wide, 20 metres (60 ft) high. Nonetheless, there was only room for 300 of the senators' chairs and, as there were 600 senators, if only half turned up, it still looked full. Everyday dress for the senators was a toga over a tunic and a golden ring on one hand. Meetings were held with the doors open, so that the public could be kept informed. Still recognisable is the base for the statue of the goddess of Victory.

Map, page 100

BELOW: pollution turning marble into limestone.

In front of the Curia lies one of the most sacred objects of Ancient Rome, the **Lapis Niger** (Black Stone), which is supposed to mark the tomb of Romulus, the mythical founder of the city. The remains of a monument from the 6th century BC have been excavated from under the Lapis Niger and while they do not conclusively prove the existence of the grave, they are evidence that Romulus was already venerated in early Rome.

Behind looms the **Arco di Settimio Severo** (Arch of Septimius Severus) AD 193–211. The arch is 25 metres (75 ft) wide, 10 metres (30 ft) deep and 20 metres (60 ft) high. It was built in AD 203 to honour the tenth anniversary of the emperor's ascent to the throne. There are inscriptions celebrating the victories of the emperor and his two sons, Geta and Caracalla. Later Caracalla had his brother murdered in the arms of their mother and then placed him under *damnatio memoriae* (exile from memory) by ordering the deletion from monuments of all inscriptions to Geta and replacing them with laudatory titles to himself. You can still see the chisel marks on the inscriptions, which were originally inlaid with metal. The reliefs on the arch depict the campaigns of Septimius Severus against the Arabs and the Parthians. In earlier years, the arch was topped by a statue of the emperor in a four-horse chariot.

Beside the arch is the Umbilicus Urbis, a navel-shaped piece of stone that was once part of a 3rd-century BC temple and marked the heart of the city. Here also stood the Miliarum Aureum, a bronze-covered column marking the start of all the imperial roads leading from Rome or, conversely, marking the end of all those roads leading to Rome. Beside it stood the **Rostra**, the speaker's platform of the Roman Forum. It was built in its present shape by Augustus, and had sufficient room for the emperor and his immediate party.

During the Middle Ages, part of the Arch of Septimius Severus, which was half buried in rubble, was used to house a barber's shop.

ABOVE: Forum fragment.
BELOW: the Arch of Septimius Severus.

You can still see the drilled holes for the mounting of ships' ramming beaks taken from the Latins at the sea battle of Actium in 338 BC – these beaks were called "rostra", hence the platform's name. Trophies from Cleopatra's fleet are reputed to have been displayed here as well.

Behind, to the right, is the **Tempio della Concordia** (Temple of Concordia), dedicated to the end of the Class Wars in 367 BC. Commissioned by the Emperor Tiberius (AD 14–37), it was decorated with artworks from various countries. The Senate sometimes met here. Cicero stood on this spot, wringing his hands and urging the citizens to unite against the "public enemy", Catiline.

Many dead emperors were automatically deified and had temples consecrated to them. All that remains of the temples of Vespasian (AD 69–79) and his son Titus (AD 79–81) are three Corinthian pillars at the back of the Rostra. Titus may have only ruled for two years, but he went down in history for conquering Jerusalem. The Emperor Vespasian's name is permanently linked with pragmatism. To restore the state finances after the disastrous extravagances of Nero (AD 54–69), he taxed urine – a useful raw material for dyeing heavy woollens. When asked how he could make money with such a stinking substance, he replied *pecunia non olet* – money doesn't smell!

The curved podium of the **Tempio di Saturno** (Temple of Saturn), in the northwestern corner of the Forum, contained the Roman state treasury in its basement. Eight upright pillars are all that remain. Saturn, next to Jupiter, was one of the longest-serving gods in Rome. His temple was consecrated in 498 BC and last renovated at the start of the 4th century. The *Saturnalia* – when masters and slaves were briefly equal and gifts were exchanged – was celebrated in Rome at the end of each year.

Map, page 100

Letters in stone, Roman Forum.

BELOW: the Roman Forum.

Vestal Virgin statue.

BELOW: House
of the Vestals,
Roman Forum.

The Forum boasts countless memorials, monuments, temples and halls. In front of the Rostra is the base of the **Decennalia Column**, raised in AD 303 to celebrate 10 years of rule by the two emperors Diocletian and Maxentius. The relief on the base shows the *Souventaurilia*, the ceremonial state sacrifice of a boar, ram and bull. Next to it is the **Column of Phocas**, the most recent of the classical monuments in the Roman Forum. This column was put up in AD 608 by Smaragdus, the Byzantine Exarch (governor) for Italy, in honour of the Eastern Emperor Phocas. Next to it, a bronze inscription commemorates one of the sponsors of the paving of the Forum, L. Naevius Surdinus, in the last decade BC. A fig tree, an olive tree and a vine, which used to grow here, together with a statue of Marsyas, symbolised the justice of the city.

On the south side of the Forum stood the **Basilica Giulia** (Basilica Julia), 100 by 50 metres (300 by 150 ft), the symbol of Julius Caesar's family. The Basilica, with its five naves, was a venue for court cases, the seat of the Roman office of weights and measures, and a meeting place for bankers. On the opposite side of the road from the Basilica are seven votive columns erected in Diocletian's time to honour victorious generals.

Next to the Basilica stands the **Tempio di Castore e Polluce** (Temple of Castor and Pollux), which commemorates a legend about two young riders who intervened in a decisive battle between Latins and Romans in 499 BC, securing victory for the Romans. Later the Romans saw the youths watering their horses at the Lacus Juturnae, recognised the divine twins Castor and Pollux, and promptly built the temple.

The church of **S. Maria Antiqua** was built on a site that, it is claimed, was frequented by a dragon in the early 4th century. The fire-breathing dragon was

eventually killed by Pope Sylvester I, who invoked the help of God, and the church was built to celebrate the settlement's freedom from the monster.

Another legend, this time concerning the murder of Julius Caesar in the vicinity of the Theatre of Pompey in 44 BC, is commemorated by the **Tempio di Cesare** (Temple of Caesar). According to the story, the grief of the people was so great when Caesar died that they kept his funeral pyre burning for days. After the cremation, Caesar's ashes were washed with milk and wine, then buried. After his deification, the temple was built on the site of the pyre.

Behind the Temple of Caesar lie the irregular remains of the walls of the **Regia**, the residence of the kings before the Republic. Later, the Regia was the residence of the *Pontifex Maximus*, the Highest Priest, a title that passed to the Pope, who still holds it today.

The Foro Romano: east

Nearby is the round **Tempio di Vesta** (Temple of Vesta), goddess of the hearth and patron of the state. Here the Vestal Virgins kept the eternal fire of Rome burning and watched over the **Palladion**, a sacred image of Minerva, saved, according to legend, from blazing Troy by Aeneas. The Vestals entered divine service as young girls and lived a chaste life for at least 30 years in the **House of Vestals**, the rectangular building next to the temple, where statues of the Vestals surround a pond.

Opposite is the **Tempio di Antonino e Faustina** (Temple of Antoninus and Faustina), dating from AD 141. Its reconsecration as a church saved it from destruction and it is the only Forum building that indicates the monumental size of Roman temples. It was built to honour the emperor and his wife.

Map, page 100

The Vestals had seats of honour in the circus and theatre, and, in the city, where wheeled vehicles were forbidden, they alone had the right to travel in a carriage. If they lost their virginity, they were walled up alive (their blood couldn't be spilled) and their lovers strangled.

BELOW: reproduction antiques for sale.

The **Basilica di Costantino e Massenzio** (Basilica of Constantine and Maxentius) was begun by the Emperor Maxentius (303–312) and completed by the Emperor Constantine (306–330). It was designed as a hall of three naves, 100 by 60 metres (300 by 180 ft), but only the northern nave now remains. The central nave, 35 metres (115 ft) high, was crossed by cruciform vaults, each resting on eight side pillars, one of which has been outside the church of S. Maria Maggiore since 1613. In Renaissance times the basilica was the model for the new church of St Peter, and both Bramante and Michelangelo studied its form. In the western apse, a **Colossus of Constantine** was discovered in 1487. Bits of the huge statue – including feet and hands – can be found in the courtyard of Palazzo dei Conservatori. Next to the basilica is the round 3rd-century AD **Tempio di Romolo** (Temple of Romulus), which is now part of the church of SS. Cosma e Damiano. Beneath the temple are the remains of tiny rooms believed to have been part of a brothel dating from the time of the Roman Republic.

From the basilica, you can turn straight to the **Arco di Tito** (Arch of Titus), the oldest triumphal arch in Rome, built by Domitian to celebrate the victories in Palestine of his brother, Titus, and their father, Vespasian. The seven-armed candlestick is easily recognisable among the spoils from Jerusalem. Between the Arch of Titus and the Colosseum is the **Tempio di Venere e Roma** (Temple of Venus and Rome), which was originally built by Hadrian (AD 117–138) and rebuilt by Maxentius in 307 after a fire. The building, 110 by 53 metres (361 by 174 ft), was the largest temple in Rome and comprised two shrines placed opposite one another, surrounded by pillared halls in the Greek manner. Hadrian was an ardent admirer of Greek culture.

TIP

You can take a picnic into the Forum/Palatine area. Officially, it's not allowed, but if you are discreet and tidy, there will be no problem.

BELOW: the House of Vestals, with columns from the Temple of Castor and Pollux.

Palatino

From the Arch of Titus, the road leads up to **Palatino** ➏ (Palatine Hill; open Apr–Oct, daily 9am–6.30pm; Nov–Mar, daily 9am–one hour before sunset; entrance fee; tel: 06-699 0110), where the palaces of the Roman emperors stood *(see inside back cover)*. Legend claims that this is where Romulus founded the city, and remains of early 8th-century BC huts have been excavated here. In republican times, the Roman nobility lived on the hill. Augustus had a series of houses built here for himself and his wife Livia. Their wall paintings are worth seeing. Tiberius (AD 14–37) commissioned another great palace. Most of it lies unexcavated under the Farnese Gardens.

Also underneath the Farnese Gardens is a long tunnel built by Nero, which may have been a secret route to other parts of the Palatine. You can still see the remains of stucco on the ceiling and parts of the original marble floor towards the end of the tunnel. South of the gardens lay the **Domus Flavia**, built by the emperor, Domitian, who is said to have lined his throne room with mirrors in order to see approaching enemies from any angle. The room with a pattern traced on its floor was the courtyard, behind that was the dining-room, and the room to the right was the nyphaeum where diners retired for breaks during banquets. Next to this palace was the **Domus Augustana** (House of Augustus), also built by Domitian, and the oval building next to that may have been a stadium built for the emperor's private games. To the south are the Baths of Septimius Severus.

The remains of the Palatine palaces overlook the **Circo Massimo** ➐ (Circus Maximus). Not much of this 6th-century BC stadium remains, but you can make out the track, which was used mainly for chariot races, and there are traces of seating to the south (the tower is a medieval addition).

Map, page 100

Domus Flavia detail.

BELOW: view of the Forum: to the right Tempio di Antonino e Faustina.

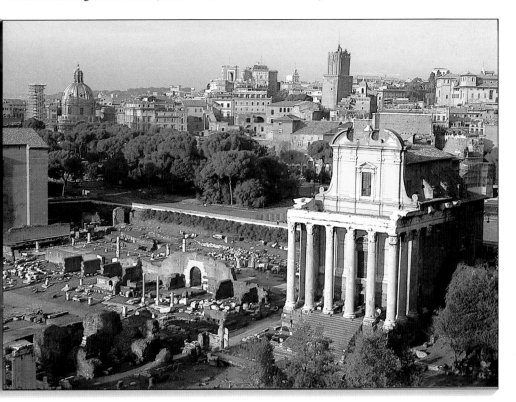

The Colosseum.

The Colosseum

The **Colosseum** ❽ (open Apr–Oct, daily 9am–7.30pm; Nov–Mar, daily 9am–3.30pm; last entry 1 hour before closing; entrance fee; tel 06-700 4261) is the most impressive of the ancient Roman buildings. Originally called the **Amphitheatrum Flavium**, it held gladiatorial combats featuring criminals, prisoners of war, slaves and, sometimes, volunteers. The Emperor Vespasian ordered it to be built on the site of the artificial lake of Nero's **Domus Aurea** (Golden House). The elliptical site measures 190 metres (570 ft) long by 150 metres (450 ft) wide. Following Roman architectural taste, Tuscan, Ionic and Corinthian pillars were placed one above the other. In AD 80, Titus opened the Colosseum with 100 days of games. More than 5,000 animals are supposed to have been slaughtered. The theatre had 80 entrances and could seat between 55,000 and 73,000 spectators. Today, the walls of the various dungeons, cages and passageways, gruesome reminders of the centuries-long slaughter that took place here, can be seen through the caved-in floor of the arena. The **Ludus Magnus**, the nearby training ground of the gladiators, complete with its own miniature amphitheatre, was connected to the arena by a tunnel.

The amphitheatre was filled early in the morning, mostly by men. The lower seats were reserved for senators, civil servants in official dress and the Vestals – other women sat at the top. On hot days, legionnaires would spread an awning over the theatre. Shortly before the games began, the emperor and his followers would enter the amphitheatre, and the spectators would show their reverence by clapping, cheering, waving cloths and chanting their sovereign's honorifics.

If one of the gladiators tried to retreat back into the underground chamber, he was pushed forward with whips and red-hot irons. A trumpet call started

BELOW: the Arch of Constantine.

the games and spectacles began with cries of "Hail Caesar, those about to die salute you". The gladiators mostly fought to the death. A wounded gladiator could beg for mercy by lifting a finger of his left hand. If the crowd waved handkerchiefs, he was saved. Thumbs down meant death. After the gladiators came the wild beasts, which were made to fight one another or human beings – armed or unarmed. The latter was considered particularly exciting.

Gladiatorial combat was banned in AD 438, and the last-recorded animal show was in 523. The reserved seats in the lower tiers still bear the names of 195 senators from the time of Odoacer (AD 476–483). In later times the amphitheatre became the fortress of the Frangipani family and a quarry for Palazzo Venezia, Palazzo della Cancelleria, the harbour of Ripetta and St Peter's. The holes in the masonry testify to the shortage of metal in the Middle Ages: the clamps were knocked out and recycled. In 1744, Benedict XIV consecrated the arena to the memory of Christian martyrs who died in it (though modern research has failed to prove wide scale sacrifice of Christians).

Nearby is the **Arco di Costantino** (Arch of Constantine), which was built in 312 after the victory over Maxentius at the Ponte Milvio. The fact that most of the sculptures come from monuments dating from the days of Trajan, Hadrian and Marcus Aurelius is evidence of a drop in the level of craftsmanship by the time of Constantine. In 1988, restorers working on this recycled material came upon an inscription from the Colossus of the Emperor Nero, which was, according to the writer Gaius Suetonius Tranquillus, 35.5 metres (117 ft) tall.

In the presence of this kind of architectural grandeur – and so much of it – it is hardly surprising that Mussolini sought to borrow from past glories to inspire his new empire. ❏

Map, page 100

BELOW: restoration on the Arch of Constantine.

THE COLOSSEUM: BREAD AND CIRCUSES

"While the Colosseum stands, Rome shall stand;
when the Colosseum falls, Rome shall fall;
when Rome falls, the world shall fall."

The Venerable Bede's 8th-century prophecy has been taken to heart and the Colosseum shored up ever since. The ancient amphitheatre is the city's most stirring sight, a place of stupendous size and spatial harmony. The Colosseum was begun by Vespasian, inaugurated by his son Titus in AD 80, and completed by Domitian (AD 81–96). Titus used Jewish captives from Jerusalem as masons. The Colosseum had 80 numbered arched entrances, allowing over 50,000 spectators to be seated within ten minutes. "Bread and circuses" was how Juvenal, the 2nd-century satirist, mocked the Romans who here sold their souls for free food and entertainment.

FALL AND RUIN

With the fall of the empire, the Colosseum fell into disuse. During the Renaissance, the ruins were plundered to create churches and palaces all over Rome, including Palazzo Farnese, now the French Embassy. Quarrying was only halted by Pope Benedict XIV, in the 18th century, and the site consecrated to Christian martyrs. The Colosseum was still neglected on the German poet Goethe's visit in 1787, with a hermit and beggars "at home in the crumbling vaults". In 1817 Lord Byron was enthralled by this "noble wreck in ruinous perfection" while Edgar Allan Poe, another Romantic poet, celebrated its "grandeur, gloom and glory".

During the Fascist era, Mussolini, attracted to the power that the Colosseum represented, demolished a line of buildings to create a clear view of it from his balcony on Palazzo Venezia. An ambitious restoration programme was undertaken to ensure that the Colosseum was fit for Holy Year in the year 2000.

△ **ALL AT SEA**
Renaissance historians believed that, in ancient times, Roman arenas were sometimes flooded to stage mock naval battles, but there is scant evidence to suggest such a display ever took place in the Colosseum.

▽ **GLADIATORIAL COMBAT**
The price of failure: the Gate of Life was reserved for victorious gladiators, with vanquished gladiators doomed to the Gate of Death.

△ **BEHIND THE SCENES**
From the higher tiers stretch views down to the arena and a maze of passages. The arena was encircled by netting to prevent beasts escaping. The moveable wooden floor was covered in sand, the better to soak up the blood. Below, the subterranean section concealed the animal cages and sophisticated technical apparatus, from winches and mechanical lifts to ramps and trap doors.

▽ SOCIAL STRATA

Although supremely public, the Colosseum was a stratified affair. The podium, set on the lowest tier, was reserved exclusively for the emperor, senators, magistrates and Vestal Virgins. Above them sat the bourgeoisie, with the lower orders restricted to the top tier, and the populace on wooden seats in the very top rows.

◁ IMPERIAL COINAGE

Bearing the head of Emperor Vespasian, the coin depicts no grape-sucking degenerate but a professional soldier who consolidated Roman rule in Britain and Germany. As the founder of the Flavian dynasty and emperor between AD 69 and 79, he began the stadium.

◁ ROMANTIC ROME

This 18th-century view by Giovanni Volpato reflects the nostalgic sensibility of the Romantic era. Visitors on the Grand Tour were beguiled by the ruins bathed in moonlight or haunted by the sense of a lost civilisation. In Byron's words, "Some cypresses beyond the time-worn breach/Appeared to skirt the horizon, yet they stood/Within a bowshot – where the Caesars dwelt".

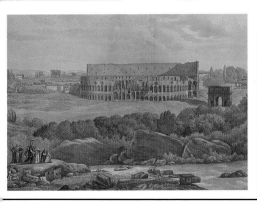

ENTERTAINMENT FOR THE MASSES

The Roman appetite for bloodshed was legendary, with the barbaric *munera*, or blood sports, introduced as a corrupt version of Greek games. The animals, mostly imported from Africa, included lions, elephants, giraffes, hyenas, hippos, wild horses and zebras. The contests were also a way of eliminating slaves and proscribed sects, Christians and common criminals, political agitators and prisoners of war. Variants included battles involving nets, swords and tridents, mock hunts and freak shows with panthers pulling chariots or cripples pitted against clowns. Seneca, Nero's tutor, came expecting "fun, wit and some relaxation" but was dumbfounded by the butchery and cries of: "Kill him! Lash him! Why does he meet the sword so timidly?"

In AD 248, the millennium of the founding of Rome was celebrated by contests involving 2,000 gladiators and the slaying of tame giraffes and hippos as well as big cats. Although convicted criminals were routinely fed to the lions, Christian martyrdom in the arena is less well documented. However, St Ignatius of Antioch, who described himself as "the wheat of Christ", was dutifully devoured by lions in AD 107. Gladiatorial combat was banned in AD 404, while animal fights ended in the following century.

THE CENTRO STORICO

Map, page 120

*People have lived in the historic centre of Rome since
the Middle Ages, and this tangle of streets and alleyways
holds many treasures*

The area known as the **Centro Storico** (Historic Centre) is within the city walls and has been inhabited continuously from the Middle Ages, when Rome's population numbered a few tens of thousands, right through to modern times. Roughly speaking, it is contained by the great bend of the Tiber west of Via del Corso.

In ancient times, the area centred on the **Campus Martius** (Field of Mars), an army training ground dedicated to the Roman god of war. It lay outside the *Pomerium*, the sacred boundary of the city, because, until early imperial times, security demanded that no armed man was allowed inside the city. It was here, usually in front of the nearby Temple of Apollo (of which three particularly beautiful pillars survive next to the Teatro di Marcello), that returning generals reported to the Senate.

Ancient relics

By imperial times, the city had spread far beyond the ancient city walls. Building space around the central Fora was scarce, so even public buildings were moved out of town. In Julius Caesar's time, the wealthiest citizens built great complexes on the Field of Mars, including Pompey's imposing theatre complex that spread from Campo de' Fiori to the temples at Largo Argentina. It was in this complex that Julius Caesar was killed in 44 BC, when the Senate used it as a meeting place during renovations to senate house in the Forum.

In the following century, the Emperor Domitian built a stadium seating 30,000 people here (AD 86). Its remains lie under the baroque Piazza Navona. Amongst the area's other ancient traces is the massive mausoleum of Augustus, dating from 28 BC.

Rome's population shrank in the Middle Ages due to devastating plagues and the relocation of the empire's capital to Constantinople. Those who remained moved towards the Tiber for defence purposes, drinking water following the destruction of the ancient aqueducts and because it was a transport route safe from bandits. The river also turned floating mills, which were tied up between the banks.

The ruins in the area also provided building materials for new houses, churches and papal complexes. Some of the ruins were used as forts or – like the Pantheon – churches. Almost all the major medieval, Renaissance and baroque buildings in the Centro Storico are expressions of either an increasingly powerful church or reflect the intense competition for power and prestige among Rome's major families.

But the Historic Centre has more to offer than just churches and Renaissance palaces. Its tangle of streets and alleys has been the home of the craft guilds since the

PRECEDING PAGES:
Ponte Sant'Angelo. **LEFT:** Campo de' Fiori. **BELOW:** detail on the Fountain of the Moor, Piazza Navona.

streets or quarters were full of *botteghe* (workshops) of the same trade. This still holds true – though the trades have changed – around Via dei Coronari and Via dell'Orso, where there are antique shops and fairs, and Piazza della Fontanella Borghese, which has a print market. One of the most interesting streets from this point of view is Via dei Cestari (connecting the Pantheon and Largo Argentina), which is lined with shops selling religious raiments and equipment for the Catholic priesthood. Many facades incorporate old guild signs or pieces of ancient marble.

The Pantheon

The highlight of the Centro Storico is the **Pantheon** ❶ (open Mon–Sat 8.30am–7.30pm, Sun 9am–6pm; free; tel: 06-6830 0230), the best-preserved ancient building in Rome. This temple to all gods was turned into a church in 609, thus saving the original building from being torn down. Only 15 metres (45 ft) above sea level, the Pantheon is now the lowest point in Rome and it used to flood regularly. The ditch around it shows just how much the rubble has raised Rome over the centuries: in ancient times one looked up to the Pantheon, not down. The dome of the Pantheon is 1.6 metres (5 ft) bigger than the dome of St Peter's.

Pantheon ceiling.

The Pantheon was begun in 27 BC by the statesman Marcus Agrippa and completely rebuilt by Hadrian (AD 117–138) after a fire. Corinthian columns support a roof with a triangular pediment and the brick walls are 6 metres (20 ft) thick. Beneath the porch are huge bronze doors 8 metres (24 ft) high. Its 45-metre (135-ft) dome is a perfect hemisphere, a symbol of beauty and harmony. The circular hole (oculus) in its centre is still the only source of light and, sunshine or rain, can create spectacular effects.

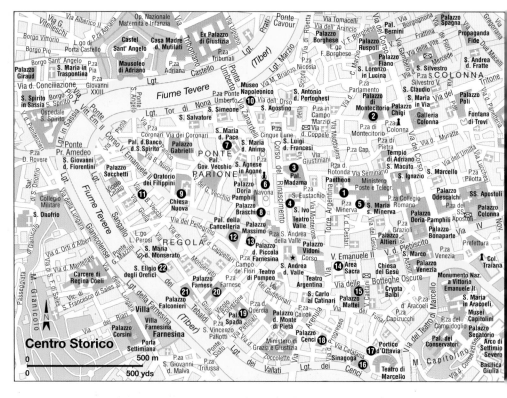

Originally, the dome was covered in bronze inside and out, but Emperor Constans II is said to have stolen the outer layer to use in Constantinople in 667, and Pope Urban VIII of the Barberini family had the inner layer melted down in 1620 in order to make cannons for Castel Sant'Angelo and Bernini's baldacchino (canopy) in St Peter's. This act inspired the famous quip that "what the Barbarians didn't do, the Barberini did".

As with many ancient monuments, the Pantheon served as a fortress in the Middle Ages, and the notches cut in the portico columns are said to have supported stalls for a fish and poultry market. The marble floor is an 1873 restoration of the original. On opposite sides of the room are the tombs of the first kings of Italy and of the artist Raphael (1483–1520). The famous inscription on his tomb by Cardinal Pietro Bembo was translated by Alexander Pope:

> *Living, great nature feared he might outvie*
> *Her works; and dying fears herself to die.*

One of the most impressive sights in Rome, the Pantheon is definitely worth a visit. The Pantheon area is also café territory, where you can buy ice-cream and coffee. Giolitti or La Palma are good places to stop for an ice-cream and the Tazza d'Oro or Caffè San Eustachio are good for coffee.

Another ancient relic that was adapted to modern usage lies in the nearby **Piazza di Pietra**, east of Piazza della Rotonda. **Palazzo della Borsa** takes its name from its one-time role as Rome's stock exchange. Prior to that, the building, with its eleven ancient columns, was a customs house, and originally, in the 2nd century AD, it was the **Temple of Hadrian**, having been dedicated by Antoninus Pius. Behind Largo Argentina, south of the Pantheon, you can see the remains of **Agrippa's Baths** on Via Arco della Ciambella.

Map, see opposite

At his own request, Raphael was buried in the Pantheon. He had lived for many years with his model, La Fornarina, but she was banned from his funeral – possibly because the artist had been engaged for many years to the niece of his patron.

LEFT: mounted carabinieri in front of the Pantheon. **BELOW:** the daily news on Piazza Navona.

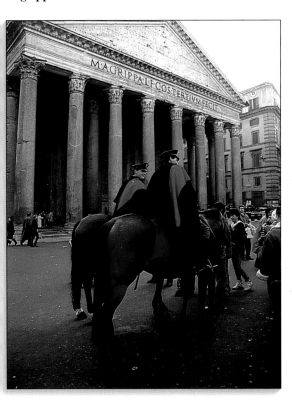

Rome is still, of course, the centre of Italian government and there are two important government offices in heavily guarded old *palazzi* in this area. Behind Piazza Colonna is **Palazzo di Montecitorio** ❷, where the Chamber of Deputies has met since 1871. Before that, the palazzo was the Papal Tribunal of Justice. Bernini drew up plans for the building in 1650, and Carlo Fontana saw the design and building through to completion in 1697. Virtually all that remains of the 17th-century design is the convex curve of the facade, designed to make the building look even bigger than it is, and the rusticated columns. The Egyptian obelisk in front of the palazzo dates from the 6th century BC. It was used by Emperor Augustus for an enormous sundial he laid out in 10 BC. The sundial was discovered in the crypt of the nearby church of San Lorenzo in Lucina.

Since 1870, the Senate has occupied the elegant **Palazzo Madama** ❸ between Piazza della Rotonda and Piazza Navona. The palazzo was built for the Medici family in the early 16th century and several of its members lived here before becoming pope, including Leo X (1513–21) and Clement VII (1523–34). Catherine de' Medici lived here before marrying Francis I of France in 1533. The palace gets its name from the Habsburg Madama Margherita (1522–86), the illegitimate daughter of Emperor Charles V and the wife of Alessandro de' Medici.

Opposite Palazzo Madama, the baroque church of **S. Luigi dei Francesi** (open daily, except Thur pm) contains works by Giacomo della Porta and Domenico Fontana, but it is the three Caravaggio paintings in Capella Contarelli (the fifth chapel on the left) that make it particularly worth visiting. These show scenes from the life of St Matthew: his calling, his martyrdom and him with the angel, the last forming the altarpiece.

ABOVE: Shrine opposite S. Luigi dei Francesi.
BELOW: cool refreshment in the city centre.

Palazzo della Sapienza housed Rome University until it moved to the Stazione Termini area in 1935. In the square is Borromini's **Sant' Ivo ❹** (1642–60; open Sun 9am–noon only), a Roman baroque church with a striking white spiralling bell tower and unusual facade. On the main altar is a 1661 canvas by da Cortona showing St Ivo and other saints surrounded by angels.

Southeast of the Pantheon, **Santa Maria Sopra Minerva ❺**, though it has a plain 17th-century facade, was built in 1280 on the site of an 8th-century church. One of the few Gothic churches in Rome, its alterations over the years include the decoration of its interior in the 19th century. As well as housing the tombs of several popes and St Catherine of Siena (the patron saint of Italy who died in the Dominican convent here in 1380), the church contains a Michelangelo sculpture and works by Filippino Lippi, Romano and da Sangallo. Outside, the jovial little elephant with an ancient Egyptian obelisk on its back was designed by Bernini in 1667.

Around the corner on Via del Pie' di Marmo is the massive foot of an ancient Roman statue. Beyond this stands the church of **Sant'Ignazio**, built between 1627 and 1685 to honour the founder of the Jesuit order and decorated in splendid Counter-Reformation style with plenty of gold embellishments and statuary, as well as Andrea Pozzi's fantastic *trompe l'oeil* views of heaven.

Piazza Navona

Piazza Navona ❻ stands on the Emperor Domitian's ancient stadium: the stand forms part of the foundations of the flanking houses and you can see one of the original entrances to the north. Its baroque aspect dates from the 17th century, in particular the reign of Innocent X. Some say that the piazza's name comes from

Map, page 120

ABOVE: vaulting in Santa Maria Sopra Minerva.
BELOW: the Fountain of the Four Rivers, in front of S. Agnese in Agone.

the word *nave*, alluding to its ship-like shape. Others claim the name comes from a succession of mutations of *in agone*, a phrase denoting the Greek-style athletic contests held here: *in agone* became *nagone* became *navone* became *navona*. Likewise, the names Via Agonale and San Agnese in Agone would have come from the same source.

Domitian's successors altered the stadium considerably. When the Colosseum was damaged by fire, an amphitheatre was built into the stadium, which was modernised by Septimius Severus. When Rome fell, the stones and marble were used to build houses and churches.

The stadium was originally 50 by 275 metres (150 by 825 ft), with the seats rising to 35 metres (105 ft). It is thought that it was used for athletic contests and horse races, and that it was still in use when the Goths invaded in the 5th century. However, the plundering of its fabric began under Constantius II (third son of Constantine the Great), who carried off works of art and decorative features in 356 to adorn his new residence in Constantinople.

There are still plenty of baroque glories on Piazza Navona, including the Borromini facade of **Sant'Agnese in Agone**. Here, it is said, the saint was pilloried and stood naked in the stocks until her hair miraculously grew to cover her modesty. There are underground chambers in this church, reached through a door set in the right wall of the second altar, where you can see the ruins of the stadium of Domitian, a Roman mosaic floor and medieval frescoes on the wall. There is also an altar showing a marble relief of the miraculous modesty of St Agnes by Alessandro Algardi.

To the left of the church is **Palazzo Pamphilj**, designed by Rainaldi in the mid-17th century. It is now the Brazilian Embassy. Of the fountains in the square,

BELOW:
Piazza Navona.

two include work by Bernini. He designed the **Fontana dei Quattro Fiumi** (Fountain of the Four Rivers) with symbols of the Ganges, the Danube, the Plate and the Nile. The statue representing the Nile is blindfolded because the source of the river was then still a mystery.

To the south of the square is the **Fontana del Moro** (Fountain of the Moor), the central figure of which (even though it looks more like a Triton than a Moor) was designed by Bernini. The **Fontana del Nettuno** (Fountain of Neptune) was originally just a large basin. The sculptures were added in the 19th century to create symmetry – although nothing else around is symmetrical.

The piazza remains today one of the most animated squares in Rome, invariably full of people wandering among stalls set up by hopeful artists or stopping for a coffee in one of the many bars. From December until Epiphany, the square becomes a gigantic Christmas market, called the Befana after the witch who brings Italian children either presents or coal, depending on how good they've been, at Epiphany. All sorts of Christmas decorations are sold, including baroque-style nativity scenes, along with toys and "coal" sweets.

Located just off the square is the church of **Santa Maria della Pace ❼**, which was rebuilt in 1482 and then restored in 1656. During the restoration, the church's convex baroque facade was added. The church contains Raphael's frescoes of *The Four Sybils* and four prophets painted by his pupils. Apparently, when the banker Chigi, who was paying for the work, received Raphael's bill, he was horrified and asked Michelangelo for an evaluation. The latter valued each of the heads at 100 *scudi*. The financier was even more alarmed: "If he wants me to pay for the clothes as well, I'll be ruined!" he exclaimed. The nearby **Santa Maria dell'Anima** is the German-speaking church of Rome and was

Map, page 120

Santa Maria dell' Anima houses a 15th-century statue of the Madonna della Pace – Our Lady of Peace. According to legend, when a stone struck the statue, it bled.

BELOW: pavement art on the Corso Vittorio Emanuele II.

started in 1500, although the present building was heavily restored in the 19th century. Apart from a Romano altarpiece, most of the works of art inside were done by pupils and followers of Caravaggio, Michelangelo and Raphael. Just north of Piazza Navona, on Piazza Sant'Apollinare, is **Palazzo Altemps**, one of the many sites of the Museo Nazionale Romano *(see page 181)*.

Piazza di Pasquino

TIP

Don't think that
Rome's best-known
original-language
cinema, the Pasquino,
is in Piazza di
Pasquino – it's not,
it's in Travestere.

Off the southern end of Piazza Navona is **Piazza di Pasquino**, named after the 16th-century tailor and wit who said "what the Barbarians didn't do, the Barberini did". The strange fragment of ancient statue, leaning against the wall, is also named after him. The statue was found in Piazza Navona and brought here in the 15th century when it became one of Rome's "talking statues". There were several of these across the city, including Marforio in Piazza del Campidoglio. At night, discontented citizens would express their disgust with the status quo by pinning their criticisms to these statues. The penalty for leaving messages was death, regardless of rank and including clerics, but there is no record of the death penalty being carried out.

Pasquino leans against a wall belonging to **Palazzo Braschi ❽**, one of the last papal palaces to be built in Rome, in the 18th century. The palazzo is home to the newly renovated Museo di Roma (open Tues–Sun 9am–7pm; entrance fee; tel: 06-6710 8346), which relates the history of the city.

Palazzo Massimo alle Colonne, next to the Braschi, belongs to the oldest family in Rome. Part of it was designed in 1536 by Baldassare Peruzzi, who created a fine curved portico of Doric columns to screen the building. If you look at the palace from Via del Paradiso, the columns can still be seen clearly.

BELOW: Oratorio
dei Filippini.

Behind the palace, in Piazza de' Massimi, is an ancient column that may have been brought from the remains of the nearby Stadium of Domitian.

Further down the Corso Vittorio Emanuele II is the **Chiesa Nuova ❾** (New Church), which was designed by Filippo Neri in the 16th century. The church contains the remains of the saint in an urn in the Santuario Terreno (ground-floor sanctuary), but the sanctuary opens only on 25 and 26 May, on the feast of St Philip. The urn is decorated with a silver bust of the saint by Algardi, and there is a chapel with a painting of *St Philip and the Angel* by Guercino. The main body of Chiesa Nuova has ceiling frescoes by da Cortona. In **Piazza della Chiesa Nuova** is a 17th-century fountain that came from the Campo de' Fiori. On the rim of its basin is the inscription: *Ama Dio e non fallire – Fa del bene e lascia dire* (Love God and don't fail – Do good and make sure people talk about it).

Situated next to the church is Borromini's facade (1637–43) for Filippo Neri's **Oratorio dei Filippini** – part of Palazzo dei Filippini. Neri founded the Oratorio in 1575 as the centre of his new, democratic religious order. This was where his followers (called Filippini) discussed religion and held musical services (hence the name). Behind the Oratorio is a clock tower designed by Borromini in 1648, with a mosaic by Pietro da Cortona and a particularly beautiful *madonelle*. The nearby **Palazzo del Governo Vecchio**, which was finished in 1478, was the residence of the Governor of Rome from 1624 until the middle of the 18th century.

In the next piazza along Corso Vittorio Emanuele II is **Palazzo del Banco di Santo Spirito**, which served as the mint until 1541. Its facade (dating from the 1520s) is by Antonio da Sangallo the Younger. Via Banco di Santo Spirito leads to the lovely **Ponte Sant' Angelo**, the three central arches of which date from

Map, page 120

BELOW: hidden secrets.

the bridge Hadrian built in AD 136 to link his mausoleum – which is now the Castel Sant' Angelo – to the centre of the city. Most of the present bridge dates from the 17th century, but it was altered in the late 19th century to accommodate the new Tiber embankment. The glorious angels along the parapet were designed by Bernini in the 1660s. Each figure holds an implement from Christ's passion, and their eye-rolling, ecstatic expressions have earned them the nickname "the breezy maniacs".

On the southern end of the next bridge upriver, Ponte Umberto I, is another victim of restoration, the **Museo Napoleonico** ❿ (open Tues–Sun 9am–7pm; entrance fee; tel: 06-6880 6286). The museum contains memorabilia belonging to the Bonaparte family, including a cast of the right breast of Pauline Bonaparte (Napoleon's sister) made by Canova in 1805, when he started work on the reclining nude of her that is now in the Galleria Borghese. **Via dell'Orso**, next to the museum, used to be lined with inns and was a favourite haunt of the courtesans of Rome. Today, the area is more famous for its antique shops, especially those along Via dei Coronari, which holds an antiques fair every May and October.

Centro Storico: south

The southern part of the Centro Storico stretches from the river to Corso Vittorio Emanuele II and from the bridge of the same name to Via Arenula. Corso Vittorio Emanuele II was built in 1880 over the ancient tract of Via Trionfale and the winding medieval Via Papale. After Unification in 1870, the new rulers tried to turn the street into one of their grand avenues. Their attempts resulted in the destruction of the well-balanced architecture of the squares. Even so, a number of important buildings survived.

The Museo Napoleonico also houses the Praz Collection from the 20th-century Italian literary figure and critic, Mario Praz. The Fondazione Primoli, which has a precious collection of 19th-century photographs, is also housed here.

BELOW: memorial to an artist who "died for freedom" in May 1944.

To avoid walking along the busy Corso, cut down **Via dei Banchi Vecchi** ⓫.
At No. 22 is the fanciful facade of **Palazzo dei Pupazzi**, built in 1504 and decorated with elaborate stucco designs by Mazzoni. This street leads to Via del
Pellegrino, which winds its way past artisan workshops, bookshops and antique
dealers to **Palazzo della Cancelleria** ⓬.

This palace, begun in 1485, is partly attributed to Bramante, especially the
inner courtyard and the adjoining 4th-century basilica of **San Lorenzo in
Damaso**, which he modified. Bramante had a reputation for destroying medieval
monuments in Rome (for example the ancient St Peter's basilica), earning him
the nickname *Maestro Ruinante* (Master Ruiner). The palace was built for
Cardinal Raffaele Riario before being confiscated by the Pope and used as the
Apostolic Chancery. Unfortunately, the palace is not open to the public on a
daily basis, but it is occasionally used as a venue for classical concerts.

South of the Cancelleria is the lively square of **Campo de' Fiori** (Field of
Flowers), so named because it used to be a meadow that sloped down towards
the Tiber. Used as an execution ground by the popes until well into modern
times, in its centre there is a statue of Giordano Bruno, who, in 1600, was burned
at the stake for claiming that the earth moved around the sun and not the other
way around. According to the report of the Compagnia of monks, "at 2am the
condemned man Bruno, Giordano… an unrepentant heretic, was surrendered
to us …he was led to the Campo de' Fiori, there stripped naked and burned alive
at the stake, adhering to his obstinacy to the last moment, and in it ending his
his miserable and unfortunate life".

The Campo de' Fiori is the most secular of Roman squares, for although it is
as old as Rome itself, it has never been dedicated to any cult and to this day is

**Map,
page 120**

BELOW: statue of
Giordano Bruno,
looking towards
the Vatican.

free of churches. Its present aspect dates from the end of the 15th century when the whole area was reshaped. Today, the Campo flourishes, thanks to a perfectly balanced infrastructure. It has everything from a butcher's and a baker's shop to clothes boutiques, a cinema and a bustling morning food market.

At night time, the Campo plays host to hundreds of trendy Romans and visitors, who frequent the bars and restaurants or simply hang out under the statue of Bruno, sipping beers until late into the night. Then the Campo has only a few hours to breathe before the marketeers arrive to set up their stalls at the crack of dawn. The streets around Campo de' Fiori still retain the names of trades originally practised in them. **Via dei Baullari**, the luggage-makers, leads to **Piazza Farnese**; **Via dei Giubbonari**, named after the sellers and makers of *gipponi* bodices, is still lined with clothes shops, including some of the cheapest in town. **Via dei Cappellari** was where the hat-makers congregated, but is now full of furniture restorers, gilders and carpenters practising their trade out on the street.

Turning back up Via dei Baullari to Corso Vittorio Emanuele II, you come to **Palazzo della Piccola Farnesina** ⓭ in Piazza San Pantaleo. Built for a French prelate, Thomas Leroy, in 1523, it is decorated with fleurs-de-lis. When building the Corso, this little palace was cropped and given a new facade overlooking the thoroughfare. The original facade is on Via dei Baullari and is now the entrance to the **Museo Barracco** (closed for restoration until mid-2003, call ahead to ask about current status; tel: 06-6880 6848), which houses a collection of ancient sculptures donated to the city in 1902 by a politician named Baron Giovanni Barracco. It includes Egyptian, Syrian, Babylonian, Greek and Roman pieces.

Further along the Corso Vittorio Emanuele II, the church of **Sant'Andrea della Valle** has a huge dome by Maderno that is decorated with frescoes by

BELOW LEFT: the Gesù church.
BELOW RIGHT: market stall, Campo de' Fiori.

Lanfranco and Domenichino. It also has a stunning white facade completed by Rainaldi to a Maderno design. Inside, the first chapel on the left is known as the **Chapel of Tosca**, because it is where the two main protagonists from Puccini's opera pray in Act 1.

**Map,
page 120**

The church stands over some of the remains of the **Teatro di Pompeo**, a huge theatre built in 55 BC as part of a plan to introduce some high-minded culture to Rome. However, the Romans did not take to the idea. They preferred the blood-and-guts entertainment of gladiators, fake battles and animal fights. Next to the theatre was the **Curia Pompeia** where Julius Caesar was stabbed to death in 44 BC. Remains of the theatre can be seen in the cellars of the surrounding houses, in the restaurants Da Pancrazio and Da Costanzo, and also in the breakfast room of **Hotel Teatro di Pompeo**. The streets behind Campo de' Fiori still follow the semi-circular curve of the theatre.

Rossini's "Barber of Seville" debuted in the Teatro Argentina in 1816. Unfortunately, it was not well received, which led the composer to insult the audience. They, in turn, were enraged and pursued him through the streets of Rome.

To the east, along the Corso Vittorio Emanuele II, is **Largo di Torre Argentina**, one of the busiest crossroads in the city and a major bus interchange. Its architecture – *palazzi* of varying heights, banks and insurance companies – isn't very exciting. Only the **Teatro Argentina**, the official seat of theatre in Rome, radiates much atmosphere. National and international performances, plays and concerts are held here.

The real attractions, however, lie in the middle of the square several metres underground. During attempts to improve the road system in the 1920s, archaeologists excavated four temples (street levels in ancient times were some 10 metres/ 30 ft below today's level). The **Area Sacra** ⓮ dates from Republican times, around the 3rd and 4th centuries BC. It is not known to which gods the temples (three square and one round) were consecrated, so they are known sim-

BELOW: the synagogue in the Ghetto.

*Ceiling detail in the
Gesù church.*

BELOW: along
the Tiber.

ply as temples A, B, C and D. Some of the remains, inhabited by Rome's many stray cats, can be examined from above.

East of the square is the large church of the **Gesù**, more properly called Santissimo Nome di Gesù (Most Holy Name of Jesus). Built between 1568 and 1584 according to plans drawn up by Vignola, it was Rome's first Jesuit church, and its early baroque facade was a model for many later imitations. A century after completion, the church was richly decorated with a swirling ceiling fresco by Baciccia and stucco work by Antonio Raggi. The founder of the Jesuit Order, St Ignatius Loyola, lies buried in the magnificent **Cappella di Sant'Ignazio Loyola**, built by Andrea del Pozzo in 1696. Above the chapel's altar is a statue of the saint, framed by gilded lapis lazuli columns. Just south of the Gesù, at Via delle Botteghe Oscure 31, is the **Crypta Balbi**, now part of the Museo Nazionale Romano *(see page 181)*.

South of Largo Argentina is the lovely **Piazza Mattei**. In its centre is **Fontana delle Tartarughe** (Tortoise Fountain), sculpted by Taddeo Landini to a design by Giacomo della Porta. The tortoises were added in the 16th century, perhaps by Bernini, and are famous for their travels – they have disappeared several times, most recently in 1944 when a rag-and-bone man eventually found them. Opposite is **Palazzo Mattei** ⓫, which houses the Emeroteca music academy.

Jewish Ghetto

The area stretching from Largo Argentina to the river and from Via Arenula to Teatro di Marcello marks the boundaries of the old **Jewish Ghetto**. In a decree of 1555, Pope Paul IV ordered all Jews in the city, who had until then lived mostly in Trastevere, to move to the other side of the Tiber. About 8,000 Jews

were forced into an enclosed area of less than 2 hectares (5 acres). Thereupon, in the words of one contemporary commentator, " He forced them to sell all their goods and follow no other trade than buying and selling old clothes and household gear. Further, he commanded that men and women should wear a yellow hat, so as to be distinguishable from Christians." The Ghetto was torn down in 1849. Today the Jews comprise only 20 percent of the inhabitants living in the old Ghetto; nonetheless there is a **Synagogue** ⑯ here and several Jewish restaurants, a Jewish bookshop, a Jewish bakery and grocers selling kosher food.

The synagogue (guided visits only, Jun–Sept, Mon–Thurs 9.30am–7.30pm, Fri 9.30am–1.30pm, Sun, 9.30am–noon; Oct–May, Mon–Thurs 9.30am–4.30pm, entrance fee; tel: 06-684 0061) was consecrated in 1904. Its extreme height was a deliberate message to the Vatican across the Tiber. On 13 April, 1986, Pope John Paul II and Rabbi Elio Toaff held an historic meeting here marking the first time that a Bishop of Rome had prayed in a Jewish house of worship. Inside the synagogue (make sure you carry some form of ID, as security is strict) is the **Museum of Jewish Culture** (same hours as synagogue).

On the facade is a plaque commemorating the deportation of the Jews by the Nazis. The German officer Kappler – later linked with a massacre in the quarries of the Ardeatine – ordered the Jews of Rome to pay a ransom of 50 kg (110 lbs) of gold. With the help of priests, this sum was delivered, but the *Wehrmacht* still surrounded the Ghetto and deported any Jews they could find.

Sant'Angelo

The medieval name of the area, Sant'Angelo, comes from the church of Sant'Angelo in Pescheria. This was one of several churches in which the Jews

Map, page 120

BELOW: the Portico of Octavia.

were forced to attend penitential sermons. The church was built in the recesses of the **Portico d'Ottavia** ⓱ (Portico of Octavia), which was built by Augustus and dedicated to his sister. The portico was a covered walkway, ornately decorated with Greek statues and paintings, enclosing the southern end of the **Flaminia Circus**. In the Middle Ages, it was used as a covered fish market and there is a Latin inscription which says that all the fish exceeding the length marked have to be decapitated and their heads given to Conservatori, as this was considered the best part for making fish soup. The single street that now runs in front of the Portico was originally three narrow streets, but these were destroyed in the 19th century when the curfew on the Ghetto was lifted.

Because of its association with the fishing activities of the nearby river port, the church of Sant' Angelo in Pescheria has many aquatic flora and fauna inlays.

At the other end of the street is the **Casa di Manilo**. Lorenzo Manilo had this house built in 1468 and adorned it with a classical plaque. The Latin inscription dating the building employs the ancient Roman calendar that used the founding of Rome as its starting point. According to this, the year 1468 was 2221. Original Roman reliefs are embedded in the facades, as well as a fragment of an ancient sarcophagus. The shop on the corner is a famous Jewish bakery.

Heading towards the river, you come across **Palazzo Cenci** ⓲, the family palace of the infamous Beatrice, who attracted sympathy for killing her brutal father, but was nevertheless condemned to death for witchcraft and murder, and was beheaded at Ponte Sant'Angelo in 1599. Only parts of the original medieval building remain. The present facade and details are baroque. Note the architectural detail of the indented balcony on the front facing Via Arenula.

Crossing back over Via Arenula, Via degli Specchi leads to **Palazzo Monte di Pietà**, which was set up as a pawnshop in the 16th century and is still used as an auction house open to the public every morning. From here, turn left and then

Below: Piazza Farnese.

right into Via Capo di Ferro. On your left, the large building with the facade covered in stucco reliefs by Mazzoni is **Palazzo Spada ⑲**. The Spada family bought the palace in 1632 and Borromini restored it, adding the ingenious corridor to the courtyard. Borromini raised the floor and shortened the columns to create a false sense of perspective, making the corridor appear much longer than it actually is. At the end, a statue was placed against a painted garden backdrop. The statue is less than a metre (3ft) tall but from afar it seems to be life-size. The *palazzo* is also home to the **Galleria Spada**, which has a fine collection of paintings, including work by masters including Rubens, Guercino, Tintoretto, Artemisia Gentileschi and Reni.

The end of the street opens into **Piazza Farnese ⑳**, with its twin fountains incorporating two huge basins from the Baths of Caracalla. Palazzo Farnese was commissioned by Cardinal Alessandro Farnese in 1517 but only completed in 1589. Progress was so slow that people thought the Farnese had run out of money and one day a malicious notice appeared on the building asking for donations. The original designs were by da Sangallo, but Michelangelo took over the work. When he died, Vignola and della Porta finished it off. Annibale Caracci frescoed the main salon over the central doorway. In 1874 Palazzo Farnese became the French Embassy, and it is now closed to the public.

Via Giulia

The road to the left of the palace leads to **Via Giulia**, named after Pope Julius II who commissioned it it as a monument to the Apostolic Church. When Bramante began work on it in 1508, the intention was to make it Rome's most important thoroughfare, connecting the Vatican with Ponte Sisto and the Ripa Grande

Map, page 120

ABOVE: Mascherone Fountain, Via Giulia.
BELOW: emblem of the Falcone family on Palazzo Falconieri, Via Giulia.

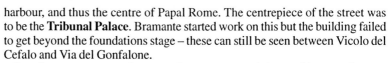

Map, page 120

harbour, and thus the centre of Papal Rome. The centrepiece of the street was to be the **Tribunal Palace**. Bramante started work on this but the building failed to get beyond the foundations stage – these can still be seen between Vicolo del Cefalo and Via del Gonfalone.

In subsequent years, the street became a prestigious address and many famous people lived in its sumptuous palaces, including Antonio da Sangallo, Raphael and Benvenuto Cellini. The parties in Via Giulia were among the best in Rome and on one occasion wine gushed from the Mascherone Fountain for three full days. All this is hard to believe now, as the street is quiet, in parts traffic-free, and lined with expensive antique shops and art galleries. The elegant arch crossing the street was designed by Michelangelo and was intended to connect Palazzo Farnese with the Villa Farnesina across the Tiber, but the bridge was never built.

Morbid fascination

Next to the arch is the church of **Santa Maria dell'Orazione e Morte** with a facade by Ferdinand Fuga (1623). The walls and the ceiling are covered with reliefs and mosaics. Grotesque and fantastic arabesques of human bones, children's skulls, collar bones and ribs form the decoration of the walls. The historian Gregorovius commented: "But that Art has here done such a deed, that it has taken that which appears to the living as most gruesome and which the earth should cover in kindly darkness, and made it into pictures and graceful arabesques, is truly too repellent and morbid."

Adjacent to the church is **Palazzo Falconieri** ㉑, which was remodernised by Borromini for the Falcone family and is framed by two falcon's heads on female busts. It is now the Hungarian Academy, and occasionally opens for exhibitions and concerts. Further down Via Giulia, in Via Sant' Eligio, is the little 16th-century church of **Sant' Eligio degli Orefici** ㉒, which was designed by Raphael – under the influence of Bramante – and has a dome by Peruzzi.

RIGHT: ivy-clad facade in Via Giulia.
BELOW: detail on the church of Santa Maria Dell'Orazione e Morte.

An exception to the refined character of the street is the derelict church of **San Filippo**. In a spectacular plan of Mussolini's, this church was to have been torn down and a panoramic road was to have swept across the river and up to the Gianicolo Hill. A little further along is the large fortified building of the **Carceri Nuovi** (New Prison), built in 1655 to replace the gruesome prisons of Tor di Nona and the nearby torture chambers of the Savella family, who until then were the papal gaolers.

Continuing along, past the blocks of the **Tribunal Palace**, you come to several important Renaissance palaces, including da Sangallo the Younger's palace at No. 66 and one of Raphael's houses at No. 85. The street ends with the church of **San Giovanni dei Fiorentini**, built in various stages by Sansovino, da Sangallo the Younger, della Porta and Maderno. The facade was added in the 18th century.

Inside, there is a delightful sculpture of St John by the Sicilian Mino di Reame over the sacristy door and an impressive apse altar by Borromini with a marble group, the *Baptism of Christ*, by Antonio Raggi. Both Borromini and Maderno are buried in the church. ❏

TOURING THE VATICAN

*The Vatican City is a shrine to the power
of the Catholic Church through the ages,
and to its impeccable artistic taste*

Map,
page 142

The fabulous extravagance of the Catholic Church through the ages is celebrated without restraint in the Vatican State. St Peter's alone is impressive, with its huge dimensions, dome by Michelangelo and an interior sumptuously bedecked with Bernini's glistening creations. Then there are the Vatican Museums, mile on mile of rooms and corridors containing historic treasures, the Sistine Chapel and the Raphael Rooms.

The Vatican, with the Pope as supreme ruler, is the smallest independent state in the world (it has a population of roughly 500). Established in 1929, it has its own stamps, currency, media, railway and police force – the Swiss Guards.

In ancient times, Nero's Circus occupied the site and St Peter, apparently, was crucified upside-down here and buried close by. The early Christians built a modest little chapel to commemorate the saint and a couple of hundred years later Constantine built his huge basilica.

Piazza San Pietro ❶ was created by Bernini between 1656 and 1667 for Alexander VII. Its two semi-circular wings represent the outstretched arms of the church, embracing and protecting the congregation. In the centre are fountains by Maderno and della Fontana, and an Egyptian obelisk, originally from Heliopolis, placed here by Sixtus V.

St Peter's ❷ (Basilica di San Pietro; open daily 7am–7pm, until 6pm in winter, no bare legs or shoulders allowed) is an architectural botch. The original Constantinian church was of the typical basilican form – a Latin-cross with a nave, side aisles and a crossing. However, in 1452, Nicholas V, deciding that the church was in need of restoration and enlargement, initiated a programme of building. In 1506, Bramante, under Julius II, started work on a new centrally planned Greek-cross church, but after his death, Raphael, da Sangallo and Fra Giacondo took over, and reverted to a Latin-cross church. In 1546, Michelangelo opted once again for the Greek-cross and designed the dome.

After Michelangelo's death, della Porta and Fontana continued his work until Pope Paul V decided that the Latin-cross was more appropriate. Maderno added the extra bits that were necessary for the change and completed the facade. In 1629, Bernini constructed the twin towers framing the facade designed by Maderno, but they were torn down when one tower was found to be causing the Basilica to crumble.

Inside St Peter's

Passing into the **portico**, Bernini's statue of Constantine on a galloping horse is on the left. Look up, opposite the 15th-century bronze central doors, to see a restored remnant of the original 13th-century mosaic, *La Navicella*, by Giotto.

PRECEDING PAGES: taking a nap after the papal audience. **LEFT:** Piazza San Pietro.

SWISS GUARDS

Founded in 1506 by Pope Julius II, the first members of the Swiss Guards were recruited from Switzerland, hence their name. They were enlisted from the mercenaries of the cantons of the Swiss confederacy because they had established a reputation for themselves as excellent infantrymen following their victory over the Burgundian cavalry in 1476. However, their role now, as papal police corps, is – in the main – ceremonial. They wear a distinctive and picturesque dark blue, yellow and red uniform – the colours of the Medici popes – consisting of pantaloons gathered below the knee and a full-sleeved jacket, which is alleged to have been designed for them by Michelangelo. They are armed with a halberd (a tall spear that includes an axe blade and a pick) and a sword.

TIP

The best stop for the
Vatican Museums is
Musei Vaticani on
Metro line A.

Once inside the Basilica, turn right for *La Pietà*, Michelangelo's remarkable rendering of the Madonna and dead Christ, which he sculpted when only 25.

In the centre of the Basilica, directly under the dome is the **baldacchino** by Bernini. This huge bronze canopy rises over the holiest part of the church, the legendary tomb of St Peter. The twisted columns are replicas of the ones which Christ apparently leant against in the Temple of Solomon. Bernini added the vine leaves and the bees, symbols of the Barberini coat of arms. According to legend, the expression on the woman's face that is carved into the marble bases becomes increasingly agonised as you pass from left to right, but culminates in a scene of calm in which a baby's face replaces the woman's. It is said that Bernini was alluding to the Pope's niece, who, at the time, was suffering a difficult pregnancy and the coat of arms in its various states of agitation represents the womb.

On the apse wall, framed by the baldacchino, is another Bernini creation, the **Cattedra Petra**. The gold-covered wooden chair (reputedly used by Peter when preaching his first sermon) miraculously floats above the hands of the four fathers of the Church, above whom is the Holy Trinity. The gold seems to flow from the central yellow window, where the dove of the Holy Spirit is painted.

Bernini also produced some of the monumental **tombs** in the church, such as the spectacular one in memory of Alexander VII, on which a gilt skeleton brandishes an hourglass, reminding us that death comes to us all – it is only a matter of time.

Other papal monuments fill the aisles, including, in the left aisle, the Monument to Innocent VIII Cybo by Pollaiuolo (1498), the only surviving decoration from the old basilica and the first to show a pope sitting on his throne.

Around the baldacchino, in the pillars supporting the dome, are four huge statues of saints. Above them little niches house their sacred relics. Over Bernini's

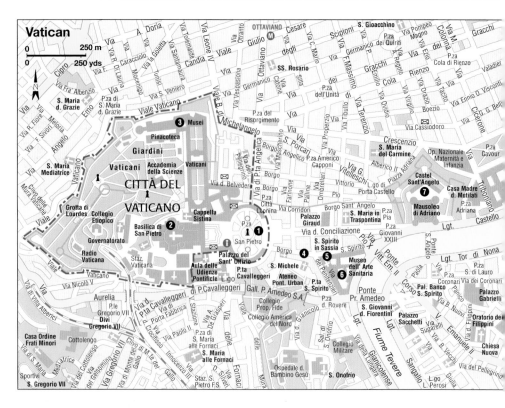

Longinus, for instance, is the spear which the soldier Longinus used to pierce Christ to ensure he was dead. To the right of the baldacchino, a stairway leads down to the **grottoes**, containing the tombs of several popes including that of Adrian IV, the only English pope.

Halfway down the nave is the 13th-century statue of St Peter by Arnolfo di Cambio, which is so venerated that its foot, kissed by pilgrims for over seven centuries, is almost worn away. Look closely and you will see the lengths of other basilicas marked along the nave floor, all much shorter than St Peter's.

On the right side of the portico is the entrance to the **dome** (open daily 8am–5.45pm; until 4.45pm in winter; closed during ceremonies in the Basilica; entrance and elevator fee). The long climb to the top is rewarded by extensive views across the city. At night, the dome is illuminated by a pale blue light, while a pastel-pink light bathes the Basilica.

The **Vatican Gardens** can be seen from the dome, but if you want a closer look you will have to book in advance (tel: 06-6988 4466; fax: 06-6988 5100; entrance fee; tours at 10am on Tues, Thur and Sat). Highlights not visible from the dome include the **Casina di Pio IV**, a little house covered in pretty plaster-work, and a couple of fountains – the galleon, which as its name suggests is a miniature reconstruction of a ship spouting water, and the eagle.

It is possible to take a guided tour of the necropolis beneath the Basilica, believed to be the site of the **tomb of St Peter**. Advance booking is required from the Vatican's Ufficio Scavi (Excavations Office), located just off the piazza and open Mon–Sat 9am–5pm. Alternatively, you can send them a fax or e-mail (fax: 06-6988 5518; e-mail: scavi@fsp.va) with your request, specifying the language required. Children under 15 are not allowed.

Map, see opposite

BELOW: conferring en route.

If you would like to see today's Pope, papal audiences are usually held in the Vatican on Wednesdays at 10.30am, except in the height of summer when they are held at the Pope's summer residence at Castelgandolfo outside Rome. (Apply for free tickets in writing to the Prefettura della Casa Pontifica, 00120 Città del Vaticano, or go to the office the Mon or Tues before the audience – you will find it through the bronze door watched over by Swiss guards to the right of the Basilica. For more information, call the office on 06-6988 3114.) The Pope also usually comes to a window above the piazza on Sunday mornings to give a blessing.

*Stera con Stera
sculpture, Vatican
Palace.*

The Vatican Museums

Passing round the monumental walls designed by Michelangelo, you will reach the entrance to the **Vatican Museums ❸** (open Easter Week and mid-Mar–Oct, Mon–Fri 8.45am–3.45pm, Sat & last Sun of month 8.45am–1.45pm, Nov–mid-Mar, Mon–Sat and last Sun of month 8.45am–1.45pm, last admission 1½ hours before closing; closed on Catholic holidays; entrance fee, free last Sun of month; tel: 06-6988 4947). Leading up to the ticket offices is the entertaining **spiral ramp** (1932), which will make your head spin if you try to work it out. On entering the museums, decide what you want to see and then follow the colour-coded route taking in the items on your list. The routes vary in length from 90 minutes to 5 hours, but be warned: the museums are large and the Sistine Chapel is about 20 minutes' walk from the entrance.

The most direct route to the Sistine will take you up the **Simonetti Staircase** and past a little octagonal room, the **Sala della Biga**, containing a 1st-century sculpture of a chariot and two horses. The long corridors, lined with candelabras, tapestries, Greek and Roman sculpture and a series of 16th-century painted maps

of Italy, stretch out from here. In a room off to the right are some 1st-century BC frescoes, including the well-preserved Aldobrandini wedding fresco.

The Raphael Rooms

The first is the **Hall of Constantine**, the last one to be painted and, since Raphael was virtually on his deathbed, mainly the work of Raphael's pupils. The frescoes depict scenes from the life of Constantine, including his vision of the True Cross at the Battle of the Milvian Bridge. The **Room of Heliodorus** was decorated by Raphael from 1512 to 1514. The subject matter alludes to events in Pope Julius II's life. *Expulsion of Heliodorus*, with angels shooing a thief out of the temple, refers to Julius's success in expelling the enemy from Italy; Julius appears on the left. Even the famous *Mass at Bolsena*, depicting the miraculous bleeding of the sacrament in 1206, was relevant to contemporary political events. Julius II stopped off to venerate the sacrament in Orvieto on his way to attack Bologna. A bolder statement is made in the *Liberation of St Peter* fresco, where Julius appears as the saint himself.

The next room, **Sala della Segnatura**, was probably where the pope's council met to sign official decrees. The frescoes (1509–11) mix pagan and Christian themes and parallel the triumph of ancient philosophy with that of Christian religion. In the *School of Athens* fresco, representing the triumph of philosophical truth, Raphael portrays ancient characters with the features of contemporary heroes. The bearded figure of Plato in the centre is da Vinci; Bramante appears as Euclid in the foreground and the thoughtful figure of Heraclites on the steps is Michelangelo. It has been suggested that even the classical setting referred to the state of St Peter's at the time. On the opposite wall is the *Dispute over the Holy Sacrament,* representing the triumph of religious truth as earth and heaven meet. The Parnassus fresco, representing poetic beauty, features Homer, Virgil, Ovid, Dante and Boccaccio. Note the references to classical sculpture: the *Thornpicker,* now in the Capitoline Museums, is perched on the rock and Homer's face is identical to that of Laocoön, from a 1st-century AD sculptural group.

The last room, the **Stanza dell' Incendio**, takes its name from the fresco of the fire in the Borgo. Legend tells of the terrible fire in 847 that was miraculously extinguished by Leo IV making the sign of the Cross. Parallels are made to the *Aeneid* and the burning of Troy and to Pope Leo X (appearing as Leo IV), who had smothered the raging wars. This room was painted after the first half of Michelangelo's Sistine ceiling was uncovered and direct influences can be seen in the monumentality of the figures.

Sistine Chapel

No visit to the Vatican is complete without a look inside the **Sistine Chapel**. The walls depicting scenes from the lives of Christ and Moses were painted by some of the greatest masters of the Italian Renaissance: Botticelli, Perugino, Ghirlandaio and Signorelli. However, the undisputed highlight is Michelangelo's ceiling.

To paint the ceiling, Michelangelo worked upside-down single-handedly for four years. The frescoes, now restored, are much brighter than they once were

Map, page 142

Museum entrance.

BELOW: the Simonetti Staircase.

Map, page 142

TIP

If you're travelling with children, the Castel Sant'Angelo, with its ramparts, trap doors, prison chambers, draw-bridges and cannon-balls galore, will keep them amused.

RIGHT: Castel Sant' Angelo, formerly the mausoleum of the Emperor Hadrian.

because several layers of dust and dirt have been removed. The ceiling depicts scenes from Genesis, starting with God dividing light from dark and ending with the drunkenness of Noah, seen in reverse from the entrance. The sides show the ancestors of Christ (in the triangles) and, on marble thrones, the prophets and the classical sybils who prophesised Christ's coming. Above these are the *ignudi*, nude figures holding up festoons with papal symbols and medallions. In the four corners are scenes of salvation, including the dramatic hanging of Haman and Judith swiping off Holofernes's head. A stylistic difference is noticeable between the part of the ceiling nearest the entrance and the rest. Perhaps because Michelangelo had a chance to see the results of his work, he painted the second half (away from the entrance) bolder, with larger figures and brighter colours.

The ceiling has no fixed point of view, no single system of perspective and no one clear meaning. Critics cannot agree if the ceiling is a neo-Platonic statement or a theological programme devised with the help of religious experts, including perhaps Julius II. Some critics say the overall theme is salvation, reaching its climax in the *Last Judgment* fresco on the end wall (painted by Michelangelo between 1535 and 1541, and beautifully restored in 1994). It depicts a harrowing image of the souls of the dead rising up to face the wrath of God. The good are promoted to heaven, while the damned are cast down into hell.

Other highlights

The **Chapel of St Nicholas** has some exquisite frescoes by Fra Angelico, representing scenes from the lives of St Laurence and St Stephen. Frescoes by Pinturicchio and his pupils can be seen in the **Borgia Apartments**; these rooms house part of the modern art collection, which includes work by Paul Klee, Francis Bacon and Max Ernst. (Note, however, that the collection is rarely shown in its entirety.) The one-way system will take you back along the vast **Vatican libraries**. Across the courtyard is the entrance to the **Museo Chiaramonti**, with rows of classical statues, and the **Museo Pio-Clementino**, with some of the best works of antiquity. Here are the **Belvedere Torso**, which influenced Michelangelo, and the **Laocoön**, a 1st-century AD piece found in 1506, depicting the Trojan priest and his two sons struggling with two snakes. Also look at Bramante's spiral staircase, just before the octagonal courtyard.

Near the exit is the **Pinacoteca**, home to work by Giotto, Bellini, da Vinci, Raphael, Caravaggio and others. If you have time, try and fit in three other museums: the **Egyptian Collection**, the **Etruscan Collection** and the **Gregoriano Profano Museum**, which includes the Athlete mosaics from the Baths of Caracalla.

Castel Sant'Angelo

The **Castel Sant'Angelo** ❼ (open Tues–Sun 9am–8pm, last entry 1 hour before closing; entrance fee; tel: 06-681 9111), with its magnificent position along the Tiber, is a symbol of Rome. Construction started on it in 123 AD and, 16 years later, it became Hadrian's mausoleum. It has since been a fortress, a prison and the Pope's hiding place in times of trouble. Thanks to patronage from the popes, many of the rooms – such as the Sala Paolina, painted in 1544 – are beautifully frescoed. ❑

THE BORGO

The criss-cross of medieval streets around the Vatican was known as the Città Leonina after Leo IV, who built the fortified walls and connected the Vatican to Castel Sant'Angelo by an overhead passageway in the 9th century. The area is now torn in two by Via della Conciliazione, which ruins the effect of Bernini's piazza, but does allow for a full view of St Peter's with its dome. Across the boulevard is the Borgo Santo Spirito ❹, where the Saxons had a religious school (Borgo comes from the Saxon *burg*). The church of Santo Spirito in Sassia (meaning "nearby the Saxons") ❺ was built for the Saxons in 689 and rebuilt in the 16th century. Next door is the Ospedale Santo Spirito, set up by Pope Innocent III in the 13th century as a hospice for Rome's unwanted babies. Inside, there are many frescoed rooms and a Museum of Sanitary Art ❻ with an ancient Red Cross carriage and a reconstruction of an old laboratory.

THE DIZZYING HEIGHTS OF THE VATICAN

The Sistine Chapel left Tchaikovsky spellbound, feeling "for the first time in my life, a real artist's enthusiasm for painting"

Sensory overload, known as "Stendhal's Syndrome", is a natural response to the majesty of St Peter's and the rich Vatican collections. Every literary visitor has left lyrical or laconic descriptions of the Vatican. However, Henry James found St Peter's a sanctuary from modernity, "when you are weary of the swarming democracy of your fellow-tourists". A character from his *Portrait of a Lady* calls St Peter's "too large – it makes one feel like an atom". Today's visitors may sympathise with the sentiments of Elizabeth Clark, a visitor in the 1950s: "It is a terrific rush to get your money's worth in paint, philosophy, allegory and general information."

CITY STATE

Europe's smallest sovereign state (108 acres/43 hectares) is ruled by the Bishop of Rome, better known as the Pope. A population of 2,000 works in the enclave, from the clergy to ambassadors, Swiss Guards and gardeners. The Vatican boasts its own civil and judicial systems, railway and radio stations, newspaper and car number plates, passports and post office. Visitors are impressed but Romans are sceptical of the world of cassocks, censers and encyclicals. The Vatican City watched millions of pilgrims flock to Rome to celebrate Christ's millennium in Holy Year, the year 2000. In a city that has seen it all before, Romans claimed to be suitably underwhelmed. "Faith is made here and believed elsewhere" runs the cynical city saying.

▷ ETRUSCAN ART
Known as the Mars of Todi, this 5th-century BC bronze is a high point of the Etruscan art collection. The Vatican Museums contain one of the world's greatest collection of antiquities.

▷ MODEL MAP-MAKING
This fresco of Venice, in the Gallery of Maps, is one of many plans created for Gregory XIII depicting the regions and cities of Italy. Another map shows Avignon, which had been the papal residence in 1309–77.

▽ RAPHAEL ROOMS
In 1509, while Michelangelo worked on the Sistine Chapel ceiling, Raphael started to decorate Pope Julius II's apartments. This detail is from the *Battle of the Milvian Bridge*, which was completed in 1525 by Raphael's student, Giulio Romano.

GARDENING FOR THE POPE

Visitors can glimpse the extensive Vatican Gardens from the Gallery of the Candelabra in the Vatican Museums, or from the dome of St Peter's. In the 1960s, writer John Updike was dazzled by the "precipitous paracola" of the view, "a map and postcard combined". By contrast, Oscar Wilde was unimpressed by "that waste, desolate park, with its faded Louis XIV gardens, its sombre avenues, its sad woodland".

The formal grounds also contain a cabbage patch, essential fare for a Polish Pope. The gardeners, like most Vatican employees, are poorly paid but compensated with fringe benefits (such as discounted Vatican shopping and subsidised rents).

To book a tour through the Vatican Gardens, contact the tourist office, tel: 06-6988 4466, fax: 06-6988 5100.

△ GALLERY OF MAPS
This superb, barrel-vaulted gallery is frescoed with maps of Italy. Most were designed by a 16th-century monk and cartographer. Also known as the Hall of Cartography, the gallery is close to the Etruscan Museum and Gallery of the Tapestries.

▷ SISTINE CHAPEL
The newly restored Michelangelo frescoes are controversially colourful. However, even a century ago, Maupassant found them garish, reminiscent of a fairground.

◁ BORGIA APARTMENTS
Lucrezia Borgia in the guise of St Catherine, in a fresco by Pinturicchio. The decoration of these intimate rooms was commissioned by Pope Alexander VI (1492–1503).

VIA DEL CORSO

Map, page 154

Next to the best designer shopping in Rome are the famous Spanish Steps and the former home of John Keats, who was sent to Rome for the good of his health but died there the following year

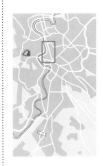

The **Via del Corso** links Piazza del Popolo, for centuries the main entrance to Rome for travellers coming from the north, with Piazza Venezia, long one of Rome's central squares. The name "Corso" dates from the 15th century when Pope Paul II introduced horse racing *(corsi)* along its length. Pope Alexander VII straightened it in the 16th century.

The races were imitations of the ancient games (with all their atrocities) and it wasn't only horses that ran: there were races for prostitutes, children, Jews and cripples. The German poet, Goethe, who lived at No. 19, was one of many visitors to witness the races, which he described in his travel book, *The Italian Journey*. The races were finally banned at the end of the 19th century.

These days, the only people racing along the Corso are politicians being whisked at high speed to Palazzo Chigi in Piazza Colonna, the prime minister's official residence, and the neighbouring Palazzo Montecitorio, the meeting place for the chamber of Deputies, the Italian Parliment. Piazza Colonna marks a divide in the street: the stretch from here to Piazza Venezia is lined with mighty palaces, mainly homes to banks, whereas the stretch to Piazza del Popolo is a partly pedestrianised area where shoppers browse windows displaying *svago* (leisure) and fashion wear. In the early evening and on Saturdays, Romans swarm into town to stroll up and down this stretch of the Corso and the surrounding streets.

PRECEDING PAGES: Piazza del Popolo. **LEFT:** painting portraits on the Spanish Steps.

Piazza del Popolo

At the top of the street is **Piazza del Popolo ❶**, one of the most impressive squares in Rome. The paving was allegedly paid for by taxes levied on prostitutes and Piazza was used for executions at one time. In the 19th century, the square was remodelled by Valadier, who added the elegant *pincio* ramps and created the oval form. The most striking feature of this elegant square is the obelisk. Stolen from Egypt by the Emperor Augustus, it once decorated the Circus Maximus where it was used as a turning point during chariot races.

The obelisk divides twin churches designed by Rainaldi. Although they appear identical, one is octagonal and the other dodecagonal. To the side of Porta Flaminia is the plain facade of the church of **Santa Maria del Popolo**, built in 1472 over a pre-existing 11th-century chapel. Inside are two fine paintings by Caravaggio, a chapel designed by Raphael and Bernini, an apse by Bramante and frescoes by Pinturicchio.

Three streets lead off from the piazza. The central road is the Corso. **Via di Ripetta** leads towards the Mausoleum of Augustus and the Ara Pacis. **Via del Babuino**, which is lined with interesting design and antique shops, leads to Piazza di Spagna. Parallel to this street is **Via Margutta**, a pretty, narrow street with

OBELISKS

There are a number of notable obelisks in Rome. Many were brought back by triumphant armies and erected in public places to show the power of the empire, but some – such as the one at the top of the Spanish Steps – are Roman imitations of Egyptian originals. The oldest, and tallest, obelisk is the one in Piazza di San Giovanni in Laterano. Erected at the Temple of Ammon in Thebes in the 15th century BC, it was brought to Rome in 357 AD on the orders of Constantius II. Made of red granite, it stands 30m (100 ft) tall. The obelisk in Piazza del Popolo is the next oldest, dating from the 12th or 13th century BC. The most recent is the Obelisk of Axum, next to the United Nations building near the Circus Maximus, which was brought back from Ethiopia by Mussolini's army in 1937.

artists' studios, galleries and workshops. Twice a year, the street holds a special art show dedicated to the works of 100 painters.

The Spanish Steps

Halfway along the Corso is **Via Condotti**, designer-label heaven. This street, plus the parallel streets of **Via Borgognona** and **Via Frattina**, which are linked by the equally sumptuous **Via Bocca di Leone**, are home to all the top fashion outlets. Matching the expensive shops are some of the best hotels in Rome.

On the Spanish Steps.

Towards the end of Via Condotti is the world-famous tourist trap **Caffè Greco**, said to have been opened by a Greek merchant in 1760. The great and the good down the centuries have frequented this café, including Baudelaire, Wagner, Taine, Listz, Stendhal, Goethe, Byron, Keats and Shelley.

Piazza di Spagna ❷ focuses on the **Spanish Steps**, so-called because there has been a Spanish Embassy to the Holy See in Palazzo di Spagna since the 17th century. The French, meanwhile, owned the land around the convent of Trinità dei Monti at the top of the steps, so they claimed the right to pass through the square and named part of it French Square. This petty rivalry between the French and Spanish reached a climax with the building of the Spanish Steps.

The original design was intended to sing the praises of the French monarchy and there was to have been a huge equestrian statue of Louis XIV. However, the Pope was against this idea and so when de Sanctis finally started building the steps in the 18th century, the only reference made to France was the little fleur-de-lis on the pedestals.

BELOW RIGHT:
inside Santa Maria
del Popolo.

The cascade of Spanish Steps is perennially crowded with visitors. In spring, the crowds are joined by pots of blossoming azaleas and, at Christmas, by a

Nativity scene. In front of the steps is the fountain by Bernini's father Pietro. The **Barcaccia** is a half-sunken boat fed by water from the ancient aqueduct *Acqua Vergine*. At the top of the steps is the Trinità dei Monti, which remains French to this day and is worth visiting mainly for the the view over the city from its entrance and the damaged *Descent from the Cross* by da Volterra.

Next to the stairs, in the pink house, is the **Keats-Shelley Museum** (open Mon–Fri 9am–1pm & 3–6pm, Sat 11am–2pm & 3–6pm; entrance fee; tel: 06-678 4235), where Keats lived in 1820 when he was sent to Rome on account of consumption – Keats's doctor thought that Rome's warm, dry climate would benefit his condition. Keats died the following year, aged just 25. In 1906, the house was bought by an Anglo-American association and turned into a museum and library dedicated to Keats and fellow Romantics who had made Rome their home for a while. The few rooms open to visitors have personal objects and documents from the lives of Shelley and Byron, but the focus is on Keats – his prints, paintings, books and death mask are on display.

On one side of the square is **Palazzo di Propaganda Fide**, the missionary centre of the Catholic Church since 1622, with a grand undulating facade by Borromini. Above is the **Colonna dell'Immacolata Concezione** erected in 1856 to celebrate Pius IX's proclamation of the dogma of the Immaculate Conception.

Monuments to Augustus

Two ancient monuments on Via di Ripetta date from the time of Augustus. In honour of the peace Augustus established throughout the empire, the Senate built an altar of peace, now incongruously placed in a modern glass building next to the Tiber (1970). Near the altar stands Augustus's tomb.

The **Ara Pacis Augustae**, an altar built in 13 BC to commemorate the era of peace that followed Augustus's victories in Gaul and Spain, is screened off in the building's centre. Particularly impressive is the frieze of the inauguration on the outer side of the screen. The part furthest from the river shows the imperial family – led by the somewhat decayed figure of the emperor – and the family's household. The man with the axe was the official sacrificer and behind him stands Agrippa. Many of those in the inaugurational frieze brought their children to the ceremony, some of whom seem bored by the event. (The altar is currently closed for restoration until at least mid-2004. Check with the tourist office for more details.)

Behind the altar is the **Mausoleo di Augusto ❸** (not open to the public), which was restored by Mussolini. The mausoleum was built between 28 and 23 BC – long before it was expected to be occupied. Covered with statues and faced with marble, it was one of the most magnificent sights in Rome. The emperor was buried inside the central chamber while members of his family were allocated rooms around him. As with many ancient remains, it served as a medieval fort and was even a theatre for a while in the 19th century.

The Corso

Halfway along the Corso is **Piazza Colonna ❹**, which has the street's only relic from its classical incarnation, the **Colonna di Marco Aurelio** (Column of Marcus

ROMAN FASHION

Italy's fashion industry is revered the world over, and while most business in centred on Milan, there are a handful of top designers who have made their base in Rome. The most famous of these is probably Valentino, who opened his Roman studio in 1959 and has enjoyed success ever since. His high-profile clients have included Sophia Loren, Audrey Hepburn and Jackie Kennedy. Other top Rome-based names to look for include Sorelle Fontana, Fendi and Laura Biagiotti. Of course, all the other well-known Italian designers, among them Versace, Armani and Trussardi, have shops in Rome, mostly around Via Condotti, as well. However, those who cannot afford top designer names should not be put off shopping for clothes. All Italian women like to look their best and there are plenty of boutiques selling clothes with less frightening price tags. Remember, too, that Italy produces stunning leather accessories.

Map, see opposite

TIP

The Museo di Palazzo
Venezia plays host to
many of the major
touring exhibitions
that come to Rome.

BELOW: Ara Pacis
Augustae. **RIGHT:**
a distant view of
the Vittoriano.

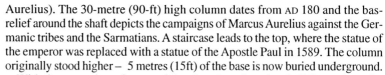

Aurelius). The 30-metre (90-ft) high column dates from AD 180 and the bas-relief around the shaft depicts the campaigns of Marcus Aurelius against the Germanic tribes and the Sarmatians. A staircase leads to the top, where the statue of the emperor was replaced with a statue of the Apostle Paul in 1589. The column originally stood higher – 5 metres (15ft) of the base is now buried underground.

With the exception of some of the churches, the other buildings along the Corso were built in the last three centuries. On the other side of the Corso from Piazza Colonna is **Santa Maria in Via Lata**, which has an impressive facade by da Cortona. In a side street next to the church is one of Rome's "talking" fountains, the *Facchino* (or water-bearer). In the days before freedom of speech the *Facchino* and other "talking statues" were hung with satirical and subversive messages and fulfilled much the same function as a newspaper. Another noteworthy church is **San Marcello ❺**, further along the Corso towards Piazza Venezia, which has a Van Dyck crucifix in the sacristy.

The palace on the right at the end of the Corso is **Palazzo Doria Pamphilj ❻** (entrance on Piazza del Collegio Romano; open Fri–Wed 10am–5pm; private apartments closed for restoration until 2003; entrance fee; tel: 06-679 7323), which contains one of the best art collections in Rome with over 400 paintings from the 15th to 18th centuries. The gallery walls are plastered with pictures, including the famous Velasquez portrait of Innocent X and canvasses by Titian, Caravaggio, Lotto and Lorrain. The other gallery on the Corso is in **Palazzo Ruspoli ❼**, close to Via Condotti, where important temporary exhibitions are frequently held.

The white monstrosity in front of the gallery is the 19th-century **Vittoriano**, otherwise known as the Altar of the Nation or *macchina da scrivere*, the typewriter. Before this "enormous white cancerous tumour", as the poet Gabriele d'Annunzio called it, was built to mark Unification (it is named after Victor Emmanuel II of Savoy, the first king of a unified Italy), the site was occupied by a tightly-knit housing quarter dating from medieval Rome. Visitors can climb up the monument for wonderful views of the city (open Tues–Sun 10.30am–4pm; free).

If all roads lead to Rome, all roads in Rome lead to **Piazza Venezia ❽**, the hub of the city's road network since 1881. Some 800,000 Romans squeeze their cars past here every day. Before the Altar of the Nation, **Palazzo di Venezia** was the most important building on this square. Built by Cardinal Barbo in 1455 and enlarged when he became Pope Paul II, it was later handed over to the Venetian ambassadors and then the Austrians until Mussolini decided it would make a perfect office. He used to speak to the crowds from the balcony, the very balcony from which Pope Paul II watched the races along the Corso.

This palace now holds the **Museo del Palazzo di Venezia ❾** (open Tues–Sun 9am–7pm; entrance fee; tel: 06-6999 4319), which has an exceedingly wide range of attractions, including medieval paintings, sculptures and artefacts, terracotta models for statues (some by Bernini), ceramics, bronze sculptures, and glass, silver and ivory objects. The museum has a permanent collection of Renaissance arts and crafts. Behind the Palace is the church of **San Marco** with a lovely mosaic in its 9th-century apse. ❏

VILLA BORGHESE

Once the country estates of wealthy Romans, these gardens have been swallowed up by the city and turned into into public parks filled with elegant architecture and fine museums

Map, page 160

This chapter covers Via Veneto, which leads north from the city centre to the Villa Borghese Gardens. It also includes the northeastern part of the city lying between the two ancient Roman roads of Via Nomentana and Via Salaria.

Since ancient times, wealthy Romans have built their country estates in this area. Nowadays, the extending city has encroached on these villas and many of the gardens have become public parks. The surrounding greenery, the elegant architecture and the proximity to the city centre have made the area a prestigious and desirable residential area.

Via Veneto

The southern end of **Via Veneto ❶** (officially Via Vittorio Veneto, after the victory over the Austrians in World War I) begins in **Piazza Barberini**, a busy square with a cinema and fast-food joints. In its centre is Bernini's **Fontana del Tritone** (Triton Fountain) and, on the corner with Via Veneto, his **Fontana delle Api** (Bee Fountain), featuring a bee of incredible dimensions, immortalising yet again the Barberini coat of arms.

Via Veneto itself, lined with plane trees and pavement cafés, was once the symbol of Roman fashion and style. However, the glorious days of *la dolce vita*, immortalised on screen by Fellini, are long gone. Anita Ekberg now lives in retirement in the Castelli Romani, and the intellectuals have drifted to Piazza del Popolo and the area around Piazza Navona. Some fashion designers remain loyal to Via Veneto, however, and hold their *Super-Sfilata* fashion show in the Excelsior Hotel.

For a macabre diversion, examine the remains of 4,000 Capuchin monks in the crypt of the church of **Santa Maria della Concezione** (crypt open Fri–Wed, 9am–noon, 3–6pm; donations expected; tel: 06-487 1185) at the southern end of Via Veneto at No. 27. Here, bones and skulls are ornately displayed, setting a new style in interior design.

Gardens of Sallust

The **Horti Sallustiani** (Gardens of Sallust) lay between Via Veneto and the Villa Borghese Gardens. Gaius Sallustius, an historian and war profiteer who made enormous fortunes out of the campaigns of 40–30 BC, embellished his home with magnificent gardens. Soon hailed as one of the wonders of the world, they were quickly appropriated by the Empire. Vespasian and Titus preferred this part of Rome to the Palatine.

Fountains, pools and mosaic floors once drew awed visitors. Now the gardens lie 15 metres (45 ft) below street level, buried by the rubble from collapsed houses

LEFT and **BELOW:** grand architecture and sculpture in the Villa Borghese Gardens.

Triton Fountain on Piazza Barberini.

and the building activity of the 19th century. Archaeological finds from the gardens include the obelisk at the top of the Spanish Steps and those on show in the **Museo Nazionale Romano ❷** *(see page 181)*.

The colourful life of the gardens ended when the Goths, under Alaric, stormed the Holy City by the nearby **Porta Salaria** in 410. In the Middle Ages, the family of Ludovisi-Boncompagni injected new life into the gardens by planting 30 hectares (74 acres) of vineyards and hosting garden festivals.

They lasted until the uninhibited property boom of the 1880s, which spelt demolition for the gardens.The *Società Generale Immobiliare*, backed mainly by German and French capital, made an irresistible offer to the Ludovisi princes and the villa was split up. All that remains is the 16th-century **Casino dell' Aurora** in the gardens of the Swiss Cultural Institute.

The other part of the gardens spared by developers is behind the American Embassy, which is housed in **Palazzo Margherita**, completed in 1890. A Ludovisi prince had this gigantic building constructed as a substitute for his lost garden, but his money ran out and he had to sell it to the Savoy royal family, who moved the queen mother in. It bears her name to this day.

Villa Borghese

At the northern end of Via Veneto, outside the **Porta Pinciana**, is the **Villa Borghese**, which was founded at the beginning of the 17th century by Cardinal Scipione Borghese Caffarelli, a nephew of Pope Paul V. The family later extended their property by buying some nearby land, so that 100 years ago the park encompassed 75 hectares (190 acres), which the Borghese frequently opened to the public. Property developers cast a greedy eye on the villa in the

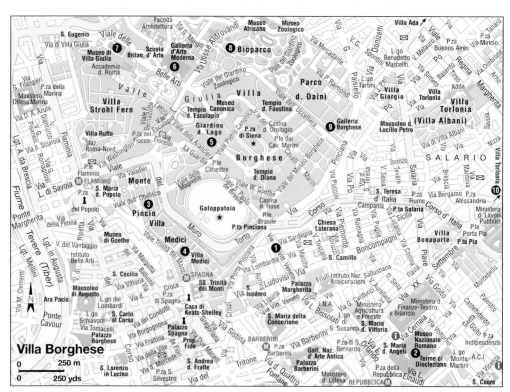

late 19th century and their plans provoked the first battle to save the Romans' traditional society promenade. Eventually, in 1901, the state bought the Villa and, two years later, gave it to the people. The Villa Borghese, along with the Pincio Gardens and the Villa Giulia, is now home to three museums worth visiting and the city zoo.

The Villa Borghese Gardens are laid out among hills with winding paths and attractive *casine*, or flowerbeds, hidden here and there. On Sunday, the people of Rome take over the park. Every corner is full of squawking children at play, while their fathers sit with transistors pressed to their ears so as not to miss a single goal.

A wide *viale* leads downhill from the Porta Pinciana, passing on the left the **Galoppatoio** (horse track) and on the right a statue of Goethe. Veer left at Piazzale Canestre into Viale delle Magnolie and head over the bridge, crossing the busy Viale del Muro Torto into the **Pincio Gardens** ❸, which were designed by Valadier in the 19th century. Look out for the fanciful water clock and the **Casina Valadier**, an elegant café visited by the intellectuals of the Roman *belle époque*. Nowadays, it is a pricey bar and restaurant.

Further down the Salita del Pincio is the majestic **Villa Medici** ❹. Rebuilt in the 16th century for the Crescenzi family, it was then passed to the Medici family, before being confiscated by Napoleon in 1803 and made into the home of the French Academy. Its doors open to the public for occasional exhibitions and concerts. There are also guided tours of the gardens on Saturday and Sunday mornings (call ahead, tel: 06-67 611).

Backtrack and cross the bridge to where a wide *viale* leads up to **Piazza di Siena** on the right. This oval track is the site of the International Horse Show in

Map, see opposite

BELOW: Casina del Lago in the Villa Borghese Gardens.

May – an important social and sporting event. Top-quality show-jumping is spiced up with a cavalry charge by the mounted *carabinieri*.

To the left is the pretty **Giardino del Lago ❺** and its tiny lake, in the middle of which stands a reproduction of a Greek temple of Aesculapius. Rowing-boats may be hired for a brief paddle. Nearby, you will find the **Fountain of Fauns**, created in 1929 by Giovanni Nicolini.

Two sloping ramps lead down to Viale delle Belle Arti. Opposite is the white neoclassical facade of the **Galleria Nazionale d'Arte Moderna ❻** (open Tues–Sun 8.30am–7.30pm, Sat until 11pm in summer; entrance fee; tel: 06-322 981), which has a permanent collection of 19th- and 20th-century pieces, and frequently hosts travelling exhibitions of international importance.

Next door, in the appropriately named **Piazza Winston Churchill**, is the **Accademia Britannica** (British Academy), designed by Lutyens and home to visiting scholars. Around the bend, in the beautiful 15th-century **Villa Giulia ❼**, built for Julius II, is the **Museo Nazionale Etrusco di Villa Giulia** (open Tues–Sun 8.30am–7.30pm; entrance fee; tel: 06-320 1951). Etruscan finds from northern Latium and Umbria are exhibited here, including the sarcophagus of the married couple – *degli Sposi* – from the excavations in Cerveteri, dating from the 6th century BC. They form one of the finest collections of Etruscan art in the world, rivalled only by the Vatican collection.

Retracing your steps along Via delle Belle Arti will bring you back into the park. The romantic Pincio Gardens, with views over Piazza del Popolo and the city, offer far better evening strolls.

The road leading uphill to the left ends at the entrance to Rome's zoo, or **Bioparco ❽**, as it is now called (open Mon–Fri 9.30am–6pm, Sat, Sun & pub-

BELOW: Galleria Nazionale d'Arte Moderna.

lic holidays 9.30am–7pm, last entry 1 hour before closing; entrance fee; tel: 06-360 8211). In the past the zoo had a reputation for being somewhat neglected, but in recent years the management have made some worthy and fairly successful attempts to phase out the caging of exotic animals and keep other specimens in more humane, purpose-built 'environments' that more closely resemble their natural habitats. Recent acquisitions include two beautiful giraffes.

From here, Viale dell'Uccelliera leads to the **Galleria Borghese ❾** (open Tues–Sun 9am–7pm; reservations advisable, especially in high season; entrance fee; tel: 06-328 10). This houses one of the world's great private art collections, assembled by Cardinal Scipione Borghese Caffarelli in the 17th century. The entrance is at Piazzale Scipione Borghese 5 *(see page 164 for more details)*.

Via Salaria

To the northeast, Via Salaria crosses the suburbs and leads out to the Sabine Hills. This old Roman road is named after the salt *(sale)* which was transported into Rome from these hills. Just before the Salaria Bridge (built in 1874) is the hill of Monte Antenne, named after *Ante Amnes* ("before two rivers": the Tiber and the Aniene).

This is where the Sabine settlement of the *Antemnae* is said to have stood and, from here, the Romans, under Romulus, are supposed to have kidnapped the Sabine women. Via Salaria was an important street and, in the early years of Christianity, many churches and catacombs were built here.

At No. 430 is the entrance to the **Catacombe di Priscilla** (open Tues–Sun 8.30am–noon & 2.30–5pm; entrance fee; tel: 06-8620 6272). These catacombs were started in the 1st century in the gardens of Priscilla Acilii's estate and were greatly extended in the 4th century. Some popes were buried here, which

Map, page 160

A Caravaggio at the Galleria Villa Borghese.

BELOW: at the zoo.

Map,
page 160

explains why there are good-quality frescoes and stucco decorations. The catacombs extend under the park of Villa Ada, which is now the Egyptian Embassy but was King Vittorio Emanuele II's hunting lodge. It is surrounded by a beautiful park which is open to the public. This park, along with the Villa Doria Pamphilj, is the largest area of greenery in Rome.

On the other side of the Villa Ada is the chic residential area of **Parioli**, where the main attraction is the **Mosque**, built by the Italian post-modern architect Portoghesi in 1992. Rome's first mosque, it serves a Muslim population of 100,000.

Coppedè's creation

To the east of Via Salaria, either side of Via Po, is the fashionable area known as **Quartiere Coppedè** (or Quartiere Dora), after the Florentine architect who designed many of the buildings in this part of the city.

Of particular interest is **Piazza Mincio**, a square with an unusual fountain of frogs, that Gabriele d'Annunzio described as "a genuine disgrace to Rome". Coppedè, whose buildings were the last notable architecture of pre-Fascist Rome, intended this square to show a harmony between the individual details of each house and the great tradition of Florentine craftsmanship.

Via Nomentana

Further east, on Via Nomentana, is the **Villa Torlonia** ❿, the last great villa built in Rome. The Torlonia family contracted the French architect Valadier to design the villa, which also had a small lake, guest house, sports field and Temple of Saturn. The villa later became one of Mussolini's private residences. Now, the buildings are in a state of neglect, but the gardens are still open to the public.

Located beneath the villa, the Jewish Catacombs, two cemeteries dating from the 3rd and 4th centuries, extend for about 9 km (6 miles), but they are in bad repair and closed to the public.

Behind the Villa Torlonia, at the end of Via G.B. di Rossi, is the **Villa Massimo**, now the German Academy.

Continuing down Via Nomentana, you come to the church of **Sant'Agnese fuori le Mura**, built over a complex of catacombs next door to the circular mausoleum built for Constantine's daughters, Costanza and Helen. The interior vaulting of the mausoleum is decorated with exquisite 4th-century mosaics depicting scenes of the *vendemmia* (grape harvest), and in the apses of the chapels are 6th- and 7th-century mosaics representing biblical scenes.

The neighbouring church, built over the catacombs where St Agnes was buried, dates from the 4th century, although it was rebuilt and decorated with a Byzantine-style apse mosaic in the 7th century and has been restored several times since. The relics of St Agnes, who was martyred in AD 304, are housed in the high altar. Every 21 January, the saint's day, two lambs are blessed and shorn to make woollen robes for the Pope *(palliums)*.

Via Nomentana leads to the ancient Nomentum (modern Mentana) and is joined by Via Salaria. Before leaving Rome, the street crosses the Aniene River, where the picturesque bridge, originally dating from the 2nd century BC, is still in use. ❑

RIGHT: on the lake in the Villa Borghese Gardens.

GALLERIA BORGHESE

The Galleria Borghese is housed in an early 17th-century *palazzina* that was designed by a Dutchman, Jan van Santen. It is divided into two sections: the sculpture collection, on the ground floor, is called the Museo, while the art collection is known as the Galleria and is on the first floor. Unfortunately, between 1801 and 1809, the Borghese sculpture collection was severely depleted, when more than 200 pieces were sold to the Louvre in Paris. However, there are still some marvellous pieces to be seen. They include some of Bernini's best work, such as *Apollo and Daphne* and *Pluto and Persephone*, as well as Canova's famous statue of Pauline Borghese, Napoleon Bonaparte's sister, posing as Venus. The Galleria is filled with paintings by the most famous Italian masters of the 16th and 17th centuries: Perugino, Raphael, Botticelli, Caravaggio and Titian.

TRASTEVERE

*Trastevere was not originally part of Rome, but the beginning
of Etruscan country. Consequently, it is very different
and maintains an atmosphere all of its own*

Map,
page 168

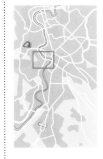

Across the river from the Centro Storico – "trans Tiberium" – lies **Trastevere**. In ancient times, it was mainly settled by sailors and foreigners. For example, in the 1st century BC, Rome's first Jews settled in Trastevere, where they were joined in AD 70 by slaves and captives brought back by Titus after the sack of Jerusalem. As a result of its isolation, the area has kept its character over thousands of years.

Today, however, Trastevere is facing changes following the gradual exodus of its long-standing inhabitants. Wealthy Italians and foreigners are slowly, but steadily, changing the character of life in this quarter, and there is less and less room for the old Trasteverini. However, Trastevere has kept some of its peculiarities, even if the old *trattorie* and *osterie* are giving way to pizzerias. During the day, Trastevere is left to its sleepy self: residents exercise dogs and do their daily shopping, while the children play and the elderly sit in the roads outside their houses, chatting and chopping vegetables in preparation for the next meal. In the evenings, especially in summer, the main streets and squares are packed with locals and tourists, who flock to eat, drink or stroll among stalls selling ethnic jewellery and fortune-tellers shuffling their cards.

LEFT: the church of Santa Maria in Trastevere.
BELOW: bar in Trastevere.

Isola Tiberina

The most picturesque route into Trastevere is from the Jewish Ghetto, through **Isola Tiberina ❶**, an island in the middle of the Tiber that is linked to both banks by bridges. This island has been associated with good health since 293 BC, when a serpent, which was being brought from the shrine of Aesculapius (the Greek god of healing) in the hope that it would avert an outbreak of plague, escaped from the ship in which it was being transported and swam ashore. According to legend, a shrine was built on Tiberina at the spot where the snake reached solid ground and the sick came to visit the shrine in the hope of being cured. In the 10th century, the German Emperor Otto III built the church of St Bartholomew over Aesculapius's shrine.

Whether or not there is a grain of truth in the snake story is unclear. There is, however, another story surrounding the island, which claims that it was formed when sacks of grain were thrown into the river in a revolt against the Tarquinian kings.

We know for certain that there has been a hospital on the island since the Middle Ages, run by the *Fatebenefratelli* (the "do good brothers", named after the chant they sang to beg alms for the sick).

The two bridges linking Isola Tiberina to the shore are among the oldest structures still in use in Rome. The **Ponte Fabricio** (leading to the north bank) was built, as the inscription says, in 62 BC by the civil engineer

Lucius Fabricius, and the **Ponte Cestio** was built in 42 BC by Lucius Cestius and restored in AD 370. However, the central arch is all that remains from that date – the rest is a late 19th-century reconstruction. Off the eastern end are the remains of the first stone bridge in Rome, now known as the **Ponte Rotto** (Broken Bridge), built in 142 BC. Most of what remains today is a 1575 rebuilding by Gregory XIII, which was washed away in 1598. The modern bridge behind it, Ponte Palatino, is sometimes called the English Bridge, because it is the only stretch of road in Rome on which cars drive on the left.

The Ponte Cestio leads straight to the church of **San Benedetto in Piscinula**, in Piazza in Piscinula. It may not be as big as St Peter's, but it has the oldest bell in the city, dating from the 10th century. From here, it is a short walk to Piazza di Santa Cecilia and the church of **Santa Cecilia ❷**. In AD 230, St Cecilia, the patron saint of music, was killed here by a combination of suffocation and attempted decapitation. In 1599, her tomb was opened and her body, in a semi-foetal position, was found in a miraculous state of preservation. A sculpture by Maderno, modelled on sketches made of the body, stands on the altar. The excavations under the church of Santa Cecilia can be visited during church opening times (daily 9.30am–12.30pm & 4–6.30pm), while upstairs in the gallery is a veritable masterpiece of Gothic art, the remains of Cavallini's fresco *The Last Judgement* (gallery open Tues & Thur 10am–noon, Sun 11.30am–12.30pm).

Something old, something new

Like every old quarter of Rome, Trastevere had to make sacrifices when the capital started expanding after 1870. For example, the broad swathe of the **Viale di Trastevere**, first dedicated to the king and then "to labour", cuts magisterially

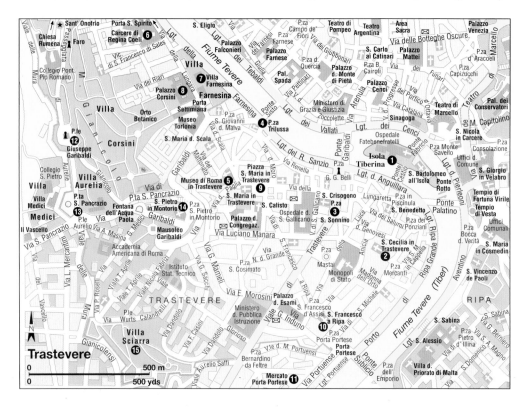

through the patchwork of Trastevere's little streets. At its northern end, on the banks of the Tiber, is **Piazza G.G. Belli**, named after the most important 19th-century Roman poet, Giuseppe Gioacchino Belli (1791–1863) whose statue is found here. Behind Piazza Belli is **Piazza Sidney Sonnino ❸**. The 13th-century **Torre degli Anguillara** is where Dante stayed during the Holy Year of 1300. Across Viale di Trastevere is the 18th-century church of **San Crisogono**, which is built over one of the oldest sites of Christian worship in Rome – originally a private house dating from the 2nd or 3rd century. There are also remains of an 8th-century church and 11th-century frescoes in San Crisogono's basement.

Another popular poet admired for his satirical wit was Carlo Alberto Salustri, known as Trilussa. A monument to him occupies the riverside square to the north, **Piazza Trilussa ❹**. Trilussa died in 1950, but even after death he seems to be addressing an audience: his statue bends forward slightly and one hand is out-stretched. The **Museo di Roma in Trastevere ❺** (Rome's Folklore Museum; open Tues–Sun 10am–8pm; last entry 30 minutes before closing; entrance fee; tel: 06-581 6563) on Piazza Sant'Egidio includes a reconstruction of part of Trilussa's house, as well as a collection of historic prints and artefacts.

Opposite the fountain on Piazza Trilussa is the end of the Ponte Sisto, a footbridge linking Trastevere with the end of Via Giulia. From Piazza Trilussa, go along Via Benedetta to the lower end of **Via Garibaldi**, which leads to the Gianicolo (Jan-iculum Hill). This route was used in the Middle Ages by pilgrims en route to the Vatican, before they turned right through the **Porta Settimiana**, a gate erected by the Emperor Septimius Severus and replaced by Pope Alexander VI in 1498.

The true Trasteverini know this route – Via della Lungara – for another reason. It runs straight to the old Roman prison, the **Regina Coeli ❻** (Queen of Heaven).

**Map,
page 168**

Garibaldi
Monument on
Piazzale Garibaldi.

BELOW: Tiber Island.

The euphemistic name came from its previous occupants, Carmelite nuns. Traditionally, it was said that if you wanted to be a true Trasteverino, you had to go down to the dungeons at least once to "make your mark".

Of rather more interest to most visitors are Palazzo Corsini and the **Villa Farnesina** ❼ (open Mon–Sat 9am–1pm; entrance fee; tel: 06-6880 1767). The villa was commissioned in 1508 by a wealthy Roman banker called Agostino Chigi. It was decorated by some of the best artists of the time: the frescoes in the downstairs rooms include the *Galatea* and *Three Graces* by Raphael (who is said to have used Chigi's mistress as one of his models) and works by Peruzzi. Upstairs is a fine *trompe l'oeil* depicting contemporary views of Rome by Peruzzi, and the magnificent *Wedding of Roxanne and Alexander* by Sodoma.

Santa Maria in Trastevere.

Across the road from the villa is **Palazzo Corsini** ❽ (open Tues–Sun 8.30am–7.30pm; entrance fee; tel: 06-6880 2323). It was built for Cardinal Domenico Riario in the 15th century, and Queen Christina of Sweden lived and died here after her conversion to Catholicism in 1654. Today, it houses part of the **Galleria Nazionale d'Arte Antica** (the rest is in Palazzo Barberini), which includes works by Rubens, Van Dyck, Caravaggio and Reni.

Behind Palazzo Corsini is the **Orto Botanico** (Botanical Garden; open Tues–Sat 9.30am–6.30pm in summer, until 5.30pm in winter; entrance fee; tel: 06-4991 7106), originally part of the palace's grounds but now open to the public and a peaceful spot for a stroll in summer. There are about 7,000 plants on display, including a scented garden for the blind and a collection of medicinal herbs. On the slopes leading up to the Gianicolo is a series of tiered fountains.

Via della Scala leads through Piazza Sant'Egidio to **Piazza Santa Maria in Trastevere** ❾, the heart of the neighbourhood. This pedestrianised square is one of

BELOW: Porta Portese, the biggest flea market in Rome.

the most peaceful in Rome. Many people while away their day in one of the cafés or sitting against Fontana's Fountain (1692), where musicians perform in the summer. The piazza takes its name from the basilica on the east side of the square, one of the oldest in Rome and probably the first to be dedicated to the Virgin. Its present appearance dates from the 12th century, although the portico (which has been cleaned and treated to protect it from the ravages of Rome's pollution) was added in 1702. The 12th- and 13th-century mosaics, both inside and outside the church, are spectacular and it is worth taking a pair of binoculars to enjoy their details. *The Life of the Virgin* series is by Cavallini (1291). Today, the church is used for smart weddings and funerals or for visits by important members of the church.

The comparative tranquillity of this square is broken only when the Festa dei Noantri turns the whole of Trastevere into a noisy theatre and market-place during the last two weeks of July. There's a completely different atmosphere in the nearby **Piazza San Cosimato**, where the daily food market is surrounded by shops, bars, restaurants and a hospital.

The nearby church of **San Francesco a Ripa ⑩** existed as early as the 10th century, but its present appearance dates from 17th-century renovations. Inside, there are a couple of masterpieces: Bernini's *Blessed Ludovica Albertoni* and Il Baciccia's *St Ann and the Virgin Mary*.

Trastevere's market

On Sunday mornings, the big draw in Trastevere is the **Porta Portese ⑪**, one of the largest flea markets in Europe, with over 4,000 stalls. When it was established after World War II, it was a centre for black marketeering. Although its traders are now (for the most part) legal, it is still very popular with Romans and visitors alike,

**Map,
page 168**

TIP

Arrive before 8am if you want to rummage for bargains or to see the market before it gets completely packed.

BELOW: the park on Gianicolo Hill.

Map, page 168

TIP

Walk the 1.5 km (1 mile) crest of Gianicolo, along Passeggiata di Gianicolo for panoramic views across the city.

RIGHT: Villa Farnesina.

and has a great atmosphere. The market stretches from Porta Portese itself to **Viale di Trastevere** and reaches nearly as far as Trastevere station. Almost anything you could imagine is on sale here, from the sublime to the ridiculous: antiques, flowers, spare parts for cars, second-hand and new clothes, foodstuffs, comics, china and other household wares. Stallholders flock here from all over Italy and beyond. Some of the more exotic goods for sale include silk shirts from China, all manner of items from Russia, woven fabric and clothes from Latin America, and incense and spices from India. This is the most interesting market in Rome, even if the prices – particularly for antiques – have risen sharply in recent years.

The Gianicolo (Janiculum Hill)

Behind, and above, Trastevere is the **Gianicolo**. After the liberation of Rome from papal rule in 1870, this hill became a gathering place where anticlerical citizens of Rome could honour their hero, Giuseppe Garibaldi. A monument to Garibaldi was built at **Piazzale Garibaldi** ⑫ and, a little further north, another was built for his wife, the intrepid Anita, who is portrayed charging into battle on her horse. South of Garibaldi's monument is **Porta San Pancrazio** ⑬, a partial reconstruction of the gate built in the time of Urban VIII. As on in the Pincio gardens in Villa Borghese, there are busts of some of the heroes of the Risorgimento who came to Rome.

Today, citizens are fond of strolling in the park, watching puppet shows and buying from the stalls that line the path. The lighthouse dates from 1911 and was a gift to Rome from Italians who had emigrated to Argentina.

Also on the hill is the church of **San Pietro in Montorio** ⑭, constructed in the 15th century near what was then believed to be the site of St Peter's crucifixion. The chapels within the church contain works by Vasari, del Piombo and Bernini. In the church courtyard, Bramante's *Tempietto*, one of the gems of the Renaissance, was erected in 1502. Although tiny, it is a perfect example of the classical proportions used by Renaissance architects.

Via Garibaldi continues up the hill, past a memorial to those who died liberating Rome, to the **Fontana dell' Acqua Paola**, a fountain commissioned in 1612 by Pope Paul V to grace the end of an ancient aqueduct built by Trajan. Designed in the shape of a church facade, there is something surreal about the way the water gushes out from under the fountain's three arches.

South of Gianicolo Hill is a smaller park, full of statuary and shady trees, called the **Villa Sciarra**, which was the garden of a 16th-century villa. Larger expanses of verdure lie further west in the biggest public park in the city, the **Villa Doria Pamphilj**, laid out in 1652 by Camillo Pamphilj, nephew of Pope Innocent X. He also paid for the building of the summer residence in the park, the **Casino del Bel Respiro**. In the 1960s, the park was bought by the state and opened to the public.

As the Villa Doria Pamphilj is some way from the city centre, and is too large to be overcrowded with monuments, much of the natural landscape remains unspoilt and it is, therefore, a peaceful place for a walk or in which to enjoy a picnic. Some of the formal gardens, including artificial lakes and carefully placed trees, have survived, but other parts remain inaccessible, hidden and overgrown. ❑

BRAMANTE'S TEMPIETTO

When the centre of the Renaissance shifted from northern Italy to Rome at the end of the 15th century, the atmosphere of the Eternal City injected a fresh impetus for the architects of the day to rediscover the styles and motifs of Antiquity. Donato Bramante had learned his trade in the north and moved to Rome in 1499. The Tempietto di San Pietro in Montorio (1502) was almost his first commission in Rome, but it bears little resemblance to anything he had produced while working in Milan. This is the first monument of the High Renaissance style.

Set in an Early Renaissance courtyard, the Tempietto possess a gravity all of its own. On closer inspection, visitors will see that there is very little surface decoration and that the style of the colonnade – Tuscan Doric – is also unadorned. It supports a classical entablature, which lends further weight and severity to the building. These features, combined with the perfect classical proportions, make the Tempietto a quite brilliant homage to Antiquity.

THE AVENTINE HILL AND TESTACCIO

The most southerly of Rome's hills, the Aventine has always been a popular residential area. It is also, however, home to a good number of religious shrines

The Aventine is now one of the most desirable places to live in Rome, being both conveniently located close to the city centre and surprisingly peaceful. In the 3rd century BC, the hill was included within the city walls – mainly for strategic reasons – and was virtually uninhabited until the plebs, in conflict with the nobility, retreated to this area to organise the first general strikes.

During the Republican years, the Aventine Hill was the site of secret meetings and midnight rituals of the Dionysian and Bacchian cults. The wild, drunken orgies were discovered in 186 BC and thousands of participants were put to death. Imperial Rome constructed magnificent temples on the hill and the aristocracy built their luxury villas. In many of these palatial buildings, Christians secretly set up their first meetings. The area continued to prosper until 410, when Alaric and the Goths destroyed the hill, leaving it uninhabited. In the following centuries, several churches were built on sacred sites. It is only in recent years that the Aventine has regained its smart appeal.

High on the Aventine is the **Parco Savello**, laid out in the 1930s with orange trees and a view over the river towards the Vatican. The gardens flank the ancient

BELOW: sunset from the Aventine.

basilica of **Santa Sabina** ❶, restored to its near original state in 1936. Perhaps for this reason the stark interior is reminiscent of the austere 1930s Fascist architecture. The church is remarkable for the elegant 5th-century columns that line the aisles, the ancient wooden doorway with some important early carvings, the marble inlaid floor and the 13th-century cloister.

Next door is the church of **San Alessio** ❷. A pretty courtyard leads into a baroque-clad interior with a gilt-covered relic of a staircase, under which St Alessio passed the last 17 years of his life. A *carabinieri* van, guarding the Arabian Embassy opposite, divides this church from Piranesi's whimsical square, **Piazza dei Cavalieri di Malta**. The square is flanked on two sides by walls with almost abstract compositions of the order's coat of arms. The final side is the entrance to the **Villa del Priorato di Malta** ❸. Peek through the keyhole and you'll see the dome of St Peter's looming at the end of a tree-lined avenue.

Down the hill and to the northeast is the church of **Santa Prisca** ❹, built on the remains of a 3rd-century house allegedly belonging to Prisca and Aquila, Christian cousins famous for having invited St Peter to dinner. Further down the hill, you will come to the Viale Aventino, which divides the main Aventine Hill from the smaller one known as *Il Piccolo Aventino*. On your right are the remains of the city walls from the Servian period (4th century BC).

Crossing Piazza Albania, the little church of **San Saba** ❺ is on Via San Saba. The ancient porch leads up to a lawn and the pretty church, with a selection of ancient fragments displayed in its portico, preserves some 13th-century Cosmatesque work and 14th-century frescoes inside.

Heading south along the Viale Aventino, which is known as the Viale della Piramide Cestia at this point, you come to **Porta San Paolo** ❻, originally called

Map, page 177

BASILICA
DI
S.SABINA
SEC.V (422-431)

BELOW: Basilica of Santa Sabina.

Porta Ostiense, because it opened out on to the road to Ostia. Its name was changed after St Paul walked through its portals. It was here that the courageous Italian troops fought their first battle of World War II against the German army on 9 September 1943.

The port of Testaccio

The area to the west of the Porta San Paolo is called **Testaccio** and, in Roman times, it was the site of the Port of Rome. The name, Testaccio, comes from the Latin word *testae* (meaning "shards"), referring to the many broken pieces of amphorae which are to be found at the 35-metre (105-ft) high Monte Testaccio (meaning "hill of shards"). The amphorae, which were used to carry imports of oil and wine, were left in this heap once the goods they contained had been unloaded at the port. Today the hill, all that remains of 400 years of trading oil and wine, is closed to the public, but occasionally the gate is left open and you can climb to the top for a view of the Tiber valley.

Porticus Aemelia was constructed in 193 BC, when the old harbour opposite the Bocca della Verità proved to be too small. Trading ships would have docked in Piazza dell'Emporio where the amphorae would then be unloaded. The harbour warehouses must have been massive, as it is known that 294 pillars supported the roof alone. Important remains can be seen in Via Branca, Via Rubattino and Via Florio, as well as on the banks of the Tiber in front of Lungotevere Testaccio. Today, Piazza dell'Emporio is marked by a modern fountain representing amphorae.

During the Middle Ages, the wine festival processions of the *ottobrate* marched through these streets every October, and at carnival time the uninhibited *Giochi di Testaccio*, the Games of Testaccio, acquired something of a reputa-

tion. The games were held from the 12th to the 15th century and began with a procession, headed by the Pope borne aloft. A bear (a symbol of the devil) and a stallion (a symbol of lust) were slaughtered. Games included jousting, human races, animal races and a bizarre fight between 13 bulls and two pigs dressed in red velvet. All the animals were killed by representatives of the various *rioni* (districts of the city), who then partook of a meaty feast. Surrounding boroughs were forced to supply the jousters and fighters, and the games were financed by Jews. In the 15th century, the Pope moved the games to Via del Corso and, instead, Testaccio hosted popular October picnics, with wine that was kept fresh in the grottoes around the Monte.

Around the year 1890, construction workers came to live in Testaccio. To house them, the Piedmontese rulers built beautiful tenement blocks in the Art Nouveau style that was fashionable at the time. Spacious architecture opens on to pretty courtyards with elegant entrances. However, Testaccio manages to preserve its working-class appeal and the large, boisterous covered food-market is a testimony to this. The inhabitants are also supposed to be the most loyal supporters of the Roma football team.

In Piazzale Ostiense, near Porta San Paolo, you will find the well-preserved **Piramide di Caio Cestio ➐**, the pyramid tomb of the Roman officer Gaius Cestius, who was inspired by the pyramids while serving in

Egypt and was buried here on his death in 12 BC. In the great rush to build the Aurelian Walls, the tomb was simply bricked in to save time, but it is now separate. Not far away is the **Cimitero Protestante** (Protestant Cemetery), also known as the Cimitero Accatolico, where the Italian Communist Party founder Antonio Gramsci, poets Shelley and John Keats, and the son of the German writer J.W. von Goethe are buried.

Walk north from Porta San Paolo, along **Via Marmorata**. En route, you will see reminders of the booming trade in marble which made Rome's palaces so celebrated. The fine stone imported from the Roman Empire was unloaded here and it was the site of the marble guilds right up until modern times, when marble from the ancient ruins was reworked. A "census of pillars" at the beginning of the 19th century recorded that there were still more than 8,000 marble pillars scattered throughout Rome.

Turn left into Via Galvani and, between Monte Testaccio and the river, you will find the derelict remains of the **Mattatoio**, a slaughterhouse dating from 1891, when the cattle market was moved here from Piazza del Popolo. Until a modern "meat centre" was built outside the city in 1975, the Mattatoio was the main source of revenue for Testaccio. In recent years, the complex has had other uses. Half of it is now used as a garage for the traffic police; the other half is home to *Villaggio Globale*, a social centre which organises a variety of cultural events and pays particular attention to Rome's immigrant communities.

In general, Testaccio is now one of the most culturally active areas in Rome, with several theatres, a cinema, a music school and some of the most interesting nightlife in town. For example, some of the old wine grottoes built into the Monte have been transformed into clubs, discos and late-night bars. ❑

Map, below

Ceremonial gathering, Porta San Paolo.

BELOW: Keats' grave in the Protestant Cemetery.

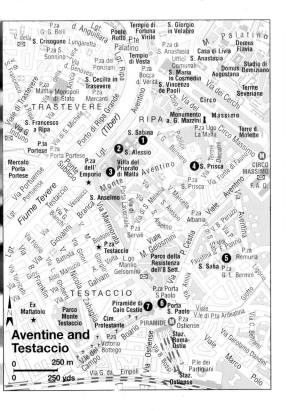

Aventine and Testaccio

TERMINI AND SAN LORENZO

*This area comprises the city's main station and the
surrounding streets, down to Porta Maggiore and along
the Aurelian Walls to Santa Croce in Gerusalemme*

One of the few successful pieces of post-war architecture, the graceful ticket
hall of **Stazione Centrale di Termini** alleviates the Fascist giantism that otherwise pervades the station. Outside, **Piazza dei Cinquecento**, is one of the
biggest piazzas in the city (around 400 sq. metres/4,300 sq. ft), yet the size doesn't
create a correspondingly big impression, for some grandiose urban planning has
determined that it should be the main bus terminus. Food stalls and vendors add to
the general clutter, and the area turns a bit seedy when the sun goes down.

During the building of the first station, which opened in 1867, the **Mura Serviane** (Servian Walls) were uncovered. These are believed to date to the reign of
King Tullius Servius in the 6th century BC. During the construction of the present
station building, which was completed after World War II, parts of Roman
houses and baths were found with their mosaic floors intact.

Baths of Diocletian

PRECEDING PAGES:
a feather in the cap
for the city of Rome.
BELOW: flower stall
in San Lorenzo.

At the northern end of the square are the extensive remains of the **Terme di Diocleziano** (Baths of Diocletian; tel: 06-4782 6152), dating from the 4th century
which were the largest and most beautiful of the city's 900 bath houses at that time.
The *esedra*, the open space surrounded by porticos and seats where the Romans

would chat, gave its form to **Piazza della Repubblica**. The **Fontana delle Naiadi** (Fountain of the Naiads) in the centre of the square, dating from *circa* 1900, caused a scandal when it was unveiled, because of the "obscene" postures of the nymphs.

Map, below

For years the baths were the only home of the **Museo Nazionale Romano ❶**, but recently the museum has undergone a huge transformation. It is now divided into four sites including the original *Terme*, where you can still see some of the museum's ancient artefacts, and marvel at Michelangelo's 16th-century cloister.

The bulk of the collection is now on show at the nearby **Palazzo Massimo alle Terme** (tel: 06-4890 3501) on the west side of Piazza dei Cinquecento. The other two sites are Palazzo Altemps *(see page 126)*, which houses the famous Ludovisi sculpture collection, and the Crypta Balbi *(see page 132)*, which documents the changing face of Rome through history (all sites: open Tues–Sun 9am–7.45pm; last entry 45 mins before closing; entrance fee).

In the 16th century, the church of **Santa Maria degli Angeli** was built inside the *tepidarium* of the Diocletian Baths to a design by Michelangelo. The spacious interior (nearly 100 metres/300 ft long) exploits the massive vaulting of the ancient building. Highlights include a painting by Domenichino of the Martyrdom of St Sebastian and an elaborate sundial on the nave floor. At the northwest corner of the ruins is the **Aula Ottagona** (open Tues–Sat 9am–2pm, Sun 9am–1pm; free). Once used as a planetarium, the octagonal hall has been converted into a display space for several fine sculptures discovered during the excavations of the baths.

Towards Porta Maggiore

Located directly south of the station is **Piazza Vittorio Emanuele II ❷**, which was constructed towards the end of the 19th century, in the wake of Unification,

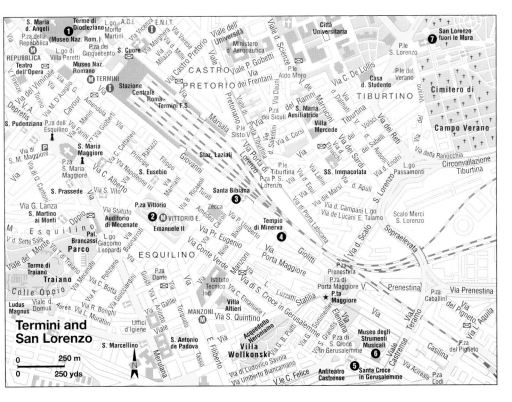

in order to accommodate new government ministeries. It was modelled on squares in Turin, which is why the surrounding area has become known as the Quartiere Piemontese. En route to the square, on Via Carlo Alberto, look out for the **Arco di Gallieno** (Arch of Gallienus), erected in honour of Emperor Gallienus (253–68) on the site of a gate in the ancient Servian Walls.

In the northern corner of the square itself are some ruins of a 3rd-century fountain, which was decorated with the marble Trophies of Marius (now found on the Campidoglio). Adjacent is the **Porta Magica** (Magic Gate), which is inscribed with symbols that have never been deciphered. However, there is speculation that they may be a formula for the fabrication of gold.

The square used to host a huge, bustling and historic daily food market which was relocated in 2001 to former barracks located not far away on Via Principe Amedeo (between Via Ricasoli and Via Lamarmora). Thanks to the area's important immigrant community, it is Rome's only real multi-ethnic market and the place to go for cheap prices and stalls piled high with Mediterranean and African fruit and vegetables, oriental rices, meat and fish, eastern spices and pulses.

Several blocks east of Piazza Vittorio Emanuele is the little church of **Santa Bibiana** ❸, rebuilt in the 17th century and one of Bernini's first architectural projects. Note, too, Bernini's statue of St Bibiana above the altar. Heading south towards Porta Maggiore, you will pass the round remains of the 4th-century **Tempio di Minerva Medica** ❹ on your left .

Porta Maggiore is a wonderfully preserved 1st-century gate, which also served as an aqueduct. In fact, you can still see the channels that carried the water. Just outside the gate is the tomb of baker Marcus Virgillius Eurysaces, dating from about 30 BC, but its style is remarkably similar to 1930s' Fascist architecture. An inscription states that Eurysaces supplied the state with bread and little reliefs show the baker's slaves in action.

In 1917, a well-preserved 1st-century basilica was discovered under Porta Maggiore (ask at the tourist office about arranging a visit). The shrine has been attributed to a group of rich Romans, followers of a Neo-Pythagorean cult who believed in the immortality of the soul.

South of the Porta Maggiore, along Via Eleniana, is the splendid white facade of **Santa Croce in Gerusalemme** ❺. This early church was established in AD 320 by St Helena, Emperor Constantine's mother, to house fragments of the True Cross that she acquired on a visit to the Holy Land. They are still here, along with an impressive collection of other relics, all held in a modern chapel off the left aisle. The apse is decorated with Romano's 15th-century fresco depicting the story of St Helena. The saint is also venerated in the underground chapel, adorned with exquisite ceiling mosaics.

Next door is the **Museo degli Strumenti Musicali** ❻ (open Tues–Sun 8.30am–7.30pm; entrance fee; tel: 06-701 4796), where some 3,000 pieces document musical history from antiquity to the 19th century.

Surrounding the church and museum are the semicircular remains of the 3rd-century **Amphitheatre Castrense**. The part along Via Castrense, incorporated into the Aurelian Walls by Emperor Honorius in the 5th century, is particularly well preserved.

ROME'S UNIVERSITY

The venerable Università Romana was founded in 1303 by Pope Boniface VIII. From the reign of Pope Eugene IV (1431–47) until 1935, it was based in Palazzo della Sapienza, in the heart of the city, but in 1935, when the Città Universitaria was inaugurated, it moved to its present site in the Quartiere San Lorenzo. The new campus was designed by Marcello Piacentini in 1933–35, in accordance with a plan that involved two axes intersecting at a right angle in the Piazzale del Rettorato: a design of modern classicism. However, the equilibrium was upset following World War II, when more buildings were added to the complex to accommodate the growing number of students. The interior has been as well planned as the exterior, with modern paintings by well-known Italian artists, such as Minnucci, adorning the walls. The library, Biblioteca Universitaria Alessandrina, houses 1 million books and roughly 16,000 periodicals.

San Lorenzo Quarter

Retrace your steps to the church of Santa Bibiana, then pass under the railway tracks to the ancient Porta Tiburtina and you will be in the **San Lorenzo Quarter**, which is known as the student area of Rome. The surrounding streets, named after the Italic and Etruscan tribes, are full of bars, cheap trattorias and pizzerias. The actual **Città Universitaria**, on Viale dell'Università, was constructed in the 1930s in typical Fascist style: big, white and imposing. In the summer term, you will see students sitting out on the lawns or perching on the grand staircases under imposing insignia.

The area takes its name from the ancient basilica of **San Lorenzo fuori le Mura ❼** (St Lawrence outside the Walls), one of Rome's first Christian places of worship. The basilica is actually made up of two churches joined together. The raised apse is the nave of the Constantinian basilica erected in 330 (rebuilt in the 6th century with beautiful Corinthian columns), which was deprived of its apse and which originally faced the other way. A 5th-century basilica built next door creates the present nave. The two were joined together in the 8th century. The interior is decorated with early mosaics and some beautiful Cosmatesque work. Off to the right is the entrance to the pretty cloister and underneath the church lies a labyrinth of catacombs. During World War II, the basilica and surrounding area were badly damaged by American bombings and there has been much restoration since.

While you are here, stroll around the adjacent **Cimitero Monumentale del Verano**, more simply known as Campo Verano. A huge 19th-century cemetery, it is divided into various zones and is one of the few places where social hierarchy is rigorously adhered to even after death. ❑

Map, page 181

TIP

Around the university you will find lots of cheap pizzerias, *birrerie* (pubs) and trattorias.

BELOW: in front of the Verano cemetery in San Lorenzo.

QUIRINALE

*The Quirinal has become synonymous with Italian politics,
because the Quirinal Palace is the official residence
of the President of the Republic*

Map,
page 188

The Quirinal Hill is the highest of Rome's seven classical hills. Probably named after the temple of Quirinus which once stood on its summit, it is Palazzo del Quirinale that now dominates the hill. However, there is another architectural feature in this area that is more internationally famous, thanks to the 1959 film *La Dolce Vita*. It was the **Fontana di Trevi ❶** (Trevi Fountain) into which the star, Anita Ekberg, plunged.

Ever since, tourists have wanted to make their own big splash, but a 1987 order from the Assessor for Tourism requires visitors to respect the "dignity and cleanliness of the city of Rome". In other words, you should keep the top half of your body covered and your feet out of public fountains. If you do try and put a foot in the water, a whistle blast from the city police, the *Vigili Urbani*, will stop you in your tracks. However, no-one will stop you from throwing a coin in the fountain, which is supposed to ensure your return to Rome.

The water in the fountain comes from the ancient aqueduct built by Agrippa in 19 BC to supply his baths near the Pantheon. According to legend, the water was called *Acqua Vergine*, after the young girl (*virgo* in Latin) who discovered the source of the spring. It was not until the 18th century that the actual fountain was added. Designed by Nicola Salvi, it was completed in 1762 and depicts Salubrity and Abundance, flanked by the huge central figure of Neptune, who is standing on a seashell being pulled by two seahorses and two tritons.

Close to the fountain is Palazzo Carpegna, which houses the **Galleria dell'Accademia di San Luca** (open Sept–June, Mon–Sat 10am–12.30pm; free; tel: 06-679 8850), a gallery with works by 17th-, 18th- and 19th-century artists.

PRECEDING PAGES:
the band plays
on at Palazzo del
Quirinale.
LEFT: Trevi Fountain.
BELOW: a relaxing
Roman.

Roman dada

From the Trevi Fountain, follow Via del Lavatore, which has several interesting shops, uphill. Turn right at Vicolo Scanderbeg and you will pass the **Museo Nazionale delle Paste Alimentari** (open daily 9.30am–5.30pm; entrance fee; tel: 06-699 1119). Carry on up to Via della Dataria, where you can climb the stairs to **Piazza del Quirinale**. The group of statues in the centre of the piazza are an assemblage of Roman *objets-trouvés*. The statues of Castor and Pollux (the Dioscuri) with their horses originally came from Constantine's baths and were arranged around the obelisk (taken from Augustus's mausoleum) in the 18th century. Forty years later, the large basin, previously used as a cattle trough in the Foro Romano, was also added.

On one side of the piazza stands **Palazzo del Quirinale ❷**, which was built as the Pope's summer residence in the 16th century and remained so until 1870, when it became the royal palace of the kings of Italy.

TIP

Head for the west side
of Piazza del Quirinale
for stunning views
across Rome.

*Door detail at Santa
Maria della Vittoria.*

Since 1947, it has been the official residence of the President. One section of the palace is open to the public (first and third Sunday of the month). The palace gardens, which stretch far behind the building, are only open to the public once a year, on 2 June, to celebrate the Festa della Repubblica. On another side of the square is the sugary white facade of **Palazzo della Consulta** ❸, designed by Ferdinand Fuga in 1732, which houses the constitutional court.

As you head northeast along Via del Quirinale, appreciate the fact that the gardens of the palace extend the full length of this road, some 350 monotonous metres (383 yards). On the right, as you're walking along the road, you will find **Sant'Andrea al Quirinale** ❹ (open Wed–Mon, 8.30am–noon & 4–7pm; free), one of the few churches totally designed by Bernini. His theatrical genius is demonstrated by the church's unusual oval plan, which has the main facade on the smaller side.

Further along the road is a tiny church, **San Carlo alle Quattro Fontane** ❺, designed by Bernini's contemporary and rival, Borromini. It is no bigger than one of the four massive piers at the crossing of St Peter's, yet Borromini has managed to squeeze in every geometrical shape possible, creating an undulating harmony in one of the most original church designs in Rome.

If you turn left at Piazza delle Quattro Fontane, you will be in Via delle Quattro Fontane, where the entrance to **Palazzo Barberini** ❻, the family palace of Pope Urban VIII (1623–44), is located. Three of Rome's most important 17th-century architects, Maderno, Bernini and Borromini, worked on the palace. In general, Palazzo Barberini reflects the political and economic strengthening of the papacy after the Council of Trent. In the large salon, for example, da Cortona created what is considered one of the most important

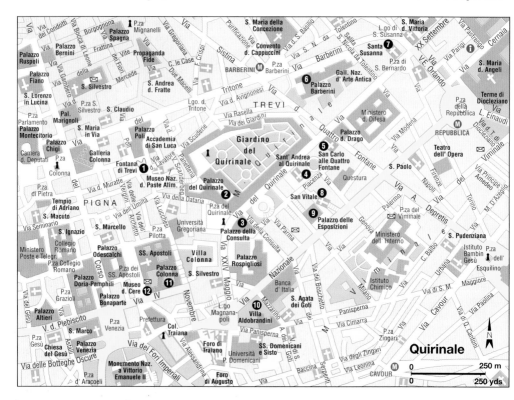

frescoes of high baroque. The message of the *Triumph of Providence* is clear. No longer are God the Father and Son in the centre, but three bees (the coat of arms of the Barberini).

Today, Palazzo Barberini contains the **Galleria Nazionale d'Arte Antica** (open Tues–Sun 9am–7pm; shorter hours in winter; entrance fee; tel: 06-482 4184), which concentrates on paintings from the early Renaissance to late baroque. Works include *The Annunciation* by Lippi, canvasses by Caravaggio, Raphael's celebrated *La Fornarina*, a Tintoretto and a portrait of Henry VIII by Holbein.

If you cross over Piazza delle Quattro Fontane, you will be on Via XX Settembre. Here you will find the church of **Santa Susanna ❼** with a baroque facade by Maderno, and the church of **Santa Maria della Vittoria**, with its wonderful chapel designed and sculpted by Bernini. The end of Via XX Settembre is marked by **Porta Pia**, Michelangelo's last architectural work.

Turning right at Piazza delle Quattro Fontane, you will reach **Via Nazionale**, built in 1870 to give Rome an appearance in keeping with its new status as capital.

At the northern end of the road is **Piazza della Repubblica**, where all the commercial buildings have palatial facades replicating the classical and Renaissance periods, in a desperate attempt to make them look of great historical importance. In the case of the Anglican church of **St Paul within the Walls**, which was built in 1880 on the corner of Via Napoli, even Gothic elements have been incorporated.

Towards the southern end of Via Nazionale stand the church of **San Vitale ❽** and the large, white **Palazzo delle Esposizioni ❾** (closed for restoration until early 2004; tel: 06-474 5903). The church, built in the 5th century and restored in the 15th century, dispensed bread to the poor every Friday until *circa* 1900, using the proceeds left in a nobleman's will. The palace, built in the 19th century, functions as an art gallery, offering temporary exhibitions, films, a bookshop, a design centre, bar and restaurant. To the side of Palazzo is a tunnel, the Traforo Umberto I, built in 1905, which cuts its way underneath the Quirinal Hill.

Across the road are the impressive **Palazzo Banca d'Italia** (1886–1904) and the **Villa Aldobrandini ❿**. In Via Mazzarino, you will find the entrance to a small public park (part of the gardens of the villa), the only patch of greenery in this area. Via Nazionale then curves around into Via IV Novembre and leads towards **Piazza Venezia**, passing on its way Trajan's Market and **Palazzo Colonna ⓫** (open Sept–July, Sat 9am–1pm; entrance fee; tel: 06-679 4362), an art gallery where highlights include Raphael's *Putti*, *The Bean Eater* by Carracci and a spectacular ballroom.

From the palace, **Via della Pillotta**, overhung by four elegant bridges connecting Palazzo with the Villa Colonna, leads to the Trevi Fountain.

At the end of Via IV Novembre, in **Piazza dei SS. Apostoli,** is the **Museo delle Cere ⓬** (open daily 9am–8.30pm; entrance fee; tel: 06-679 6482), a bizarre, dusty wax museum. The square, which marks the end of the Roman Fori, has both a Bernini-designed palace and a part 6th-century, part 19th-century church. ❑

Map, see opposite

BELOW: a Roman obelisk and statues of Castor and Pollux, by Palazzo del Quirinale.

THE ESQUILINE AND VIMINALE

*The Esquiline and Viminale were two of Rome's original seven
hills; the area covered in this chapter stretches from Via Nazionale
to Colle Oppio and from the Colosseum to Stazione Termini*

Map,
page 192

In ancient times, the Viminale was covered by a forest of bamboo trees
(vimine), hence its name, while the Esquiline was the site of communal burials for slaves, the murdered and the executed.

Augustus, following the advice of Maecenas, transformed the area into a luxury residential zone with idyllic gardens and palatial villas. Maecenas, an
extremely rich *bon vivant* and Augustus's lifelong friend, built himself a luxury
villa in the area. Virgil and Horace also lived there. On the Colle Oppio peak,
Nero constructed his extensive Domus Aurea, which was later used as the foundations for Trajan's Baths.

In the Middle Ages, the area once again declined and became a favourite haunt
for witches and magicians, who met under the cover of night to celebrate mysterious rituals. At a later date, the powerful families of Rome bought up the land
and built towers to show their might. Of the 200 towers that were built in Rome
during this period, only a few remain. **Torre delle Milizie** is behind Trajan's
Market, **Torre dei Conti** stands at the beginning of Via Cavour and two others
flank Via Lanza.

The Viminale boasts two comparatively recent additions – the 19th-century
Teatro dell'Opera and the large 1920s **Palazzo Viminale**, housing the Ministry of the Interior. These days, traffic thunders along
Via Nazionale and Via Cavour, two characterless 19th-
century thoroughfares, off which there are pretty little
streets lined with bars, restaurants and boutiques.

LEFT: Via Santa
Maria Maggiore.
BELOW: on the steps
of Santa Maria
Maggiore.

Esquiline

According to legend, in 352 Pope Liberius had a vision
of the Virgin, who instructed him to build a church dedicated to her wherever snow had fallen on the following morning. It was 5 August, but snow was found on
the Cispio peak of the Esquiline. As a result, the basilica
of **Santa Maria Maggiore ❶** was built. If you happen
to be in Rome on 5 August, go to the church to witness
white flower petals being showered through a hole in
the ceiling in simulation of the miracle.

The basilica has been rebuilt, extended and embellished since the 4th century. The sturdy baroque facade
was added in the 18th century. Inside, the coffered ceiling and elaborately decorated chapels are relatively new
additions. The ceiling is decorated with some of the first
gold brought from the New World. Especially extravagant are the two chapels opposite the altar, dating from
the 16th and 17th centuries. The apse mosaic is a 13th-
century replacement of the original by Torriti, whereas
the mosaics on the triumphal arch and the panels high
up on the nave walls are the original 5th-century ones.

South of Santa Maria Maggiore, the mosaic-filled
church of **Santa Prassede ❷** lies on Via di Santa

Prassede. It was built by Pope Paschal I in the 9th century as part of his renewal programme for the Christian church. To decorate the apse, the triumphant arch and the side chapel of San Zeno (dedicated to his mother Theodora), Paschal imported mosaic workers from Byzantium – reintroducing an art that had not been practised in Rome for nearly three centuries.

Cutting through this area is the busy **Via Merulana**, built in the 16th century to link Santa Maria Maggiore and San Giovanni in Laterano. On the right is the large 19th-century **Palazzo Brancaccio ❸**, home to the **Museo Nazionale d'Arte Orientale** (open Mon, Wed, Fri, Sat 8.30am–2.30pm, Tues, Thur, Sun & public hols 8.30am–7.30pm; closed 1st and 3rd Sun of each month; entrance fee; tel: 06-487 4415). In the gardens and public park behind the palace are remains of Nero's huge water cistern called the **Sette Sale**, built for his private house and also used to feed Trajan's Baths.

Further along Via Merulana, on the left, is the **Auditorio di Mecenate ❹** (open Tues–Sat 9am–5pm, until 7pm in winter, Sun 9am–1.30pm; entrance fee; tel: 06-487 3262), dating from 30 BC and almost certainly the nymphaeum of Maecenas's villa. It would have been a cool retreat, where he could rest and entertain friends, surrounded by painted landscapes and the sound of trickling water. The interior, a hall with an apse, conserves remains of the ancient frescoes depicting garden scenes, foliage designs, birds and small figures. One shows a tipsy Dionysus, true to his reputation, being supported by a satyr.

Returning to Palazzo Brancaccio, take Viale del Monte Oppio down the hill to the 8th-century **San Martino ai Monti ❺** – a damp, dark church dotted with mosaic remnants and classical statuary. If you wish to visit it, ask the sacristan. The original building was built in the 4th century, in the annexes of Trajan's Baths.

TIP

To see the remains of the 13th-century mosaics showing scenes of the miraculous founding of Santa Maria Maggiore, join a guided tour – they start at the front of the church (every half hour, 9am–5pm; entrance fee).

NERO'S GOLDEN HOUSE

Nero's palace – the Domus Aurea – on the Colle Oppio was designed to provide him with a rural environment in the centre of the city. The palace had its own aqueducts to supply water for the fountains, and the baths were fed by sea-water and sulphur springs. Suetonius describes the lavish interior, with "dining room ceilings composed of moveable ivory tiles pierced with holes so that flowers or perfume could be sprinkled onto the guests below". The building was decorated with whole shiploads of plundered Greek works of art, and eventually the eccentric emperor was able to say: "At last I am living like a man". Following Nero's suicide in AD 68, the buildings were quickly destroyed. Vespasian drained the artificial lake and built the Flavian Amphitheatre, named after his family, but soon called the Colosseum after the colossal 34-metre (110 ft) golden statue of Nero that once stood nearby.

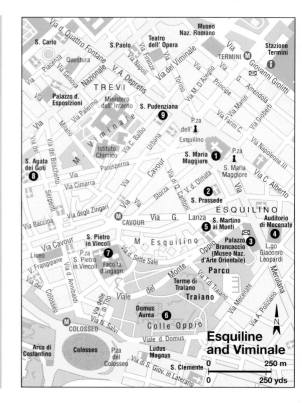

Esquiline and Viminale

South of the church is the park of **Colle Oppio** ❻, littered with rubbish, stray-cats and tramps, but there are some notable ruins and views of the Colosseum. The ruins include those of the baths built by Trajan and the underground rooms of Nero's **Domus Aurea** (Golden House; visits Wed–Mon 9am–7.45pm, by reservation only; entrance fee; tel: 06-3996 7700), which is not open for unauthorised visits.

Via delle Sette Sale leads to **San Pietro in Vincoli** ❼. This church has two major attractions: the *Moses* by Michelangelo, sitting state-like on a throne, part of the unfinished tomb that Michelangelo was painstakingly preparing for Julius II, and the chains that imprisoned St Peter in Jerusalem and Rome. Apparently, when the two chains were brought together, they miraculously fused.

Viminale

The stairway of Via San Francesco di Paola leads from the large piazza in front of San Pietro in Vincoli to Via Cavour. Cross the road, turn left and then take the first right, Via dei Serpenti, which leads to the little church of **Sant'Agata dei Goti** ❽, which is named after the Goths who invaded the city in the 5th century and celebrated the Arian cult. This cult, which denied the divinity of Christ, didn't last long and, when the Goths left in 593, the church was reconsecrated by St Gregorio Magno.

Santa Prassede doorway.

Head east along Via Panisperna, lined with boutiques, artisan shops and restaurants, and then tack to your right to discover the beautifully restored **Piazza degli Zingari**, where the gypsy *(zingari)* caravans used to congregate. Continue along Via Urbana to the ancient church of **Santa Pudenziana** ❾, which was built over a house where St Peter apparently stayed. Dating from the 4th century, this church conserves one of the earliest Christian mosaics in its apse. ❑

BELOW: the main church of Santa Maria Maggiore.

Map, see opposite

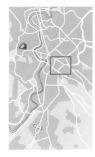

THE LATERAN

The Lateran, on the eastern extremity of the Celian Hill,
was the centre of the Catholic church until the seat of the papacy
was transferred to the Vatican in the 14th century

When the Lateran Palace was the seat and residence of the popes (from the 5th century until the papacy's temporary move to Avignon in 1309), the Lateran was the centre of the Catholic Church. On the return of the papacy to Rome in 1377, the pope's official residence was moved to the Vatican, but the Lateran retained much of its importance – popes were still crowned there up until 1870.

At the heart of the Lateran district is **Piazza di San Giovanni**, which is bordered by **Palazzo Lateranense** ❶ (Lateran Palace). Today, the main role of the palace, commissioned by Pope Sixtus V and designed by Fontana in 1586, is as the headquarters of the diocese of Rome (of which the Pope is bishop). However, it has been the site of many important church meetings, such as the one that led to the 1929 Lateran Treaty that established the current boundaries of the Vatican and stabilized its relationship with the Italian state.

PRECEDING PAGES:
Acqua Claudia
aqueduct. **BELOW:**
Piazza di San Gio-
vanni in Laterano.

San Giovanni in Laterano

Next door to the palace is the mighty basilica of **San Giovanni in Laterano** ❷ – the "mother of all churches" and the first Christian basilica in Rome. Its Apostle figures and the Christ topping the facade can be seen as far away as Frascati.

Built under Emperor Constantine, the church has stood here since 313 and, although it has burnt down twice and been rebuilt several times, it retains its original structure. Nicknamed "the gilded basilica", on account of its deep-red stone, its central doorway has the original bronze doors taken from the Roman Curia of the Forum.

The east facade through which you enter the church is the work of Galilei (1732–5), but Fontana designed the north facade when he was working on his rebuilding of the Lateran Palace. Most of the marble-clad interior is the result of remodelling carried out by Borromini (1646), but some of the works of art and church furnishings are far older. They include a fragment of fresco attributed to Giotto (1300) and a 14th-century Gothic baldacchino from which only the Pope is allowed to celebrate Mass (which he does every Maundy Thursday). The gilded wooden ceiling of the nave was completed in 1567 and had to remain unaltered when Borromini came to work on the building. Other features of note include the statues of the 12 Apostles designed by followers of Bernini, the baroque frescoes and reliefs of the transept, and the peaceful 13th-century cloisters.

San Giovanni's ceiling.

The **Battistero Lateranense** ❸ (the baptistry; open daily 9am–12.30pm & 3.30–7pm; free) was part of the original complex, but it was rebuilt in its present octagonal shape during the 5th century. In the earliest days of Christianity, all Christians were baptised here. The chapels of St John the Evangelist and Santi Rufina e Secunda (which was the original entrance) contain exquisite 5th-century mosaics.

Standing at a height of 30 metres (100 ft), the **obelisk** on the square is the tallest and oldest in Rome; it honours the Pharaoh Tutmoses III and once stood at the Circus Maximus.

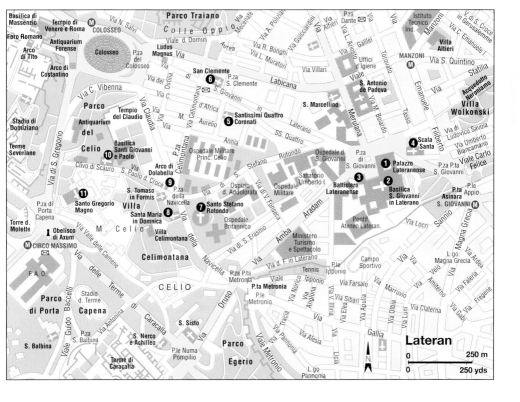

More Religious Monuments

Across the street from the Lateran Palace is the entrance to the **Scala Santa** ❹ (Holy Staircase; open daily 6.15am–12.15pm and 3.30–7pm; until 6pm November–March; tel: 06-7049 4489), said to be the stairs that Christ ascended when he was tried by Pontius Pilate. Brought to Rome from Jerusalem by Constantine's mother, Helena, they are protected under a layer of wood, but you still have to mount them on your knees, and the devout (who arrive in bus loads) do so slowly, stopping on each of the 28 steps to pray. You can cheat and walk up one of the side staircases to the top, where, in the **Sancta Sanctorum** (Holy of Holies), there is a picture of Christ, said to be the work of St Luke and an angel.

The bronze doors of San Giovanni.

West of the Basilica lie two more important churches. The **Santissimi Quattro Coronati** ❺, originally part of the fortress that protected the Lateran Palace, belongs to a community of silent Augustine nuns. The present church, built over the remains of a much larger 4th-century edifice, dates from the 11th century – the entrance to the present church lies behind a courtyard, which shows the extent of the original building. You'll have to ring a bell to summon a nun, who will give you the key to the 12th-century cloisters or to the **Chapel of San Silvestro**. This 13th-century chapel contains an endearing fresco illustrating the conversion of Constantine to Christianity by St Sylvester (who was pope at the time). You can see the emperor suffering from what looks like the advanced stages of a skin disease, then travelling to Rome to be cured by the pope. A mosaic depicts St Helena's discovery of the True Cross, which she found at the same time as she discovered the Scala Santa.

The second church is the basilica of **San Clemente** ❻ (entrance fee; tel: 06-7045 1018), one of Rome's best examples of a layered church (where one edifice has been built on top of another, older one). The three layers of San Clemente lie behind an 18th-century facade. The most recent building is the 12th-century basilica with its beautifully detailed mosaic depicting the Triumph of the Cross. Below this lies the 4th-century church, with fine 11th-century frescoes of miracles being performed by St Clement. This church is still being excavated by the Dominican monks who live here. The final layer dates from the 1st century when town houses were converted to a temple dedicated to the god Mithras. This cult was open only to men.

In San Clemente's **Chapel of St Catherine**, there are some early Renaissance frescoes of the life of St Catherine of Alexandria, which were painted by Masolino (1383–1447) and Masaccio (1401–28).

The Celian Hill

The Celian, incorporated into the city in 7 BC when the defeated citizens of the rebellious city of Alba lived there, is one of the famous seven hills of Rome. Today, it's home to Villa Celimontana, which is surrounded by the pleasant **Parco del Celio**. This park is sprinkled with ancient ruins and some fine early medieval churches. One of the most notable of the latter is the circular mid-5th century **San Stefano Rotondo** ❼ (closed Monday am). The church's soft natural lighting, from 22 windows high up in its walls, contrasts with the gruesome 16th-century frescoes of martyred saints by Pomarancio.

ROME'S PARKS

Rome has many beautiful parks, each with its own attractions. The 17th-century Doria Pamphilj, the largest of the city's public parks, has plenty of open spaces and a network of paths, so it is popular with joggers and dog walkers. Villa Borghese, which is more central than the Doria Pamphilj, is also large and is packed with activities for the kids – you can feed the ducks, hire a rowing boat or bicycle, visit the mini-cinema or zoo and enjoy the small fun fair. Then there are the Botanical Gardens, which contain more than 7,000 plant species from all over the world, including sequoias, palm trees and collections of orchids and bromeliads. There are also many smaller parks tucked away in little corners, such as the Parco del Celio. They provide some respite, as well as a perfect place for a picnic. Other green spaces include the gardens of Palazzo Farnese, the Pincio Gardens and those of the Villa Celimontana.

On the other side of Via della Navicella, beyond the 16th-century fountain made from an ancient stone boat, is the 9th-century church of **Santa Maria in Domnica** ❽. It has a magnificent altar mosaic of the Virgin and Child surrounded by saints and angels in a field of flowers – the man on his knees at the Virgin's feet is Pope Paschal I, who commissioned the mosaic and who wears the halo of a living saint. Above them are the Apostles, striding out to join Christ.

If you turn left outside the church, you'll reach Via di San Paolo della Croce where the 1st-century **Arco di Dolabella** ❾ (Arch of Dolabella) spans the road. The arch was incorporated into Nero's aqueduct (traces of which can be seen between the arch and Santa Maria in Domnica). Next to the arch is the gateway of **San Tommaso in Formis**, decorated with a 13th-century mosaic showing Christ with two freed slaves, one black and one white.

The road leads on to the church of **Santi Giovanni e Paolo** ❿, its 13th-century bell-tower built into the remains of a Temple of Claudius that stood on this site. The first church here was constructed in the 4th century, but the present edifice is mainly 12th-century and the interior, lit by numerous chandeliers, is early 18th-century. The outer wall on Clivo di Scauro contains more ancient parts and is supported by buttresses that pass high over the road running beneath.

Another notable church on the Celian Hill is **San Gregorio Magno** ⓫, founded by St Gregory in the 6th century. You can see the saint's throne (already 600 or 700 years old when he used it) in the little chapel. Much of the current building is a 17th-century restoration and the interior is mainly 18th-century, although some of the decorations, including the 13th-century Virgin on the wall of the chapel towards the end of the north aisle, are earlier. The chapels of St Silvia and St Andrea house works by Domenchino and Reni. ❑

Map, page 197

TIP

If you are thinking of spending some time on Celian Hill, take a picnic with you as there are few bars or restaurants in the area.

BELOW: mosaics in San Clemente.

THE APPIAN WAY

Via Appia, named after Appius Claudius Caecus under whose magistracy the road opened in 312 BC, was an important part of Christian Rome and is, therefore, home to many interesting sites

I n classical times, Via Appia began at the Circus Maximus and passed the Baths of Caracalla on its way to the city gate of Porta Appia (now Porta San Sebastiano) in the Aurelian Walls. Today, it is only the section of the road outside the ancient Porta Appia that is called Via Appia. The stretch leading up to the Porta San Sebastiano is called Via di Porta San Sebastiano.

The first stop on the old Via Appia is the **Terme di Caracalla ❶** (Baths of Caracalla; open Apr–Aug Tues–Sun 9am–6.30pm, Sept–Mar Tues–Sat 9am–1 hour before sunset, Mon 9am–1pm all year round; entrance fee; tel: 06-575 8626). When the baths were started in AD 212, they were the biggest in Rome, with room for 1,600 people. The interior was sumptuously decorated with marble, gilding and coloured stone. Today, only patches of mosaic survive, but the buildings are still impressive, their vaults rising to 30 metres (100 ft). Bath complexes such as this incorporated other recreational features such as gymnasiums, libraries and shops; they were also popular places with male and female prostitutes – today, only the females remain. More salubriously, the remains of the *caldarium* (hot room) are used to stage an annual outdoor opera festival in July and August.

Further along the road is the **Parco degli Scipioni ❷** and, at No. 9 Via di Porta San Sebastiano, is the **Sepolcro degli Scipioni** (closed to visitors), the mausoleum of the Scipios, a famous family in the Roman Republic. The first family member entombed here was L. Cornelius Scipio, a consul in 298 BC. By the middle of the 2nd century BC, the square tomb was full and an annexe was dug adjacent to it. Nearby is the 1st-century AD Columbarium of **Pomponio Hylas** (also closed to visitors), which stored the cremated remains of those too poor to build their own tombs. Rich Romans often had columbaria built for their freemen, but this was probably a commercial venture in which people bought a slot, much as people book graveyard plots today. To go inside, make an appointment at the Museo delle Mura.

Porta San Sebastiano

Porta San Sebastiano is the entrance to the **Museo delle Mura ❸** (open Tues–Sat 9am–7pm, Sun 9am–5pm; entrance fee; tel: 06-7047 5284), which gives a detailed account of the building of the Aurelian Walls, which were once almost 20 km (12 miles) long with 381 towers. In AD 403, their height was doubled to 12 metres (40 ft). They were then 3.5 metres (12 ft) thick and had 18 gates.

Older buildings, such as the Pyramid of Cestius, the Porta Maggiore, the Praetorian barracks, the aqueducts, the Castrense amphitheatre and Hadrian's Mausoleum, were incorporated into the walls. A walk along the top gives an idea of the view the imperial legionaries had as

PRECEDING PAGES:
Porta San
Sebastiano,
Via Appia.
BELOW: mosaic in the
Baths of Caracalla.

they watched for barbarian armies. Today, however, there are concrete blocks in every direction, except towards Via Appia, where the Campagna is almost in its original state.

When Via Appia was extended outside the city walls to Capua by Appius Claudius Caecus in 312 BC, it followed an existing route to the Alban Hills and was the most important campaign path for the conquest of southern Italy. In 190 BC, it was extended via Benevento to Brindisium (modern Brindisi), connecting Rome with the eastern Mediterranean. When the empire fell, the road decayed and was not used until the time of Pius VI.

Via Appia Antica

Beyond the gate is what is known as Via Appia Antica (Old Appian Way). The first part, with the main monuments and sights, is not a pleasant walk due to unrelenting traffic and the lack of a footpath, so be prepared for some nerve-racking moments. Half a mile down Via Appia, on the left, is the church of **Domine Quo Vadis** ❹ ("Lord, where are you going?"), where the Apostle Peter, after escaping from a Roman prison, is said to have met Jesus. Peter asked where he was going, to which Jesus replied: "To let myself be crucified a second time." Jesus is supposed to have left his footprints on the road and you can see them, preserved, inside the church.

To the left of the church is a little tarmac road, **Via della Caffarella**, that leads into the valley across Via Latina. Bear right at Domine Quo Vadis and head along Via Ardeatina, on which the mausoleum and memorial of the **Fosse Ardeatine** ❺ are located. Here, on 24 March 1944, 335 Italians were murdered in revenge for a partisan attack on Via Rasella in which 32 Nazi soldiers were killed. The vic-

Map, page 204

TIP

The No. 218 bus from Piazza San Giovanni will take you to Via Appia Antica.

ABOVE: Domine Quo Vadis. **BELOW:** the Baths of Caracalla.

tims had nothing to do with the attack, but they were rounded up in Rome, shot and buried in a mass grave. After the war, their bodies were retrieved and reburied in sarcophagi in the mausoleum, each tomb bearing the name, age and occupation of the occupant.

On the way back to Via Appia are the **Catacombe di San Callisto** ❻ (open Thur–Tues 8.30am–noon & 2.30–5pm; closed Feb; entrance fee; tel: 06-513 0151). In the **Cripta dei Papi** (Crypt of the Popes), inscriptions of at least 10 different bishops of Rome from the 3rd and 4th centuries have been discovered. Among them is the first documented use of the title "Pope" for the Bishop of Rome (dating from 298). Also open to the public are the **Catacombe di San Sebastiano** at Via Appia Antica 136 (open Mon–Sat 9am–noon & 2.30–5pm, closed Nov; entrance fee; tel: 06-788 7035) and the **Catacombe di Domitilla** (Catacombs of Domitilla; open Wed–Mon 8.30am–noon and 2.30–5pm; closed Jan; entrance fee; tel: 06-511 0342). Contrary to popular belief, the catacombs were not used for worship, nor for hiding in during times of Christian persecution; the excavated rooms were used for simple funeral ceremonies. They were built outside the city because the law forbade burials within the city limits and tended to be built in the grounds of rich Christians or Christian sympathisers. They were built in storeys underground to save space on the surface.

Among the rows of shelves for the dead, you can see a lot of little "tombs", used for the tragically high number of infant deaths, and some particularly large or imposing ones, usually belonging to martyrs who were reburied in Roman churches in the Middle Ages. Further along Via Appia, at No. 119A, are the Jewish catacombs of Vigna Randanini. They are not open to the public.

Also worth seeing are the **Circo di Massenzio** ❼ (Circus of Maxentius; open Apr–June & Sept, Tues–Sun 9am–7pm, July–Aug, Tues–Sun 9am–2pm, Oct–Mar, Tues–Sun 9am–5pm; entrance fee; tel: 06-780 1324) and the **Mausoleo di Romolo** (Mausoleum of Romulus, son

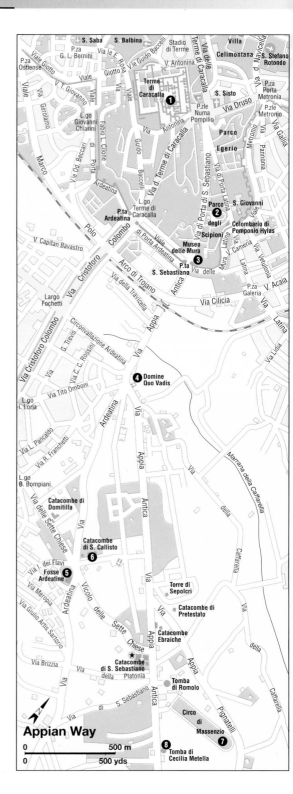

Appian Way

of Emperor Maxentius), dating from 309. The circus was used for chariot races and could seat 10,000 spectators. Maxentius's imperial palace, Villa di Massenzio, is located nearby.

The **Tomb of Cecilia Metella ❽** (open Tues–Sun 9am–5pm; last entry 1 hour before closing; entrance fee; tel: 06-780 2465) was built in 10 BC for the daughter of Quintus Metellus Creticus, conqueror of Crete. She was later the wife of Crassus, son of the famous member of the Triumvirate of Caesar's time. During the 14th century the tomb was used as a fortress by the Caetani family, relatives of the Pope, who used to boost the family coffers by extracting tolls from passers-by.

The End of the Road

Beyond this, Via Appia is far more walkable, though there are no refreshment stops. In parts, it is still paved with rounded cobbles and trees offer shade along most of the route. The roadside has the remains of many Republican tombs, built by the great families of Rome because of the ban on burials within the city. Some still have their original inscriptions and portraits of the dead in marble relief.

Beyond the crossing with Via Erode Attico, the ancient remains in the middle of farmland to the left of the road are those of the 2nd-century AD **Villa dei Quintilli**. If you look closely, you can see a nymphaneum, the arches of aqueducts and other buildings. Finally, where Via Appia joins the road that leads back to Via Appia Nuova, there is the domed **Casale Rotondo**, a late 1st-century BC tomb, with fragments of relief stuck to its sides and a farmhouse and garden built on top. From here on, Via Appia, although still lined with ancient monuments, is in too poor a state of repair to make it worth continuing, unless the walk is more important to you than its sights. ❑

Map, see opposite

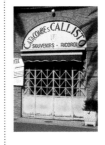

ABOVE: Catacombs of St Calixtus.
BELOW: the Tomb of Cecilia Metella.

EUR AND THE FORO ITALICO

Map,
page 210

*EUR and the Foro Italico are grouped together in this
chapter, not because they are geographically close, but because
they are both 20th-century Fascist developments*

When we think of Roman architecture, we tend to think of Ancient Rome, the Middle Ages, the Renaissance and the brief flowering of 19th-century classicism. However, Mussolini's Fascism of the 1920s and 1930s has left its imprint as well. Whole areas of the city are dominated by massive, sometimes downright obtrusive buildings with white rectangular columns and plain reddish-brown facades, decorated with statues of, often naked, athletes and grim-faced women holding ears of corn or bunches of grapes. In places, people continued to build in this style even after the war had ended and the Mussolini regime had collapsed.

Some of the most impressive examples are Stazione Centrale di Termini, the Città Universitaria in the San Lorenzo district and the former air ministry. Another is the building to the south of the Circus Maximus that is now occupied by the Food and Agriculture Organization of the United Nations, but was originally intended to be the administrative centre of the African empire of which Mussolini dreamed. And then there is the church of Santi Pietro e Paolo, to the south of the Aurelian Walls, with its dome resembling a spiked helmet. However, the two most prominent examples of Fascist architecture are the area of southern Rome known as EUR (pronounced ay-oor) and the Foro Italico near Ponte Milvio, across the Tiber to the north-west of the city centre.

Some of these projects involved the demolition of whole areas of the city. For example, a huge swathe was cut through the forums in the city centre to build Via dei Fori Imperiali as a route for military parades. Likewise, Via della Conciliazione was built at the entrance to the Vatican as a symbol of reconciliation between the Holy See and the Italian state following the destruction of the papal state in 1870. Construction of the road involved demolishing the Spina, a row of suburban houses several hundred metres long.

But most of these grand structures were built on uninhabited land on the outskirts of the city, partly as a signal of the city's expansionist intentions. Both EUR, in the south, and the Foro Italico, to the north, were built in areas which were largely undeveloped.

PRECEDING PAGES: the Foro Italico. **LEFT:** Museo della Civiltà Romana. **BELOW:** a mixed architectural legacy.

From delusions of grandeur to post-modern bureaucracy

The district of EUR owes its name to the Esposizione Universale di Roma (Universal Exhibition of Rome). This international exhibition was to have been held in 1942 to mark the 20th anniversary of Mussolini's accession, but because of World War II it never took place. The slightly hilly site, then over 2 km (3 miles) outside the built-up area of Rome, was intended to form an impressive entrance to a new town extending

all the way to Ostia. But by the time Fascism ended, all that had been built were two palaces on either side of **Via Cristoforo Colombo**. A start had also been made on **Palazzo della Civiltà del Lavoro ❶** (Palace of Civilization based on Labour), which soon became popularly known as the "square Colosseum". Today, with its six storeys and plain arcaded windows, it has become a symbol of EUR.

After the war, the city continued the work begun by the architect Marcello Piacentini, and began building housing in the empty fields between the Aurelian Walls and EUR. Today, only a small dip on either side of Via Cristoforo Colombo remains undeveloped.

The idea of a town in the countryside, with a new interpretation of the old Italian use of space, is mingled in Piacentini's plans with a monumental grandeur and a repetitive motif: square pillars, square ground plans and square roofs. The buildings radiate a cold beauty that is all the more striking because, in the city's centre, nothing is rarer than a straight line. The streets are named to honour the new ideals of the time: agriculture (*agricoltura*), industry (*industria*), humanism (*umanisimo*), technology (*tecnica*) and arts (*arte*). And, where the Fascists managed to complete their plans before the war stopped work, there are statues and mosaics glorifying workers, soldiers and miners.

EUR was one of the main focal points of the 1960 Olympic Games and the multi-purpose **Palazzo dello Sport ❷** (also known as Palaeur) was built at the top of the second hill to the south. The sports hall holds up to 20,000 people, and is used for major concerts and for party and trade union conferences. A water tower with a viewing platform and restaurant was built to the west, giving a unique view of Rome; the people of the city have christened this rather mis-

BELOW: antique statuary in the Museo della Civiltà Romana.

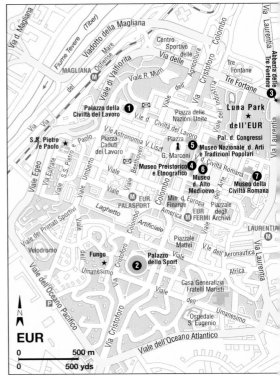

shapen building "Il Fungo" (the mushroom). In the depression between the two main hills, a three-section artificial lake was built, surrounded by beautiful greenery and with huge fountains which are only occasionally switched on.

By the time these buildings were erected, Mussolini-style architecture was passé, giving way first to glass facades and reinforced concrete, and then to post-modernism. The result is a largely unplanned mishmash of styles and shapes. Today, Via Cristoforo Colombo, which runs straight through the centre, is lined with a variety of ministries, government buildings and a large conference centre, **Palazzo dei Congressi**; this is bureaucracy writ large. It was originally intended that the whole of the government district should be located here, but the main ministries wanted to remain in the symbolic centre of the city.

It is not all modern. There is a reminder of Ancient Rome in the form of the **Abbazia delle Tre Fontane ❸**, the 8th-century abbey on the northeast slope of the EUR hill which is reached by a small path from the sports ground on Via delle Tre Fontane. This is where St Paul was reputedly beheaded: his head is supposed to have bounced three times and each time a spring welled up from the ground. As a result, three churches were built. The Cistercian monks who now live here distil a powerful spirit from eucalyptus, and sell it in a small shop open daily (but not at lunchtime).

Museums are EUR's main attraction. The **Museo Nazionale Preistorico-Etnografico "Luigi Pigorini" ❹** (Museum of Prehistory and Ethnography; open daily 9am–8pm; entrance fee; tel: 06-549 521) on Piazza Guglielmo Marconi houses a large number of prehistoric artefacts from Africa, Asia, Australia and America. Next to it is the **Museo Nazionale delle Arti e Tradizioni Popolari ❺** (Museum of Folk Art and Traditions; open Tues–Sun 9am–6pm; free; tel: 06-592

Map, see opposite

BELOW: the "square Colosseum", built in Mussolini's time.

6148), a lively portrayal of Rome's social history, including puppets, costumes, historic tools, votive objects and even an original Venetian gondola.

Opposite is the **Museo dell'Alto Medioevo** (Museum of the High Middle Ages; open Tues–Sun 9am–8pm; entrance fee; 06-5422 8199), where valuable medieval collections reflect a time when occupied Rome had little political significance, but achieved a high standard of prosperity and produced high-quality arts and crafts. The most interesting of the museums is slightly further to the east, behind the grand colonnade. It is the **Museo della Civiltà Romana** ❼ (Museum of Roman Civilization; open Tues–Sat 9am–7pm, Sun 9am–1.30pm; entrance fee; tel: 06-592 6135), which chronicles every aspect of life in Ancient Rome, using models, originals and copies of artefacts. The exhibits include entire temple frontages; the spiral reliefs from Trajan's Column, originally more than 150 metres (500 ft) long and now broken into pieces, which can be viewed from the "parterre"; Diocletian's famous emergency prices edict, a means of dealing with rampant inflation in the 3rd century; tools and other everyday items; and a 20 by 20 m (65 by 65 ft) model of Rome at the time of Constantine. This can be viewed from the surrounding balustrade and gives an impression of the size of the city at the time.

Unused roads and wealthy suburbs

If you start from EUR and go along Via Cristoforo Colombo away from the city centre, passing the junctions with Viale dell'Oceano Atlantico and Viale dell'Oceano Pacifico, you will come to an odd stretch of road. Although there are few buildings along it, this six-lane highway looks like a cross between a major city street and a long-distance *autostrada*. Street lights have been placed in the

TIP

EUR boasts two excellent *gelaterie* (ice-cream parlours): the traditional Giolitti (Casina dei Tre Laghi, Viale Oceania 90) and Chalet del Lago, next to the lake.

BELOW: modern homage to classical athletes.

fields for no apparent reason and the road continues on for 25 km (40 miles), ending by a swimming-pool on the beach at Ostia.

The reason for the road's strange appearance is the fact that a whole town was originally intended to be built between EUR and Ostia. None of it came to fruition, and the residential areas that grew up to the southwest of the city in the 1970s and 1980s wisely stayed well away from the road. The result is an expensive district in which white-collar workers live in atrium apartments and bungalows surrounded by tall hedges and walls, their tranquillity disturbed only by the occasional roar of a jet engine from Fiumicino Airport to the north.

Map, page 210

A stop along the way: San Paolo fuori le Mura

If you are returning to the city centre or the second great complex of Fascist architecture at the Foro Italico to the north, and do not want to retrace your route along Via Cristoforo Colombo, you can take a different route and see a different style of architecture. Turn left out of Piazza Navigatori along Via Guglielmo Marconi and, just before you reach the Tiber, turn right into Piazzale Edison. Here, you will find **San Paolo fuori le Mura** (St Paul's Without the Walls) one of Rome's four patriarchal basilicas and its second largest church. If you are coming into the city on the Metro from EUR centre, get out at San Paolo station.

The church was built on the site of St Paul's tomb by Constantine the Great in the 4th century, and was later extended by Theodosius. In 1823, it was almost completely destroyed by a fire, but was faithfully restored by the Roman architect Poletti. The entrance portico was added by Calderini in 1892; the facade is by Vespignani and the gold mosaics by Agricola. Inside, there are 80 monolithic granite columns, and the arches are covered in mosaics. The apse, the decoration

BELOW: in EUR.

Map, page 210

of which remained largely undamaged by the fire, has the same mysterious gold tone, though experts believe it is not as impressive as it was prior to the fire. After you leave the church, have a look at Vassalletto's beautiful early 13th-century monastery courtyard.

Monuments to the cult of the body

The **Foro Italico**, at the northern end of Rome, is very similar in style to the original EUR, but it is more practical and less doctrinaire. As you cross the Ponte Milvio, you will see a square obelisk bearing the words "Mussolini Dux". Here again, most of the buildings are rectangular with white columns and reddish-brown facades, but some, such as the great swimming-pool, have rather softer rounded edges, and there are some much more informal areas such as the tennis courts and lawns. This district was formerly dominated by the Stadio dei Marmi, built by Mussolini's architects in the style of a Greek stadium and surrounded by 60 marble figures of athletes in heroic poses. Today, it is dwarfed by the **Stadio Olimpico**, the huge football and athletics stadium immediately behind it, designed by Pier Luigi Nervi and seating 100,000 spectators. This is where the opening ceremony of the 1960 Olympics took place and when the World Cup was held here in 1990, the stadium was extended into the Monte Mario behind it; the stands have since been roofed over. The youth hostel near the stadium was once part of the Olympic Village.

The foreign ministry, known as the Farnesina, stands on a bare, empty patch to the east of the stadium, with the Viale Macchia di Farnesina running behind it. Many visitors to the ministry, with its high, empty corridors hundreds of metres long, have been reminded of Charlie Chaplin's film, *The Great Dictator*. ❏

RIGHT: entrance to San Paolo fuori le Mura.

SPORT: A NATIONAL OBSESSION

Sport, particularly football, plays a important part in the lives of the Italian people as a whole. When there's a football match in progress, do not be at all surprised to see Romans of all ages with radios pressed against their ears, eager to hear the latest result. If the home team wins, then the peace of the afternoon is likely to be broken by honking car horns and a great deal of shouting.

If you do like football, actually going to an Italian football match is an experience that should not be missed, for several reasons: the quality of play, the excitable crowds and the electric atmosphere. Rome has two teams: Roma and Lazio, who play at the Stadio Olimpico on alternate Sunday afternoons. If you do want to go and watch a match, note that seats can be very difficult to come by; the best places to buy tickets – and official team paraphernalia – are shops by the Lazio Point on Via Farina (near Termini) or the Roma Point (Piazza Colonna).

Aside from football, Rome hosts a major event on both the men's and women's international tennis circuits. Both events are known as the Italian Open and they take place at the Foro Italico during May. You will never see another tennis event like it – unlike Wimbledon, it's not a case of a polite clap here and there, the crowd clap and jeer to their heart's content.

If you visit Rome in May, don't miss Italy's international riding week, held in Piazza di Siena in the middle of the Villa Borghese park. As well as show-jumping, with the Nations Cup and World Cup events, there is the Carosello dei Carabinieri, in which more than 200 riders armed with sabres engage in mock battles and other complex manoeuvres.

Other sporting events on offer include motorbike races and greyhound racing and, if you feel like taking up the challenge yourself, Rome has several golf clubs, and many swimming-pools and health clubs.

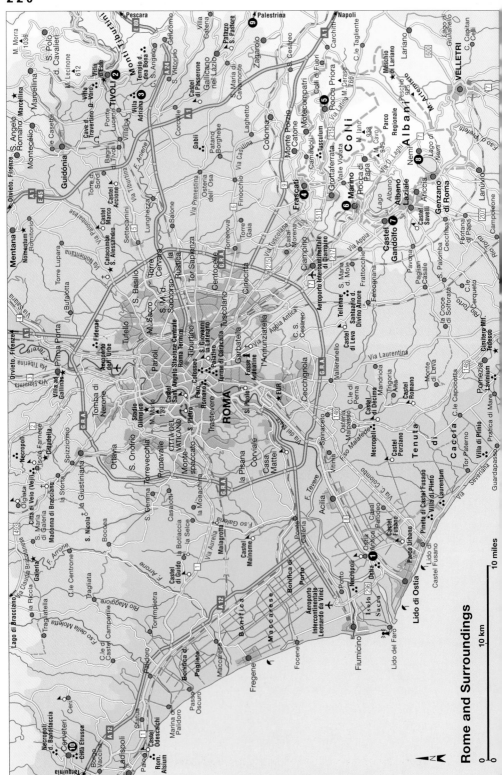

Rome and Surroundings

0 10 km

0 10 miles

EXCURSIONS FROM ROME

The countryside around Rome offers
such a variety of landscapes that it is worth
a holiday in itself

It is surprising that so few of the 2 million tourists who pour into Rome every year find their way into the "hinterland romano" – to the Etruscan graves near Cerveteri; the lakes of Bracciano, Albano, Nemi; the remains of the pre-Roman shrine in Palestrina; the fountains of the Villa d'Este; the Byzantine Greek Orthodox abbey in Grottaferrata. And there's more to Frascati than a light white wine: a former summer residence for Roman nobility, this region offers glorious scenery and, for the energetic, long country walks.

The fertile, hilly area immediately south of Rome is known as the Campagna. Now thronged with billboards featuring Asterix and Obelix, it was here that Rome fought to establish supremacy over Latium. After the defeat of Veio (396 BC), the Agro Romano was, at last, Roman. Soon, the small farms were displaced by *latifundia* (large agricultural estates), which used cheap slave labour to work the fields. Shortly before the fall of the empire, the Campagna blossomed once more, because everyone who had a chance fled the city. Most of the ruins turned up by farmers' ploughs today date from this time. After the empire's collapse, the Campagna decayed into a malaria-ridden marsh.

The "Bonifica" of the Campagna was one of the first actions undertaken by the new Italian government before the turn of the century. Earlier appeals to the popes to have the Campagna drained and cultivated had failed. At first, only a stretch of some (10 km) 6 miles around the city was drained – this area has long since been built upon. The rest of the area, which was drained after World War I, is where Mussolini built his *borgate* (satellite towns).

Despite these inroads made by the city, the Campagna still feeds most Romans. Dairy farming, market gardening, strawberries, wine, carnation growing and arable farming flourish. In spring, the fields are bursting with the bright yellow of rape-seed in flower; in autumn, whole groves of olive trees blossom. ❑

PRECEDING PAGES: wishing for luck in Tivoli; Ostia Antica archaeological site.

OSTIA ANTICA

*The wonderful ruins of the Roman town of Ostia, surrounded
by Roman pines and flat coastal plains, make a great excursion
from the dusty hustle and bustle of Rome*

King Ancus Marcius, according to legend, founded a port town in the 7th century BC and named it **Ostia ❶** after the *ostium* or mouth of the Tiber. However, the archaeological evidence dates only to the second half of the 4th century BC, when fortifications were built around the town.

Rome was very dependent on this one connection with the sea, because all its essential commodities – but especially grain – were transported from Ostia along the **Via Ostiensis**. Rome's dependence on Ostia was good news for the port's inhabitants. Imported goods from both the West and East, which Rome devoured, were traded here and the population enjoyed a luxurious standard of living. The town even had special status, with the male inhabitants being freed from military service. There was also money to be made from holidaymakers. On hot summer days, when the stone streets of Rome practically blazed, Romans fled to the fresh air of the sea resort.

However, when Emperor Augustus moved the Roman naval base to Misenium, Ostia felt the loss of free-spending sailors and all the associated trade. For a while, it remained the unloading point for the grain ships and, in AD 41–54, Claudius had new docks built, but the beginning of the end of Ostia was already evident – the harbour was silting up. Not even a new harbour basin – now the airport of Fiumicino – that was dug on the orders of Trajan (AD 98–117) could stop this process. The coastline gradually moved west and today Ostia is several kilometres from the sea.

BELOW: the
Decumanus
Maximus.

Mass exodus

At the height of Ostia's prosperity in the early 2nd century, its population was about 500,000, but its decline was steady. Emperor Constantine's decision to move the capital of the empire to Constantinople in the third century, continual pirate attacks and, in the early Middle Ages, the threat of the Saracens meant that Ostia's population was forced to leave. Soon, the only inhabitants left were malarial mosquitoes.

At that time, the coastline was about (2 km) 4 miles further inland than it is today. Luckily for archaeologists, the city was never repopulated and it has been very well preserved under a bed of sand. Although the ruins were quarried for building materials in the Middle Ages, about two-thirds of the Roman town can now be seen, thanks to extensive archaeological excavation. Since the 19th century, this archaeological treasure house has been systematically laid bare. The better finds are on display in Rome's museums.

Today, many Romans still flee the heat of the city to spend the day at the beach of Ostia Lido. The wealthy, however, have moved a bit further south, to **San Felice Circeo** and **Terracina**.

At the entrance to Ostia, visitors follow the **Decumanus Maximus**, the same main road as the Ancient Romans, which leads through the city centre. Worth noting en route are the **Terme di Nettuno** (Baths of Neptune), named after their glorious mosaic floor, and the **Teatro** (theatre), warranting a visit for the splendid views offered by its upper tiers. Underneath these tiers, there would have been taverns and shops. Beside the theatre, three large masks have been mounted on tufa – originally, they were part of the theatre's decoration. Occasionally, in summer, it is used for plays. Also worth looking at are the stalls in the **Piazza delle Corporazioni** (Square of the Guilds), where lovely floor mosaics preserve the insignias of the various guilds – most of which were associated with fitting and supplying the ships.

Map, page 220 & below

The **Decumanus Maximus** leads to the **Forum**, where citizens met to gossip and justice was dispensed by city officials, and the **Capitolium**, Ostia's largest temple, which was dedicated to Jupiter, Juno and Minerva. Beyond is the **Schola di Traiano** (School of Trajan), formerly the headquarters of a guild of merchants, and the **Basilica Cristiana** (Christian Basilica).

The workers of Ostia lived in **insulae**, blocks of flats three or four storeys high. The **Casa di Diana** (House of Diana), near the Forum, is one of the smarter ones and is well-preserved. It had a balcony on the second floor, its own private bath house and a central courtyard where there was a cistern to collect water. An interesting insight into the sort of housing used by ancient Romans, it also incorporates an old tavern on the ground floor, complete with a marble counter on which customers were served their sausages and hot wine (sweetened with honey), ovens, storage and a beer garden for outdoor drinking.

Mosaics in Ostia Antica.

A few miles away, the tombs on **Isola Sacra** (Sacred Island) give a good impression of ancient burial customs in the 2nd to 4th centuries AD. The dead of Ostia were buried in layered tombs, which can be seen outside the city, but within the fence of the excavated zone.

Medieval Ostia

Before heading either to Rome or to the beaches of Ostia, you shouldn't miss the opportunity to visit the medieval town of Ostia.

Developed around the ruins of Gregoriopolis, a fortified citadel built on the orders of Pope Gregory IV between 827 and 844, Ostia was a medieval village within defensive walls. After it had been destroyed by invading forces in 1408, Martin V built a defensive tower against the barbarians and Saracens. This tower became the centre of a castle built by Pontelli later in the same century for the future Pope Julius II, then a cardinal. However, the attacks continued and, together with the silting-up of the river and a huge flood in the 16th century, drove the inhabitants away.

You can visit the **Castello di Giulio II**, as the castle is now known, which was completely restored in the early 1990s. It has some interesting features, such as scarped curtain walls, which were innovative at the time, but became commonplace in the 16th century. You can also see the fortress's museum, its church (Santa Aurea) and the Palazzo Episcopale, official residence of the Bishop of Ostia. The latter houses notable frescoes by Peruzzi. ❑

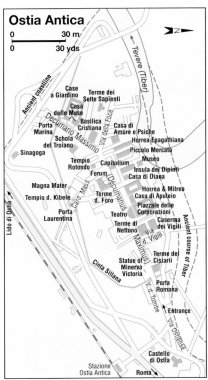

TIVOLI

Map, page 220

Travel through vineyards and past sulphurous springs to get to Tivoli, a small town pressed against a hillside that has three famous villas and was home to Borgias, Habsburgs and Roman emperors

Tivoli is one of many towns set in the hills outside Rome that has long served as a getaway for Romans – both ancient and modern – in the hot summers. Three famous villas make Tivoli a popular attraction and a worthwhile day trip out of town. There are several ways to reach Tivoli: you can either drive, take Metro Line B to Rebibbia, from where a bus that stops at Hadrian's Villa leaves every 15 minutes, or take a bus (journey time approximately 45 minutes) from the Ponte Mammolo station of Metro line B.

The primary attraction is **Villa d'Este ❷** (open Mar–Sept, Tues–Sun 8.30am–6.15pm, Oct–Mar, Tues–Sun 8.30am–4pm; entrance fee; tel: 0774-312070), which is justly famous for its wonderful fountains and waterworks. Originally a Benedictine convent, the building was converted into the Governor's Palace in the 13th century. In 1550, Cardinal Ippolito d'Este, son of Lucrezia Borgia and grandson of Pope Alexander VI, was elected governor. He then began to renovate the villa and its gardens into something befitting his aspirations to the papacy. He never became pope, but he did leave a memorial to himself in the fountains, which have delighted visitors for centuries and served to inspire waterworks all over Europe. After the decline of the Este family, the Habsburgs inherited the Villa, but they were poor caretakers. After World War I, the Italian state took it over and the Villa was restored.

LEFT: fresco at Villa d'Este. **BELOW:** tourists in Tivoli.

A walk through the terraced gardens, which were so beautifully laid out by Ligorio and Giacomo della Porta, is a delight. The **Viale delle Cento Fontane** (Avenue of a Hundred Fountains) has a row of close-set thin pipes that spray water into the air. Set in the middle of the road is the **Fontana dei Draghi** (Dragon Fountain), made in honour of Pope Gregory XIII, who was once a guest at the Villa and whose emblem included a dragon.

Located at the end of the Viale, on the right-hand side, is the **Fontana dell'Ovato** (Oval Fountain) decorated with eight nymphs. The **Fontana dell'Organo** (Organ Fountain) no longer plays music, as it once did, but it isn't hard to imagine how lovely it might formerly have sounded.

Tivoli's watery attractions don't all flow in the Villa d'Este. The town is full of ancient remains of temples and other buildings – some (such as the Temple of Vesta) are extremely well preserved, while others have been incorporated into medieval churches. The **Villa Gregoriana**, set in a steep wooded park, is also worth a visit. Here, the River Aniene plunges into the famous **Grande Cascata**. About 15 km (10 miles) further on, you reach the area where the spring for the **Acqua Vergine** rises, which feeds the aqueduct restored by the popes that leads into the Fontana di Trevi in Rome. Carry on past the **Bagni di Tivoli**, sulphurous medicinal springs, popular since Roman times.

Hadrian's Villa

Even more impressive than the Villa d'Este are the ruins of **Villa Adriana** ❸ (Hadrian's Villa; open May–Aug, daily 9am–7.30pm, Apr & Sept, daily 9am–7pm, Oct–Mar, daily 9am–1 hour before sunset, last entry 1½ hours before closing; entrance fee; tel: 0774-382733), the most magnificent country villa of Roman imperial times. Even today, after centuries of systematic despoilment and decay, it exudes an atmosphere of wealth and leisure.

Roman remains at Tivoli.

When the Roman Empire flourished, **Tivoli** (ancient Tibur), in the foothills of the Sabine Hills, was a favoured retreat for poets and wealthy citizens. Among the guests at the splendid villas were Horace, Catullus, Maecenas, Sallust and the Emperor Trajan. In AD 117, the Emperor Hadrian started to build a luxurious refuge for himself at the foot of the hill on which Tivoli stands. His plan was to rebuild the monuments that had most impressed him on his travels, particularly in Greece and Egypt. He demanded more than mere copies of the originals: he wanted to create aesthetically pleasing edifices that would contrast dramatically with functionalism and practical common sense. A notable feature of the villa was Hadrian's idea, a new concept at the time, of scattering the individual buildings over the 60 hectares (148 acres) of the park, rather than grouping them in a central complex. To protect against the weather, all the buildings were connected by covered walkways and underground passages *(cryptoportici)*.

BELOW: the Canopus in Hadrian's Villa.

The beautifully painted colonnade, Stoa Poikile, which Hadrian had seen in Athens – and is here called the **Pecile** – is one of the most noteworthy buildings. The mighty surrounding wall, 230-metres (760-ft) long, of the Pecile has survived on the north side, as has the water basin in its centre. Opposite, on the inner side stood a covered, pillared entrance. Notice the lattice-work effect cre-

ated by small blocks of tufa forming a diaper pattern. Excavations, which were first carried out to obtain marble, have turned up more than 300 statues since the 15th century. These are now on display in museums all over the world.

Well worth closer inspection is the **Teatro Marittimo** (Maritime Theatre), a circular construction consisting of a portico and a central building surrounded by a moat, and reached by two wooden swing bridges. It must have been a perfect retreat for the emperor. Passing the olive grove, you can see the **Ninfeo** (nymphaeum), a flat area between two walls that was originally thought to be a stadium. The **Terme** (Baths) consisted of the Small Baths and the Great Baths – both show the high architectural standards that were employed in the villa.

Next to the Baths is the most ambitious of Hadrian's replicas. The **Canopo** (Canopus), a copy of the famous Temple of Serapis near Alexandria in Egypt. A 15-km (10-miles) long canal, lined with luxury residences and statues, led from the River Nile to the Temple. Hadrian tried to imitate the scenario by creating a 119-metre (390-ft) long canal, by the side of which stood marble architraves and copies of Egyptian statues. The southern bank was originally occupied by a copy of the Serapis shrine, but all that remains is a large niche in the rock and a big chunk of rock lying in the water basin.

Hadrian's collection

Hadrian's eclectic collection of statuary – copies from Egypt and Greece – has helped archaeologists restore the originals. For example, Phidias's *Amazon*, now in the Villa's museum, is a copy of the original from Ephesus's Temple of Diana.

Hadrian himself didn't enjoy his collection for long – he died only four years after it was completed. ❏

Map, page 220

Tivoli caryatids.

TIP

Water pressure can vary at Villa d'Este, so call beforehand (tel: 0774-312 070) to ensure the fountains are working.

BELOW: Tivoli.

CASTELLI ROMANI

*This region, to the southeast of Rome, has been known as the
Castelli Romani since the Middle Ages – it has always been
a popular retreat for the city's inhabitants*

Map,
page 220

F or a leisurely country drive through towns and villages famous for their
food and wine and, in most cases, supplied with at least one excellent
restaurant, you could do no better than to hire a car and tour the Castelli
Romani. The alternative is to take a bus and/or a train.

Thirteen towns in the Alban Hills are known as the "Castelli Romani" (Roman
Castles). Their collective name stems from the fact that they all grew up around
the feudal castles of Roman patrician families, who sought refuge in their
fortresses when anarchy ruled in Rome. During World War II, some towns in
the Castelli were badly damaged by Allied bombing. **Frascati ❹**, seat of the
German High Command and the Queen of the Castelli Romani, suffered particularly heavy bombardment.

Frascati

By all accounts, Frascati has long been an attractive place to visit. The poet and
critic Arthur Symons, who came here in 1903, described it thus: "Frascati, as
one turns in and out of its streets, opening suddenly on vague glimpses, as if cut
by the sides of a frame, is like a seaside village; and one cannot help imagining
the wash of waves; instead of the grassy plain of the Campagna, at the end of
those coiling streets." Today, Frascati is still a delight.

One of the best times to visit the town is autumn,
when the grape harvest begins in October; a *frasca di
lauro*, a laurel twig, is displayed; the smoke of the first
woodfires mixes with the sweet scents from the vineyards; and when a fat, fresh *porchetta* (whole-roast pig
stuffed with aromatic herbs, for which the region is
justly known) lies on the counter.

Frascati, which translates as "huts of leaves", became
a town in 1197, when the ancient city of Tusculum was
destroyed and its population settled here. Later, it
became the favourite resort of the affluent.

The town's trademark is its world-famous wine – a
light, very quaffable wine with a faint, refreshing
prickle – which is a product of the rich volcanic soil. In
Italy, Frascati is drunk mostly by the "Frascatani" themselves. Much of the stuff on sale in supermarkets bears
little relation to the drink served in *cantinas*, which
ranges from pale to dark yellow. A good proportion of
the exported wine comes from neighbouring towns and
villages rather than Frascati itself, though this is not why
it is often so poor. The reason for this is that most is
based on the rather bland Trebbiano variety of grape
and only the better producers – Fontana Candida and
Colli di Catone (especially Colle Gaio) among them –
use Malvasia.

But before you get stuck into some decent local wine,
let's begin with a walk around town, starting from

LEFT: the Greek
Orthodox abbey
in Grottaferrata.
BELOW: a day's
outing.

Coin from the time
of Julius Caesar.

From both Villa Torlonia
and Villa Aldobrandini,
there are far-reaching
views towards Rome –
if it's clear, you can
even see the dome
of St Peter's.

Below: Villa
Aldobrandini.

Piazza San Pietro. From here, go through the little *galleria* (breezeway) to **Piazza del Mercato** (Market Square), where you can get a good sandwich bursting with *porchetta*. Go left past the market and you will find several wine shops in **Via Regina Margherita** that allow customers to bring *cibo proprio* (their own food). It is not all that unusual for whole families to arrive equipped with a complete evening meal.

Frascati is not only famous for its wine (and its children's carnival), but also for its many palaces and their attendant gardens. Next to the bus station, for example, lies the park of the **Villa Torlonia** (part of a 16th-century estate). And above the town rises the **Villa Aldobrandini**, built in 1602 for Pietro Aldobrandini, a nephew of Clement VIII. The most beautiful feature of the villa, and the only area that may be visited by the general public (permits are available from the tourist office), is the park. It contains a wonderful water display with Atlas balancing a "globe with a hundred thorns" on his head, and behind him a grove of bizarrely shaped oak trees.

Another unusual secret lies hidden in the vineyards south of Frascati. Here, in **Via Enrico Fermi**, Bruno Touschek, a young Jewish physicist exiled from Austria, invented the first electron accelerator. The invention of the cyclotron in the nuclear laboratory in Frascati broke new ground and paved the way for other research establishments, such as CERN in Geneva and DESY in Hamburg, in the discovery of quarks, the basic building blocks of matter.

Tusculum

The way to **Tusculum**, where Cicero wrote his philosophical *Tusculanes,* lies uphill, along about 5 km (3 miles) of asphalt road. (There are no easily accessible

footpaths, but you may still be able to find your way along the unmarked wood-land paths.)

The ancient city of the Latins (founded, according to legend, by Telegonus, son of Circe and Odysseus) was a monarchy before it came into Rome's sphere of influence in the 6th century BC. Later, in 340 BC, the city participated in the revolt of the Latins against the Romans. From the 10th to the 12th centuries, the Counts of Tusculum ruled over it – as well as Rome. In 1191, the Romans destroyed the town, as an act of revenge for its subjugation, and its inhabitants fled to Frascati. The town has never been rebuilt, so all that remains are ruins.

Map, page 220

Grottaferrata

It's only a few kilometres from Frascati to **Grottaferrata**, known for its Greek Orthodox abbey. The monastery, with its Eastern rites, was founded by St Nilus, a Greek from Calabria, who was fleeing north to find a site safe from attack by Saracens. Under Byzantine rule, southern Italy had a large Greek minority, whose descendants still survive today in a few remote areas. The fleeing monks built their monastery on the remains of a sepulchre dating from Republican times. Julius II later had the protective wall built. The church of the abbey, **Santa Maria di Grottaferrata**, has some beautiful frescoes. After visiting the abbey, you might care to try the brothers' own wine, which is on sale. Also, on Sunday mornings, the monks celebrate Mass according to the Greek Orthodox rite – it's worth making a special visit just for this because the chorales are unrivalled.

From Grottaferrata, you can see the cross on the summit of the hill at **Rocca Priora ❺**, the highest town in the Castelli at 768 metres (2,520 ft), which is often covered in snow in winter.

BELOW: Swiss Guards at the Pope's summer residence in Castel Gandolfo.

Rock of the Pope

The town of **Rocca di Papa** ("the Pope's rock") lies a few miles away, steeply uphill, on the northern flank of the **Monte Cavo**, the highest peak of the Alban Hills (949 metres/3,114 ft). This attractive medieval town has a *quartiere bavarese*, named after the Bavarian mercenaries who were stationed here by Emperor Ludwig III in the 1320s. Rome is only a few miles away and yet the city, whose lights are like a raft of glow-worms below, couldn't seem more distant. The wine of Monte Cavo is excellent and a particularly delicious local speciality, the *sfogatelli* mushroom, is worth seeking out.

From Rocca di Papa, anyone who enjoys hiking may want to climb to the peak of **Monte Cavo**, following Via Sacra through the oak woods. The top of Monte Cavo is a little disappointing, because it is covered in 2,500 antennae belonging to the state and private radio and TV channels of Rome, plus the military. These cover the remains of the ancient shrine of Jupiter, worshipped by the 47 federated Latin cities, and a more recent monastery. A struggle has been going on for some time to get all the broadcasting antennae linked up in a system of dishes – technically possible, if only the participants could agree – so that the peak would be less of a mess.

Whatever happens, the view will always be fantastic. In the distance, beyond Rome, are the **Tolfa Hills**, where the ancient Etruscans discovered iron ore, and the Etruscan plain around **Lago di Bracciano**. You can recognise the charter airport of Rome, **Ciampino**, and St Peter's if it is clear, but in high summer the city is too damp and smoggy to see anything. Further inland, looking northwards, you might just see **Terminillo**, a 2,200 metre (7,200 ft) mountain popular with winter skiers, which is only an hour's drive away.

BELOW: Lago di Albano, the crater of an extinct volcano.

Further to the east lies the massif of **Gran Sasso d'Italia**, another skier's mountain, reached by the Roma-l'Aquila motorway. To the south and southwest, beyond Lago di Albano and Rocca di Papa, lie the former Pontine Marshes, where mozzarella cheese (which is traditionally made from the milk of buffalo) is produced. You can see the coastline and, in clear weather, even as far as the islands of **Ponza** and **Palmarola**.

Map,
page 220

Marino

Close to ancient Castrimoenium lies **Marino ❻**, which is associated with the deliverance of Christianity from the Turks. In the main square, **Piazza Matteotti** (named after the socialist leader murdered by Mussolini), stands the Fountain of the Moors, which was built in honour of the *condottiere* of the papal fleet, Marcantonio Colonna, Prince of Marino, the victor of the sea battle of Lepanto in 1571. The church of the **Madonna del Rosario** is definitely worth a visit. Built in 1713, probably by Sardi, it is perhaps the most beautiful rococo church in Lazio. Dominican nuns, living here in a closed community, are responsible for its excellent state of preservation.

Summer residence

The Pope's summer residence at **Castel Gandolfo ❼** is beautifully situated about 400 metres/1,300 ft above the crater rim of Lago di Albano.

This site is associated with one of the most ancient legends of the founding of Rome. Historians agree that this was the site of Alba Longa, the city founded by Aeneas. The story is one of struggle between Alba Longa and Rome, and between the Curatian and Horatian families. Eventually, the Horatian family

BELOW: view of Nemi.

won, giving Rome mastery over Alba Longa. The latter was subsequently destroyed as a punishment for its treachery, but the temples were spared. They are rumoured to have occupied the exact spot of the present papal villa.

The Holy See acquired the "Castello" Gandolfo at the end of the 16th century, and in 1628 Pope Urban VIII commissioned Maderno to design a villa on the site of Domitian's earler villa. The gardens of the **Papal Villa** are closed to the public for security reasons. In the summer, the Pope holds the traditional Angelus prayer every Sunday at midday on the **Loggia della Benedizione**.

Stendhal, Goethe, Winckelmann and Gregorovius all had a high opinion of Castel Gandolfo and modern Romans love the place, too, particularly because it is so close to **Lago di Albano**. The clean water of this volcanic lake invites boating and swimming, but a word of caution: in the middle, where the water is 170 metres (558 ft) deep, there are dangerous currents. The water level is kept constant by the Emissarium, a tunnel cut by the Romans in the 4th century which is just under a mile (1.4 km) long and leads to the Tiber.

There is a delightful footpath, about 10 km (6 miles) long, around the lake. On Sundays, it is as crowded as the seaside.

To the southwest of the lake, the supposed tomb of the Horatian and Curatian families can be seen in **Albano Laziale** on the right-hand side of **Via Appia Nuova**, if you are travelling in the direction of **Ariccia**. The local park has remains of the **Villa of Pompey**.

Genzano

BELOW: small castle in the Castelli.

Further along Via Appia Nuova, the foundation of a medieval castle also provided the starting point for the town of **Genzano**, on the southeastern edge of

the little lake of Nemi. This town has been famous since the 16th century for its elm-lined roads and is also known beyond Lazio for the *Infiorata* – on the first Sunday after "Corpus Domini", the main street to the church of the Virgin Mary is decorated with holy pictures made out of flower petals.

The town also has an excellent reputation in Lazio for dance. It holds an important annual dance festival, which even the Bolshoi Ballet has been known to attend, and a dance centre in the town offers young artists from around Rome a place to practise.

Lago di Nemi

A 30-minute walk along the **Lago di Nemi** (sadly polluted, as a result of intensive farming and untreated sewage) leads up to the town of the same name.

Nemi ❶ is famous for its *fragole di bosco (*wild strawberries), which thrive in the warm climate along the low-lying lake shore. Set on a cliff above the lake, the small town takes its name from the goddess Diana – this area was once known as *Nemus Dianae*, the sacred grove of Diana. In her honour, the Emperor Caligula built enormous boats over 70-metres (230-yards) long. The boats were discovered in the 1920s during work on the lake and exhibited in the local museum until 1944, when both the boats and the museum were destroyed by the Germans. One-fifth scale models are on display in the nearby Nemi Museum of Roman Ships.

Follow the path to the right, under the sleepy **Palazzo Cesarini**, to a small garden watched over by a statue of Diana. This is a pleasant place to rest, and the café sells excellent vanilla ices. On a good day the views over the volcanic lake stretch to the sea. ❑

Map, page 220

TIP

If you are in Nemi in June, ask the tourist office about the Strawberry Festival.

BELOW: in the Garden of Diana, above the lake of Nemi.

Rome
Palestrina

Palestrina

*An ancient Etruscan settlement that later became a favourite
retreat among patrician Romans, Palestrina is an attractive town,
tucked away in the hills and scattered with ancient ruins*

Very little is known about the history of *Praeneste*, as **Palestrina ❾** used to
be called. Its origins lie far back in the mists of time and, according to legend, it was founded by Telegonus, son of Odysseus. When Rome was in its
infancy, Praeneste was already flourishing. The Romans conquered it in 338 BC.
Then, after the civil wars in 82 BC, the Roman general Sulla, as a punitive measure, made it into a *colonia* and settled army veterans throughout the region. It
soon became something of a resort. Horace described it as "cool Praeneste".

Praeneste was famous, but feared, for its huge temple dedicated to the goddess **Fortuna Primigenia**, the mother of all gods. The six terraces of the mighty
shrine still stand today. When the complex was richly adorned with statues and
blazing with torches, it was an impressive sight which could be seen from afar.

The statue of the goddess stood before the semi-circle that is now the entrance
to the museum. The goddess Fortuna was worshipped in the upper part of the
shrine and, for this reason, the Roman patrician family of Barberini built its
palace neatly into the upper circle of the temple. The original palace was 11th-century, but much of the present incarnation is from the 1640s.

Palazzo Barberini now houses a museum, the Museo Nazionale Archeologico. Countless busts and other objects are on display, including the badly

BELOW: the shrine of
Fortuna Primigenia,
Palestrina.

damaged remains of the statue of the goddess Fortuna. However, it is the top floor that contains one of the highlights of Palestrina: the **Nile Mosaic**. Dating from the 1st century BC, it probably decorated the floor of the buildings where the temple now stands. It shows, in detail, the Nile valley after the annual flood, a scene teeming with peasants, fishermen, priests, soldiers and wild animals.

In the lower part of the shrine, the walls of which now enclose the old town of Palestrina, lies the secretive heart of the complex. In the central **Piazza Regina Margherita**, you will find the **Seminario**, which incorporates the remains of the sacred place, the *area sacra*. Most archaeologists agree that this was the entrance to the **Oracle** – not just any oracle, but one of the most important oracles of ancient times. It was here that the citizen Numerus Sufficius is supposed to have unearthed the *sorti Preneste*, thin wooden sticks with oracular powers. To consult the oracle, you drew one of the wooden sticks out of a box and the priests then used it to predict your future.

The worship of the goddess declined with the arrival of Christianity and, with the prohibition of non-Christian worship in the 4th century, Fortuna closed her gates. In the early Middle Ages, the city was fought over by Goths, Longobards, Byzantines and papal families. The last finally conquered the town at the beginning of the 14th century and destroyed it once again.

Apart from its goddess, Palestrina is linked with the composer Giovanni Perluigi da Palestrina, who was born here in 1525. As choirmaster of St Peter's, he was responsible for a fresh expressiveness in Catholic church music, in the spirit of the Counter-Reformation. The town also has a following among food-lovers, who come in autumn to hunt the local speciality, *funghi porcini*, wild mushrooms that have been a great delicacy since Roman times.   ❏

Map, page 220

ABOVE: detail from an 18th-century map of Italy.
BELOW: the famous Nile Mosaic.

CERVETERI

*Once one of the most populated and culturally important
towns in the Mediterranean, Cerveteri is now but a
series of interesting ancient ruins*

There are more ancient remains – even older than those at Ostia – near Cerveteri ❿. These are the remains of an Etruscan settlement called Kysry, which was established in the foothills of the Tolfa range, about 45 km (28 miles) northwest of Rome and only 6 km (4 miles) from the sea. The oldest archaeological evidence in the area dates back to the 9th century BC.

In the 7th and 6th centuries BC, Kysry evolved into one of the most important and powerful cities in Etruria, with a population of around 25,000. The city boundary enclosed about 150 hectares (370 acres) and was about 6 km (4 miles) in circumference, though not all of this was heavily built upon. Revenue came mostly from the rich ore deposits in the Tolfa Hills, but also from trade with Greek cities and the Middle East, via the ports of Alsium (Palo near Ladispoli), Punicum (Santa Marinella) and, most of all, Pyrgi (Santa Severa).

Kysry was probably ruled by a king and, for a long time, the town maintained good relations with its Roman neighbours. Then, in 358 BC, Rome conquered the Etruscan town and it became known as Caere. The town grew steadily poorer, but it was not abandoned until the Middle Ages. The population then moved east to the town of Ceri, renaming their abandoned town *Caere Vetus*, which eventually developed into the modern name Cerveteri.

BELOW: the entrance
to the 7th century BC
Tomba della
Cornice, Cerveteri.

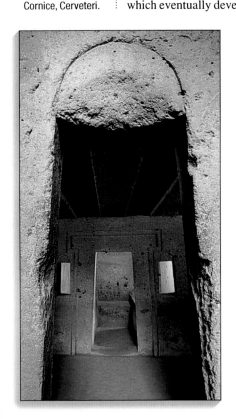

City of the dead

Nothing is left of the ancient city, but it is worthwhile going to look at the excavation of the necropolis on the hill of **Banditaccia** (open Tues–Sun until an hour before sunset; entrance fee), where an archaeological park has been set up. Here, different types of tombs are laid out along a main road and side roads, like a city for the dead, all carved into the soft tufa rock.

From the simple body tombs, covered with a mound of earth, the tumulus tombs developed in the 7th century BC. On a round foundation, up to 30 metres (100 ft) in diameter, a hill was built, where rites for the dead were celebrated. Inside the tomb, one or more burial chambers were hewn out of the rock – copies of the wooden houses of the living with windows, doors and pillars. As well as the chambers, furniture such as beds and chairs were carved out of the rock, giving a detailed impression of Etruscan everyday life.

Especially worth seeing are the 6th-century BC **Tumulo dei Capitelli** and the **Tumulus II**, containing four graves belonging to one noble family, dating from the 5th century BC to the end of the 2nd century BC. Other tombs to see include Tomba della Capanna, Tomba dei Dolii e degli Alari, Tomba dei Letti e Sarcofagi, Tomba dei Vasi Greci, Tomba della Cornice and Tomba degli Scudi e delle Sedie.

In the 6th and 5th centuries BC, the so-called cubic

graves became common. These rectangular buildings stand in regular rows of streets, reflecting the social changes that had taken place in the city. By then, prosperity had spread to the lower classes and a social levelling had taken place. The tumulus tombs, appropriate to rustic huts, were replaced by the rectangular "council houses". Graves with many chambers gave way to graves with only one. This was partly to save space, but also a sign of a failing belief in an after-life in which graves could be used as houses. Examples worth visiting can be found on **Via dei Monti Tolfa** and **Via dei Monti Ceriti.**

From the 4th to the 1st century BC, the dead were buried in underground tombs called hypogaea. Most of these were fairly plain and contained many bodies. The richer you were, the larger your burial tomb. The largest is the **Tomba dei Rilievi,** belonging to the wealthy family of Matuna, which dates from the 4th century BC. It has space for 32 bodies in all and is decorated with coloured plaster reliefs depicting assorted weapons, tools, household implements, musical instruments and furnishings.

The **Museo Nazionale Cerite** (open Tues–Sun 8.30am–7.30pm; free; tel: 06-994 1354), in the 16th-century Castello Orsini in Cerveteri, contains some of the items found in the graves, including domestic items, vases and terracotta lamps. However, finds from Cerveteri can be found as far afield as the British Museum, the Louvre, the Vatican's Museo Gregoriano and the Villa Giulia in Rome, which includes the famous sarcophagus of the married couple, the *Sarcofago degli Sposi.*

If you are travelling by car, return to Rome via **Lago di Bracciano** (Lake Bracciano), famous for fishing and watersports. In **Bracciano** itself, the 15th-century Castello Orsini-Odescalchi is worth visiting. More idyllic, however, is the medieval village of **Anguillara** on the southern shores of the lake.   ❏

Map, page 220

TIP

To reach Cerveteri from Rome, take the Pisa train which stops at the town. Alternatively, a Cotral bus leaves from Lepanto station on Metro Line A.

BELOW: tumulus tomb in Cerveteri.

INSIGHT GUIDES

TRaVeL TIPS

Insight FlexiMaps

Maps in Insight Guides are tailored to complement the text. But when you're on the road you sometimes need the big picture that only a large-scale map can provide. This new range of durable Insight Fleximaps has been designed to meet just that need.

Detailed, clear cartography
makes the comprehensive route and city maps easy to follow, highlights all the major tourist sites and provides valuable motoring information plus a full index.

Informative and easy to use
with additional text and photographs covering a destination's top 10 essential sites, plus useful addresses, facts about the destination and handy tips on getting around.

Laminated finish
allows you to mark your route on the map using a non-permanent marker pen, and wipe it off. It makes the maps more durable and easier to fold than traditional maps.

The world's most popular destinations
are covered by the 125 titles in the series – and new destinations are being added all the time. They include Alaska, Amsterdam, Bangkok, Barbados, Beijing, Brussels, Dallas/Fort Worth, Florence, Hong Kong, Ireland, Madrid, New York, Orlando, Peru, Prague, Rio, Rome, San Francisco, Sydney, Thailand, Turkey, Venice, and Vienna.

INSIGHT GUIDES
The world's largest collection of visual travel guides

CONTENTS

Getting Acquainted

The Place

Situation: 41.53°N 12.30°E
Capital of Lazio (Latium) –
17,203 sq. km/6,634 sq. miles –
and of Italy (Italia) – 301,245 sq. km/
116,280 sq. miles.
Area: centre: 21 sq. km
(8 sq. miles)
Population: central Rome: 3 million.
(Italy: 57 million)
Language: Italian
Religion: Roman Catholic
Time zone: Central European Time
(GMT + 1 hour)
Currency: euro
Weights and measures: metric
Electricity: 220 volts AC, 50 cycles.
Sockets have either two or three
round pins
International dialling code: 39 for
Italy; Rome and the Vatican 06
Port: Civitavecchia
Number of churches: 450
Patriarchal basilicas: 5
National airline: Alitalia
National flag: three vertical stripes
of green, white and red
National anthem: *Fratelli d'Italia* (by
M. Novaro, words by G. Mameli, 1847)

Geography/Population

Ancient Rome was built on and
between the famous seven hills:
the Capitoline, Palatine, Viminale,
Esquiline, Celio, Aventine and
Quirinale, and these still occupy the
centre although they are now barely
discernible as distinct hills. The
modern city has a population of over
3 million people, who live in a space
of around 21 sq. km (8 sq. miles).
The city obtains much of its water
supply from the hills to the east, as
did ancient Rome.

The inner city (area inside the
Aurelian Wall) is divided into *rioni*.
The city of Rome is considerably
larger than the built-up part, for the
41 communities of the "Agro
Romano" are also included in the
definition, so that the whole city
area covers 150 sq. km (58 sq.
miles). The province of Rome, which
includes among others the Castelli
Romani, covers 5,352 sq. km
(2,066 sq. miles).

The Vatican state covers an area
of about 40 ha (100 acres) and only
around 400 people actually
live there.

Only a minority of the population
of Rome are of Roman descent. In
1870, when the city became capital
of Italy, it had a population of barely
200,000. Since then people have
come from all areas of Italy, mostly
from the southern provinces.

The majority of Romans are
Roman Catholic (Italy is 90 percent
Roman Catholic). Judaism has
traditionally been the second religion
in the city, and today there are also
a number of Muslims and non-
Catholic Christians resident there.

Government

Ever since it became the capital in
1870, Rome has been Italy's
political centre, seat of the Italian
government, as well as capital of
the Lazio region. In addition, as the
Papal seat, it is the centre of the
vast, international administrative
web of the Roman Catholic Church.

Government administration
employs the majority (almost two-
thirds) of Rome's working
population. The Church also
employs considerable numbers,
as does the tourist industry.

The Fascist party is outlawed.
Male descendants of King Victor
Emmanuel are excluded from public
office, cannot vote or be elected,
and are banned from Italian soil.
Titles of nobility are no longer
recognised except for those that
existed before 28 October 1922.

Italy is divided into regions
(regioni), provinces *(province)* and
municipalities *(comuni)*.

Climate

The city has a mild Mediterranean
climate, the coldest month being
January with an average mean
temperature of 8°C (46°F). In
August the temperature can
reach 40°C (104°F). The wettest
month is October. On average,
the sun shines more than 180
days a year.

Average temperatures:

	Jan	Feb	Mar	Apr
°C	8	9	11	14
°F	46	48	52	57
	May	Jun	Jul	Aug
°C	18	22	25	25
°F	64	72	77	77
	Sep	Oct	Nov	Dec
°C	21	17	12	9
°F	70	63	55	48

Economy

The city has a predominantly service
economy with around 600,000
office workers compared to an
industrial workforce of 100,000.

The civil service is the biggest
employer *(see above)*. Adding to
Rome's army of civil servants are
the multinational employees of the
Food and Agriculture Organisation
(FAO), a UN body based in the city.

The numbers employed in
industry indicate its relatively slight
importance to the Roman economy.
Nearly all sections of society contrive
not to pay money to the government,
as a result of which the underground
economy, the *economia sommersa*,
is very powerful.

Planning the Trip

Entry Regulations

VISAS & PASSPORTS

EU passport holders do not require a visa. A valid passport is sufficient. Visitors from the US, Canada, Australia or New Zealand do not require visas for stays of up to three months.

Nationals of most other countries do need a visa. This must be obtained in advance from the Italian Consulate. For addresses of embassies and consulates in Rome, *see page 249.*

EXTENSIONS OF STAY

EU citizens: There are no restrictions on length of stay for EU citizens and no particular legal obstacles preventing you from taking up employment or studying in Italy. **Non-EU citizens**: It is relatively difficult to get permission to stay long term in Rome, unless you are enrolling as a student in Italy or have been offered a job by an employer who will help you to get the necessary work and residence permits. These must be obtained from the Questura *(see below).* Your own embassy will be able to provide information on current rules and on any special conditions that may apply to you.

Questura, Ufficio Stranieri, Via Genova 2 (near Via Nazionale). Tel: 06-4686 2711. Open: 7am–noon. Arrive by 7am, bringing your passport or ID and several passport-style photos of yourself. Be prepared to wait: you will have to.

Studying in Italy

If you wish to study at an Italian university, you must obtain a declaration from the Italian Consulate in your own country stating that your qualifications are acceptable. This may require translation and validation with examination or school-leaving certificates. Check with the university you plan to attend and the relevant Italian Consulate.

Accommodation

If you plan to stay longer in Rome, start looking for accommodation immediately. There is a serious shortage in Rome, so unless you have a friend of a friend who has an apartment waiting for you, finding one will take a lot of time, patience and probably money. Rents are high, and on top of the first month's rent in advance, you will often be expected to pay a deposit equal to two or three months' rent. If you find a flat through an estate agent, there will generally be another fee to pay.

You may have an advantage in being a foreigner: many Italians prefer to let to non-Italians. The rent laws give considerable rights to sitting tenants so landlords often have difficulty in regaining access to rented property. Many believe that foreigners will prove easier to get rid of, so do not over-emphasise the length of your planned stay.

Getting a job

Unless you have fluent Italian, you will find it difficult to find work. EU nationals may register with the Italian national employment offices but this is unlikely to produce results. The main newspapers carry job ads, but you may have more success by deciding on a possible type of work and then lobbying potential employers intensively. Fields to try are the tourist and catering industries, together with the language schools.

What to Wear

For most of the year, Rome is warm to hot or very hot *(see Climate, page 242)* and summer clothes are

Customs Regulations

Used personal effects may be imported and exported without formality. Importing narcotics, weapons and pirated materials is forbidden. Alcoholic drinks, tobacco and perfume can be imported in limited quantities, depending on your nationality.

Duty-free shopping for EU citizens within Europe ended on 1 July 1999. Goods on which duty has already been paid in another EU country may be freely imported, provided the amount falls within what might be reasonably described as "for personal use", for example for a wedding or a family party.

However, the recommended allowances for each person over 18 years of age are still given. They are as follows:
● 10 litres spirits or strong liqueurs over 22 percent vol.
● 20 litres fortified wine
● 90 litres wine (of which no more than 60 litres may be sparkling)
● 110 litres beer
● 200 cigars
● 400 cigarillos
● 800 cigarettes
● 1 kilo tobacco

If you are any in doubt about what you are allowed to bring back, you can check with your local customs office. In the UK, contact HM Customs and Excise, Dorset House, Stamford Street, London SE1 9NG (tel: 020 7928 3344) or any other Excise enquiry office.

For US citizens, the duty-free allowance is: 200 cigarettes, 50 cigars or 3 lb tobacco; 1 US quart of alcoholic beverages and duty-free gifts worth up to $100.

suitable. Consider wearing a hat, particularly if you are sensitive to heat. Sunglasses are essential.

If visiting churches, and particularly St Peter's, remember that bare arms or shorts (on men or women) and short skirts are not acceptable, and you will be refused admittance if you wear them. If wearing a short-sleeved or sleeveless garment, carry a light shirt/blouse or scarf with you.

The Roman heat is sometimes alleviated by a sea breeze. This can produce cool evenings even in summer, so a cardigan or jacket is useful.

Romans, like most Italians, consider clothes important. Although Romans are slightly less obsessive in this than Florentines or Milanese, most will dress smartly for an evening out, a restaurant meal or a visit to the theatre. Although this is very rarely required and Rome is accustomed to casually dressed tourists, you may wish to follow local habits.

Dress codes for discos and bars vary enormously and change with both the seasons and fashions. In general, however, dress is still likely to be slightly more formal (and occasionally far more outrageous) than would be expected in much of Northern Europe or the USA.

In summer, the likelihood of rain is slight: sometimes there is no rainfall in Rome for more than three months. If it does rain during the summer, it will probably be a downpour in a thunderstorm. There is little point in preparing for this: just run for cover. At other times of the year, some form of waterproofing (umbrella, rain jacket, plastic mac) is worth bringing, but not worth a lot of weight in your luggage. The most likely times for rainfall are autumn and spring.

In winter, warmer clothes are needed, although not a really heavy overcoat. Winter days are frequently sunny and pleasantly warm. However, indoors, you may find the heating levels are below your normal expectations. In logical response to the climate, Roman building design

Public Holidays

Banks and most shops are closed on the following public holidays:
● **New Year's Day** *(Capodanno)*: 1 January
● **Epiphany** *(Befana)*: 6 January
● **Easter Monday** *(Lunedí di Pasqua)*: varies
● **Liberation Day** *(Anniversario della Liberazione)*: 25 April
● **May Day** *(Festa del Lavoro)*: 1 May
● **Patron Saints of Rome Day** *(Santissimi Pietro e Paolo)*: 29 June
● **August holiday** *(Ferragosto)*: 15 August
● **All Saints' Day** *(Ognissanti)*: 1 November
● **Immaculate Conception** *(Immacolata Concezione)*: 8 December
● **Christmas Day** *(Natale)*: 25 December
● **Boxing Day** *(Santo Stefano)*: 26 December

Banks may close early the day before a public holiday. If a holiday falls on a Tuesday or a Thursday, then many offices may also close on the preceding Monday or the following Friday. This is known as a *ponte*, bridging the gap. Many Romans take their main holiday during August and so a lot of restaurants and shops close during all or part of the month. The population drops by 40 percent, and the city is considerably quieter, and more pleasant, than usual.

has always concentrated on keeping heat out, rather than creating cosy warm interiors. Most Italians wear wool throughout the cold months.

Health

The largest single health hazard in Rome is probably the traffic, for which inoculation is not available. A few other potential hazards are worth guarding against. In summer, heat and sunshine may pose problems for those not used to Mediterranean climates. Although some Roman hotels and restaurants now have air conditioning, many more do not. This means you will need to open the windows, and inevitably risk introducing mosquitos. Although they are not as serious a menace as in Florence, bring mosquito repellent.

You will spend much time in Rome out of doors and on the move. Moving too much in the heat of the day in midsummer is likely to produce bad temper, sunburn and even heatstroke. Come prepared, with a hat, sunscreen and loose, cool clothing. Imitate the Romans and take a long lunch break in the shade, or consider a siesta.

Tap water in Rome is generally perfectly drinkable, especially from street fountains – the water comes from the same natural springs used by the ancient Romans. Exceptions are marked *acqua non potabile*. As elsewhere in Italy, restaurant patrons tend to drink bottled water with their meals.

See *Emergencies – Medical Services (pages 249–50)* for information on hospitals, doctors and pharmacies in Rome.

Currency

The unit of currency in Italy is the euro. There are 5, 10, 20, 50, 100, 200 and 500 euro notes, and 1, 2, 5, 10, 20 and 50 cent coins.

Travellers' cheques are the safest way to carry money, but not always the most economical since banks charge a commission for cashing them, and shops and restaurants usually give unfavourable exchange rates if they accept them at all. Major credit cards are accepted by most hotels, shops and restaurants in Rome but are less easy to use in the countryside. Very few petrol stations accept credit cards or travellers' cheques. Cash is often preferred, but should not be carried about in large quantities.

Automated cash dispensers, called Bancomat, can be found throughout central Rome, and are linked with several international banking systems, including Cirrus. The transaction fee will depend on your home bank, but the rates are generally the best.

Banks are open Mon–Fri 8.30am–1.30pm and 2.45–3.45pm. You will need your passport or identification card when changing money. Remember, changing money can be a slow operation in Italy, so allow plenty of time.

Not all banks will provide cash against a credit card, and some may refuse to cash travellers' cheques in certain currencies. Generally speaking, the larger banks (those with a national or international network) will handle tourist transactions best.

Most currency exchange bureaux are open on Saturday. **Thomas Cook** at Piazza Barberini, tel: 06-4202 0150, is also open on Sunday from 9.30am–5pm for currency exchange and credit card withdrawals.

Lost Credit Cards

If you lose your credit card, call the following freephone numbers:
● **American Express**, tel: 800-864 046, or for lost travellers' cheques, tel: 800-872 000.
● **Diner's Club**, tel: 800-864 064.
● **Mastercard/Carta Si**, tel: 800-868 086.
● **Visa**, tel: 800-877 232.

Getting There

BY AIR

There are direct scheduled flights to Rome from most major European cities, Australia and a number of cities in North America. From many European countries, there are also charter flights.

Scheduled flights land at the main airport, Aeroporto Leonardo da Vinci in Fiumicino, about 30 km (18 miles) southwest of Rome. **Fiumicino airport**, tel: 06-65 951.

Charters come into Ciampino airport, about 15 km (9 miles) to the southeast of the city.
Ciampino airport, tel: 06-794 941.

From Fiumicino, there are frequent train services to the city – every 30 minutes to Trastevere station and Rome's main train station, Termini. It's a short taxi ride to most hotels from Termini and a 15-minute tram ride or slightly longer taxi ride from Trastevere station. A taxi from Fiumicino to the centre will cost about €40–45.

From Ciampino, the best way to reach the centre is by taxi. Expect to pay about €35. Alternatively you can catch a COTRAL bus (leaving every half hour) to Anagnina metro station on Line A and then take the metro to Stazione Termini. Allow at least an hour for the journey.

For details of the main airlines with offices in Rome, see *Useful Addresses, page 246*.

BY RAIL

Rome is very well served by rail connections to the majority of major European cities, and the national railway, Ferrovie dello Stato, is generally efficient and relatively inexpensive.

There are several categories of train: reservations are required for the *Pendolino* or *Eurostar*, the fastest and most luxurious trains, and optional for the *InterCity* and *EuroCity* trains. You have to pay a supplement to use these lines, but it's worth it when you consider the time saved over a slower regional train that stops at many stations.

In any case, if you plan to travel by rail during your stay, it's always a good idea to book a seat. Do this at a travel agency *(agenzia di viaggio)* in the city if you can *(see page 246)*, rather than at the station where queues can be long and service is typically slow.

If you're planning a lot of rail travel, look into various rail pass offers at home and in Italy.

Maps

Free city maps that include the metro, tram and local train routes are available from the main tourist office and the tourist information booths dotted around town *(see page 248)*. Free and extremely comprehensive bus maps are available (when not out of print) from the ATAC information booth outside Stazione Termini in Piazza dei Cinquecento, or from the central ATAC office just around the corner at Via Volturno 59 (open Mon–Fri 9.30am–1.30pm, Tues & Thur also 2.30–5.30pm).

Otherwise *Roma Metro-Bus*, which details all public transportation routes and also contains a tourist map, can be bought from news stands. All news stands and bookstores sell city maps, which often include a street index. One of the best is *Roma A–Z*.

Important: train tickets are valid for two months after the date of issue and must be stamped on the day you travel at one of the machines at the stations. You will be fined if you don't get the ticket stamped.

Stazione Termini is the main railway terminal, the meeting point of the two metro lines and the main bus stop for many city buses. All shops and services in the station close at midnight (though some trains run later) and open again around 7am. There is a branch of the tourist office opposite platform 4, and a hotel reservation booth opposite platform 20, as well as full station services (waiting area, lost property, luggage deposit, fast food, bookstore, telephone office).

The official taxi stand is in front of the station. Do not be tempted by offers of "taxi" from unofficial cab drivers loitering in the station interior. **Train enquiries**, tel: 892 021, www.trenitalia.com.
Lost property, tel: 06-4730 6682, beside platform 1. Open daily 7am–midnight.
Station police, tel: 06-488 2588.

Left luggage, on the side of platform 24 but on level –1 (below ground level). €3.09 per piece for the first 5 hours and €0.51 for every hour after that. Open 7am–midnight.

BY COACH

If you are travelling by coach, you will almost certainly arrive at or near Stazione Termini.

BY ROAD

European (EU) driving licences are valid in Italy. Travellers from other countries will normally require an international driving licence. You should carry your licence, plus the vehicle registration and insurance (Green Card) documents with you when driving. If driving your own car, you may wish to take out extra insurance to cover, for example, home recovery in case of a breakdown.

Tolls are payable on most motorways, including the A1. Tolls can be paid in cash or with magnetic cards which can be bought at service stations.

Car travellers arriving in Rome from all directions will first hit the Gran Raccordo Anulare (GRA), the ring motorway. The GRA is busy and can be alarming to drive on, but is usually the quickest way to reach one of the entry roads into the centre. During rush hour, however, there are frequently traffic jams.

The A1 Autostrada del Sole leads into the GRA from both north and south, as does the A24 from the east. If you arrive on the Via del Mare from the coast (Ostia), you can either switch onto the GRA or simply continue straight on into the centre.

When leaving the GRA, follow the white signs for the road you want (blue ones usually lead away from the centre). Look also for the city centre sign: a black point in a black circle on a white background.

Disabled Travellers

Rome does not, in general, cater well for the disabled. With the notable exception of the Vatican museum, many public buildings have little or no disabled access. Most churches and museums have steps – even outdoor archaeological sites. In addition, streets and pavements are often uneven, and pavements in the medieval centre are frequently too narrow for a wheelchair. Some trains have disabled access, but check with the railways before planning your journey. Although seats at the front of city buses are reserved for the disabled, buses and trams may be hard to use.

If travelling by car, there are free parking spaces for disabled drivers displaying an official placard, and taxis are relatively cheap compared with northern European cities.

Restaurants are usually helpful if asked, but call in advance to ask about access. A number of Rome hotels now claim to offer access to disabled travellers. Check with the individual hotel – be as precise as possible about your needs and ask detailed questions.

Children

Rome is not an obvious place to choose for a children's holiday, but, on the other hand, Italian culture is very hospitable towards children. No one will eye you askance in a restaurant, and the staff may end up vying with each other to keep the children amused. Adults give children plenty of attention and their needs will be considered. Anyone struggling with a child and luggage can be fairly certain of help.

If you have children, it may be sensible to stay either near the city centre, so it is easy to get back to the hotel during the day, or outside Rome, so you have more green space around you. If your children can adapt to the idea, afternoon siestas may help them (and you) cope with the heat in the middle of the day.

Most children enjoy Italian food (at least, the pasta and pizza variety). Restaurants do not usually open until 8pm, so if the children need to eat earlier than that, look for a bar or *rosticceria* serving snacks and meals.

Clean toilets are often hard to find. If in doubt, head for the nearest hotel reception. If no hotel is in sight, try a bar or restaurant. Changing facilities are particularly hard to find.

Children are likely to enjoy visits to the Via Appia, the catacombs and the Museum of the Walls, the Colosseum and major Roman ruins in the Forum and Baths of Caracalla, St Peter's and its dome, and Castel Sant'Angelo. Puppet theatre is also worth looking out for *(see page 259 for details)*.

If children need relief from Rome's busy streets, there are a number of green spaces within easy reach of the centre (Villa Borghese and Villa Pamphili). There are also the lakes and beaches. The Villa d'Este at Tivoli makes an attractive place for an afternoon or day trip.

Some swimming pools are listed in the *Sport* section, *page 264*. The Rome tourist office *(see page 249)* can provide a list. Some hotels have swimming pools, but these tend to be outside the centre and more expensive. Cycling in the parks can also be enjoyed by all the family: see *Getting Around (page 251)* for information on bike hire.

Women Travelling Alone

Women are likely to receive considerable male attention in Rome, especially if alone. Most of this is amiable and unthreatening, but to minimise attention, dress well and mimic Italian women's behaviour: walk tall, look no-one in the eye and act as though you know exactly where you are going.

Most of the centre of Rome is reasonably safe even at night, though the areas round the Colosseum and Stazione Termini are rather seedy.

Practical Tips

Business Hours

Business hours vary greatly, but in general, shops are open Mon–Sat 9am–1pm and 3.30–7.30pm. Many shops, especially clothes shops, close on Monday morning. Recently, more and more shops, especially in the touristy areas, have started opening on Sunday and through lunch. Hairdressers and barber shops are open all day but closed on Monday. In general, food shops are open 8am–1.30pm and 5.30–8pm, and are closed Saturday afternoons in summer and Thursday afternoons the rest of the year. Many shops close for two weeks in August. Churches generally open from 7am–7pm with a three-hour break for lunch. See *page 245* for bank opening times.

Religious Services

For many, the highlight of a visit to Rome is attending Mass in St Peter's or even a Wednesday morning audience with the Pope. Mass is celebrated daily in St Peter's in several different languages. Confessions are heard in English and many other languages in all four main Roman basilicas: St Peter's, San Giovanni in Laterano, San Paolo fuori le Mura, and Santa Maria Maggiore.

To attend an audience with the Pope, you need to write in advance to the **Prefettura della Casa Pontifica**, 00120 Città del Vaticano, tel: 06-6988 3114. Specify the date you would like to attend and give a local phone number and address (your hotel) where tickets can be delivered. The general audiences are held either in St Peter's Square or in the Audience room or, in summer, at

Pilgrimages

As befits the headquarters of a world religion, the Vatican has offices that deal specifically with pilgrimages. Contact the **general information line** for pilgrimages to the Vatican, tel: 06-6988 1162.

For information on attending **Papal Audiences** and special services, such as Christmas Mass, see *Religious Services, below*.

Castel Gandolfo, the Pope's summer residence in the Castelli Romani. There is no charge for attending an audience.

If you are in Rome for Christmas and want to attend midnight Mass or the Christmas Day service, you will need to get a ticket at least a few days in advance. These can be obtained at St Peter's or via the Prefettura and, again, are free. Apply in the same way for many of the Easter services.

NON-ROMAN CATHOLIC SERVICES

English Catholic Chiesa di San Francesco in Capite, Piazza San Silvestro 1. Tel: 06-679 7775.
Anglican Church of England All Saints, Via del Babuino 153b. Tel: 06-3600 1881.
Mosque Centro di Cultura Islamica e Moschea, Via della Moschea (Parioli). Tel: 06-808 2167.
Protestant St Paul's within the Walls, Via Napoli 58. Tel: 06-488 3339.
Synagogue Lungotevere Cenci. Tel: 06-684 0061.

Media

NEWSPAPERS

Most main European dailies are available on the day of publication from the Rome street kiosks, as is the *International Herald Tribune*.

The main Rome-based Italian newspapers are *La Repubblica* and

Il Messaggero. Other Italian newspapers such as *Il Corriere della Sera* publish Rome editions containing more local news and entertainment listings.

By far the most convenient way to find out about what's on in Rome is *Roma C'è*, a comprehensive weekly guide to everything in the city, from museums to art exhibitions, shopping, eating, movies, etc. It comes out on Wednesday and can be bought from any news stand throughout the week. Listings are in Italian, but decipherable with a little effort, and there is an abbreviated section in English at the back.

RADIO & TELEVISION

Italian airwaves are packed with radio stations. Most play pop interspersed with occasional phone-ins and lots of advertising. The national radio stations (RAI) include news, current affairs and documentary programmes, and also, particularly on RAI 3, classical music.

Reception of the BBC World Service tends to be poor, but is possible on short wave: you may have to search for a frequency. The Vatican radio station (93.3FM) has some broadcasts, including news, in English, but the rest is in Italian.

There are three state television networks (RAI) and several private channels, but a great many hotels offer satellite TV.

Postal Services

Post offices are generally open Mon–Sat 8.30am–2pm.

Stamps *(francobolli)* for postcards and standard weight letters to most destinations can be bought at many tobacconists *(tabacchi)* and bars that sell tobacco products. Often you can buy stamps from the same place you buy your postcards.

You will only need a post office for more complicated transactions, such as sending a parcel, express letter or fax, collecting *Posta Restante*, or withdrawing money from a post-office account.

Italian postboxes are red, but several blue boxes specifically for foreign letters have been set up in the centre of town. The Italian postal system has improved considerably in recent years and now runs a pretty efficient priority post *(posta prioritaria)* which gets letters and cards to their destination in 3 days for Europe and 5 days elsewhere. If posting valuables or important documents, send them registered *(raccommandata)*. If sending an urgent parcel ask for CAI-*post* or *posta celere*, a courier-style service that is slightly slower than the private companies but far cheaper.

The Vatican runs its own postal service, at one time a far more reliable option than the Italian service. When visiting St Peter's, buy Vatican-issued stamps for your postcards and post them immediately: they are only valid in the Vatican City's blue postboxes.

Faxes can also be sent from and received at most hotels (but beware of price mark-ups) and from many copy shops all over the city. Italians have become very enamoured of the fax, and it is often the most efficient means of communication.

In addition to the following post offices, there are many others all over the city: ask at your hotel or in a local bar to find the nearest – *Dov'è l'ufficio postale più vicino?*

The **main post office** is in Piazza San Silvestro, just off Via del Corso; it is open longer hours than other branches – daily 8.30am–6.30pm. It offers all services, including fax and telegram sending facilities. For more information visit www.poste.it or call the post office helpline on 160, Mon–Sat 8am–8pm.

Private courier companies:
UPS, tel: 800-013 601.
DHL, tel: 800-345 345.
Federal Express, tel: 800-123 800.
These are all freephone numbers.

Telephone Services

Several companies provide public payphones in the city, but the most ubiquitous phones are the silver ones run by Telecom, which accept phone cards *(scheda telefonica)* only. You can buy the phone cards for €2.58, €5.16 and higher denominations from *tabacchi* shops and from many news stands. Some pay phones accept credit cards, and many bars have coin-operated pay phones, too.

Additionally there are a number of far cheaper international phonecards available from many news stands, and call-centres where you can make your call and pay later, particularly in the area around Stazione Termini.

Directory enquiries (dial 12) for numbers in Italy costs €0.52 from private and public pay phones (more from a cellphone). For international directory enquiries dial 176, which will cost you €0.52 as soon as they pick up and then the going rate for the time you are on the phone. Long-distance and international calling rates are lowest between 10pm and 8am, and on Sunday. Check the front of the phone book for exact rates.

To make a long-distance call, dial 00, the country code, the area code (omitting the initial 0, if applicable) and then the subscriber number.

The code for Roman numbers is 06 (do *not* drop the zero when calling from outside Italy). Cellular and toll-free numbers have different prefixes. Numbers in Rome have four to eight digits.

International Codes

Australia	61
Canada	1
France	33
Germany	49
Ireland	353
Italy	39
United Kingdom	44
United States	1

Tourist Information

The APT offices are well stocked with information on what's going on in Rome. They also have maps, an updated list of opening times for museums and historical sites, plus a sheet of useful information and telephone numbers. Although they cannot book accommodation for you, they do have a comprehensive list of hotels in Rome and environs.

Alternatively, the **Hotel Reservation Service**, operating from a booth in Stazione Termini opposite platform 10, open daily 7am–10pm, tel: 06-699 1000, makes commission-free reservations.

The **main Rome Tourist Office** (APT) is at Via Parigi 5 (Mon–Sat 8.15am–7pm, tel: 06-488 991). The APT also runs an English-speaking tourist information service which you can call daily 9am–7pm, tel: 06-3600 4399.

Other branches are as follows:
● Largo Goldoni (Via del Corso) Tel: 06-6813 6061.
● Piazza Pia (Castel Sant'Angelo) Tel: 06-6880 9707.
● Piazza del Tempio della Pace (Via dei Fori Imperiali) Tel: 06-6992 4307.
● Piazza delle Cinque Lune Tel: 06-6880 9240.
● Via Nazionale (Palazzo delle Esposizioni). Tel: 06-4782 4525.
● Piazza Sonnino (Trastevere) Tel: 06-5833 3457.
● Piazza San Giovanni in Laterano Tel: 06-6772 0353.
● Via dell'Olmata (Santa Maria Maggiore). Tel: 06-474 0995.
● Via Marco Minghetti (Fontana di Trevi). Tel: 06-678 2988.
There is also an information booth in Stazione Termini, which is open daily 8am–9pm, tel: 06-482 4078.

The Vatican tourist office: Centro Servizi, Pellegrini e Turisti, Braccio Carlo Magno, Piazza San Pietro (south side of St Peter's Square, to the left of the church). Tel: 06-6988 1662. Open Mon–Sat 8.30am–6.30pm.

Consulates

Consulates generally have answering machines on which you can leave a message in the event of a query or problem. If your passport is lost or stolen and you need a new one, you will need to obtain a police report, have proof of your identity and have suitable photos: check your country's requirements before setting out.

Consulate Addresses

Most consulates are open in the morning on weekdays, though some open in the afternoon, too. Call ahead to check exact times.
● **Australia:** Via Alessandria 215. Tel: 06-852 721.
● **Canada:** Via Zara 30. Tel: 06-445 981.
● **Ireland:** Piazza Campitelli 3. Tel: 06-697 9121.
● **New Zealand:** Via Zara 28. Tel: 06-441 7171.
● **South Africa:** Via Tanaro 14. Tel: 06-852 541.
● **UK:** Via XX Settembre 80A. Tel: 06-482 5441.
● **US:** Via Veneto 121. Tel: 06-46 741.

Emergencies

SECURITY & CRIME

The main problem for tourists in Rome is generally petty crime: pickpocketing and bag snatching, together with theft from empty cars. Reduce the possibility of theft by taking some elementary precautions. It is best to leave money and valuables, including airline tickets, in the hotel safe. Carry your camera out of sight and always be discreet with your money or wallet.

If you are carrying a handbag, keep it on the side away from the road, and when sitting in a café, place it firmly on your lap; one Roman speciality is the motorbike snatch.

Backpacks, while convenient, make easy targets for a pickpocket: take them off or sling them under your arm in crowds.

Always keep a separate record of credit card and cheque numbers just in case. A photocopy of your passport is also a useful precaution.

On the streets and particularly near the main tourist attractions, keep an eye on beggars, particularly the small children who crowd around you with boxes in their hands (under those boxes are some surprisingly nimble fingers). Take extra care on bus routes frequented by tourists.

The area near Stazione Termini, in particular the streets to the southeast, is well-known for drug peddling and prostitution.

Put a car with a foreign number-plate in a garage overnight. Take your radio out, even if your insurance company will replace it, because fixing a broken windscreen means wasted time and trouble. Don't leave any coats, bags or other items visible in the car, and make sure the glove compartment is closed.

If you are unlucky enough to have something stolen, report the theft to the police as soon as possible: you will need the police report for any insurance claim and to replace stolen documents. For information on the nearest police station call the central police station, the **Questura Centrale**, at Via San Vitale 15. Tel: 06-46 861.

MEDICAL SERVICES

EU residents are entitled to the same medical treatment as an Italian citizen. Visitors will need to obtain and complete an E111 form (available through post offices in the UK) before they go. This covers medical treatment and medicines, although it is still necessary to pay prescription charges and a percentage of the costs for medicines.

Note that the E111 does not give any cover for trip cancellations, nor does it provide repatriation in case of illness. If you wish to provide for this, you will need to take out private insurance. Canadian citizens are also covered by a reciprocal arrangement between the Italian and Canadian governments.

If you are covered by a reciprocal scheme and need to visit a doctor while in Italy, take the form E111 (if an EU resident) or proof of citizenship and residence (e.g. passport) to the local health office (*Unità Sanitaria Locale*) who will direct you to a doctor covered by the state system and supply the necessary paperwork. Not all doctors work in the state scheme,

- **Ambulance** Tel: 118.
- **ACI (breakdowns)** Tel: 803 116.
- **General Emergencies** Tel: 113.

Loss of Belongings
- **ATAC (city buses and trams)**, Via Nicolò Bettoni 8. Tel: 06-581 6040. Open Mon–Fri 8.30am–1pm, and also 2.30–5.30pm on Wed and Fri.
- **Railways**, Ufficio Oggetti Smarriti, Stazione Termini, platform 1. Tel. 06-4730 6682. Open daily 7am–midnight.

and those who do are often busy, so be prepared to wait. A consultation with a private doctor may be quicker (and certainly requires less preparatory paperwork) but costs more. Medical standards are generally high. Standards of nursing and infrastructure are sometimes less so.

If you need **emergency treatment**, call 113 for an ambulance or information on the nearest hospital with emergency services (pronto soccorso).

The International Medical Center (tel: 06-488 2371; nights and weekends: 06-488 4051) is a private referral service for English-speaking doctors. **The Rome American Hospital** (Via Emilio Longoni 69, tel: 22 551), 30–40 minutes out of the town centre in a taxi, has English-speaking doctors and dentists.

24-HOUR PHARMACIES

Farmacia della Stazione, Piazza Cinquecento 51, on the corner of Via Cavour. Tel: 06-488 0019.
Farmacia Piram Omeopatia, Via Nazionale 228. Tel: 06-488 0754.

Other pharmacies are open all night on a rotating basis. Check listings posted outside pharmacy doors for current schedules. Purchases after midnight carry a surcharge.

Getting Around

Orientation

It sometimes seems that all Roman roads lead to Piazza Venezia. This can produce traffic chaos, but from a visitor's point of view the square is a useful orientation point at the centre of ancient, medieval and modern Rome.

To the south of Piazza Venezia, the three roads, Via dei Fori Imperiali, Via di San Gregorio and Via delle Terme thread between the greatest monuments of ancient Rome to the Terme di Caracalla.

Northwards, Via del Corso runs through the commercial heart of modern Rome to Piazza del Popolo.

To the west, Corso Vittorio Emanuele II leads through the heart of Medieval Rome and across the Tiber (Tevere) both to St Peter's and the Vatican.

Eastwards are Via Nazionale, Piazza della Repubblica and Piazza del Cinquecento to Stazione Termini.

An easy way to get an overview of the city, and also pleasant in its own right, is to walk up the Gianicolo (Janiculum Hill) behind Trastevere. There are great views of the whole city from the dome of St Peter's via the Pantheon to the Colosseum.

For more information on roads into the city from Rome's ring motorway (Gran Raccordo Anulare), see page 246.

Public Transport

The city is served by two Metro lines (A and B), which intersect at Stazione Termini, a few trams and an extensive system of buses. Public transport is quite inexpensive, but often over-crowded.

Single-use tickets are available from bars, tobacconists and newspaper kiosks that display the ATAC (city bus company) emblem, and from vending machines in Metro stations and at bus terminals. Once validated in the Metro turnstile or stamping machine at the back of the bus, a ticket is good for bus or tram rides and/or one Metro ride within 75 minutes. Riders caught without a ticket will be fined on the spot.

One-day and seven-day passes, called Biglietto Integrato Giornaliero and Carta Integrata Settimanale, are good for unlimited Metro, bus and urban train travel and need to be validated only at the first use. Month-long passes, Abbonamento Mensile, are also available. COTRAL, the regional bus company, offers a regional day-pass (BIRG), which covers your round trip and in-city travel.

For information on connections to the airports, see page 245.

BUSES & TRAMS

Bus and tram services run from 5.30am to midnight, with all-night service on 22 lines, noted by the letter "N" after the number. Bus stops are clearly marked and most also list route numbers, the main

Taxis

Licensed taxis are white or yellow with an identification number and a meter inside. Avoid unlicensed taxis. Additional charges apply for service after 10pm, on Sunday and holidays, for each piece of luggage, and for going to and from the airport. In general, cabs cannot be hailed from the street – look for them at taxi stands in the centre of town, or call for one.
- **Radio taxi telephone numbers:** 06-3570, 06-6645 and 06-4994.

Passengers are not expected to give a taxi driver a percentage tip. Instead, it is customary to round up to the next euro, and perhaps give a bit more to show appreciation.

Metro

The Metro runs from 5.30am to 11.30pm. The COTRAL buses for the Castelli Romani leave from Anagnina Station (end of line A).

destinations along each route and lines with night service. A free map of city bus routes is available from the ATAC kiosk in Piazza dei Cinquecento (in front of Stazione Termini). Board buses at either door and stamp your ticket immediately. Ring the bell to request the next stop and exit through the centre doors.

USEFUL ROUTES

Bus route 64 from Stazione Termini to the Vatican via Piazza Venezia is the most used by tourists (and consequently the most notorious for pickpockets, so watch your wallet).

Three very useful electric minibuses serve the narrow streets of the *centro storico*: the 116 passes through or alongside Campo de' Fiori, Piazza Farnese, Piazza Navona, the Pantheon and Piazza Barberini; the 119 serves the area around Piazza del Popolo and Piazza di Spagna; and the 117 goes from Piazza del Popolo to Basilica San Giovanni in Laterano.

Bus 81 runs from the Colosseum to Piazza del Risorgimento near the entrance to the Vatican Museum.

If you are visiting the catacombs, take bus 118 from the Piramide metro stop to the Via Appia.

From Piazza di Spagna to Stazione Termini, take Metro line A. For the Colosseum, do the same and change at Termini to line B.

ATAC Bus 110 leaves every 30 minutes daily from Termini station and tours the city's principal monuments. Tickets can be bought at the terminus (if you want to get on and off along the way they are more expensive) and the service operates daily from 9am– 8pm in summer, and 10am–6pm in winter. A special night-time version

of the tour departs at 9pm in summer and 8pm in winter.

ATAC (city buses, trams, metro) and COTRAL (regional buses) information: Mon–Fri 8am–6pm, tel: 800-431 784, www.atac.roma.it

Private Transport

Generally, a car is of little use within the city. Parking is hard to find, one-way systems are complex and traffic jams appear permanent. However, if you are not deterred by such problems or if you wish to make extensive trips out of town, you might want to hire your own vehicle. Cars, bikes, motorbikes and mopeds are all available for hire.

BICYCLES & MOPEDS

Romans tend to cycle, if at all, on weekends away in Tuscany with their mountain bikes. However, if you wish to set a trend, you can hire a bicycle by the hour, the day or the week. Riding in one of the parks is a more pleasant alternative to the city streets.

Bicycle rental companies include: **Bici & Baci**, Via del Viminale 5. Tel: 06-482 8433 (mopeds also). **Collalti**, Via del Pellegrino 82. Tel: 06-6880 1084.

Rome by moped or Vespa is not for beginners or the nervous. You will need to show your licence and leave a deposit.

Motorcycle rental companies include: **Moto 3 C**, Via in Lucina 13. Tel: 06-687 6455. **St Peter Motor Rent**, Via di Porta Castello 43. Tel: 06-687 5714.

MOTORING TIPS

During the day most cars in the city centre obey the traffic lights. However, many of Rome's traffic lights are often switched to flashing amber: this indicates caution, although not all drivers seem to understand this.

There are very few car parks in the city and the historic centre is closed to cars without a permit. Much of the centre is one-way or closed to traffic, and the streets that are not are liable to traffic jams, so even if you have your own car with you, you may prefer to use public transport in the centre.

There is a large car park under the Villa Borghese (entrance at the top of Via Veneto). Several of the four- and five-star hotels in the centre have their own garage or protected parking: ask when booking. Few two- or three-star hotels can help with parking.

Given the lack of parking spaces, it is not surprising that a lot of cars are towed away in Rome – over 10,000 a year – so if your car is no longer where you left it, this, rather than theft, may be the reason. The Ufficio Rimozione of the traffic police *(Vigili Urbani)* will be able to tell you if this is the case. You must pay to get your car back (fines and fees for a towed car can go as high as €160). Contact: **Vigili Urbani**, Via della Consolazione 4. Tel: 06-67 691.

A lot of cars are clamped. If this happens to you, then a note on the windscreen will give you the number to call.

If you think that your car has been stolen, you can report it at the nearest police station.

Car Rental

Car rental tends to be expensive, as is petrol. Good deals are often available at the weekend. It is usually cheaper to arrange hire cars before you leave.

All the major car rental companies are represented in Rome. Most have counters at Stazione Termini and at Fiumicino airport.

General reservation numbers:
Avis Tel: 199-100 133
www.avis.com
Europcar Tel: 800-014 410
www.europcar.com
Hertz Tel: 199-112 211
www.hertz.com

The Italian Automobile Association (ACI) provides an emergency breakdown service. If you need repairs, look in the telephone Yellow Pages *(Pagine Gialle)* for the nearest car mechanic *(Autofficine)*. The ACI will also provide information on *Autofficine*.

ACI breakdown service,
tel: 803 116.
ACI information, Via C. Colombo, 261, tel: 06-514 971; Via Marsala, 18, tel: 06-495 9352.

ON FOOT

In much of the city centre you can best get around on foot. The majority of the main sights are within walking distance of each other, or you can use public transport for longer distances.

Some parts of the centre are theoretically pedestrian only; do not rely too heavily on this, however. Moped riders in particular, but also some car drivers, often decide that they are exempt.

Cross the road with confidence, staring down nearby drivers. If you wait timidly at a pedestrian crossing for the traffic to stop, you will spend the whole day there.

Where to Stay

Areas

Rome offers countless places to stay in every imaginable category. The following list gives a selection only, concentrating on hotels in the centre.

The area around Piazza Navona, the Pantheon and Campo de' Fiori perhaps offers the best introduction to the city, since here you are right in its medieval heart and within easy reach of almost all the main sights. However, there are relatively few hotels in the area, and these tend to book up early. This area is always lively, and in Rome that means that it is also noisy.

For those who prefer a quieter location, the Aventine Hill may be ideal, although a little further from the centre. The Via Veneto area has a number of large hotels at the higher end of the scale, and a good choice. It is a convenient location, although the area is no longer Rome's fashionable centre. Around Piazza di Spagna there is a more varied selection.

Large numbers of hotels can be found around Stazione Termini. This is not the most attractive area to be based, but it is well connected with the rest of the city by public transport. A lot of the cheaper hotels are to be found in this area, but there are also a number in the middle and luxury ranges. The area south of the station is rather unsalubrious and best avoided if at all possible.

Hotels slightly out of the centre sometimes offer more facilities such as swimming pools and parking. They are also likely to be quieter.

The Roman office of the APT *(see Tourist Information, page 248)*

publishes an annual list *(Annuario Alberghi)* showing star categories, facilities and prices of all Rome hotels. This may be obtained from the Rome EPT direct or through the Italian national tourist offices. Commission-free booking is available from the Hotel Reservation Service, *see page 249*.

While hotels in Rome are rated by stars, these ratings correspond to facilities and services offered, and not to the quality, which is often disappointing compared with what you would expect from similarly rated hotels in other major European cities.

Hotel Listings

Abruzzi
Piazza della Rotonda (Pantheon) 69
Tel: 06-679 2021
Set directly opposite the Pantheon, this hotel is not quiet except in some of the less attractive rooms at the back, but you can always join the lively crowds outside. Fairly basic – bedrooms aren't en-suite – but clean and pleasant. No breakfast. €€

Ambasciatori Palace
Via Vittorio Veneto 62
Tel: 06-47 493
Fax: 06-474 3601
Central and very comfortable. The hotel's decor recalls the period of its creation, the 1920s. €€€€

Campo de' Fiori
Via del Biscione 6
Tel: 06-6880 6865
Fax: 06-687 6003
This well-located hotel has small but comfortable rooms, and a roof terrace with wonderful views across Rome. It is excellent value for money; book well in advance. €€

Cavalieri Hilton
Via Cadlolo 101
Tel: 06-35 091
Fax: 06-3509 2241
Situated right on the Monte Mario to the north of the Vatican, this luxury hotel has several amenities that more central hotels lack, a swimming pool and tennis courts among them, as well as one of Rome's best restaurants (La Pergola). A minibus service runs to and from Piazza Barberini. €€€€

Price Guide

For a double room in high season:
€€€€ = over €250
€€€ = €160–250
€€ = €80–160
€ = under 80

Columbus
Via della Conciliazione 33
Tel: 06-686 5435
Fax: 06-686 4874
On the main street in front of St Peter's, this ex-monastery has retained some of its original features including frescoes and a garden, and continues to attract visiting cardinals. A large, comfortable hotel with its own parking. €€€€

Della Lunetta
Piazza del Paradiso 68
Tel: 06-686 1080
Fax: 06-689 2028
Comfortable, if slightly basic, economical and well-located hotel between Piazza Navona and Campo de' Fiori. No breakfast. €€

D'Inghilterra
Via Bocca di Leone 14
Tel: 06-699 811
Fax: 06-6992 2243
Very old-fashioned and traditional, with unfussy service and antique furniture. This is where Ernest Hemingway, Anatole France and Alec Guinness stayed. Good position just off the Corso. €€€€

Eden
Via Ludovisi 49
Tel: 06-478 121
Fax: 06-482 1584
Near the Villa Borghese. A discreet, cosy but ultra-refined hotel with excellent service and a roof garden restaurant. €€€€

Excelsior
Via Vittorio Veneto 125
Tel: 06-47 081
Fax: 06-482 6205
This hotel is located almost opposite the US embassy and is – perhaps predictably – especially popular with Americans. For almost 100 years, the hotel has been a meeting place of actors and famous people, and in the

1950s it became a part of the *Dolce Vita* scene. Still offers the ultimate in comfort and service. €€€€

Fontana
Piazza di Trevi 96
Tel: 06-678 6113
Fax: 06-679 0024
This hotel is located in a restored 13th-century monastery near the Fontana di Trevi. Beautiful roof terrace bar. €€€

Forum
Via Tor de' Conti 25
Tel: 06-679 2446
Fax: 06-678 6479
Just off the Via dei Fori Imperiali, this luxurious if slightly old-fashioned hotel is ideally located for the Fori, and has a wonderful view of them and the city from its roof garden restaurant. €€€€

Grand Hotel de la Minerve
Piazza della Minerva 69
Tel: 06-695 201
Fax: 06-679 4165
Built inside the fabric of a 17th-century palazzo, this hotel is close to the Pantheon. Its interior was designed by Paolo Portoghesi who made use of vast areas of Venetian glass to create spectacular public spaces. Rooms are large and there are splendid views from the roof terrace. €€€€

Gregoriana
Via Gregoriana 18
Tel: 06-679 4269
Fax: 06-678 4258
The Gregoriana's attraction lies in the Art Deco-style interior, with room numbers designed by the fashion designer Erté in the 1930s. Near the Spanish Steps. Only 19 rooms, no restaurant. €€€

Hassler Villa Medici
Piazza Trinità dei Monti 6
Tel: 06-699 340
Fax: 06-678 9991
Situated above the Spanish Steps and elegantly furnished. The hotel's famous restaurant with its roof gardens and view of the city is particularly beautiful. Although some consider its grandeur slightly faded, this is still one of Rome's most alluring luxury hotels, and the last one still family-run. €€€€

Jolly Vittorio Veneto
Corso Italia 1
Tel: 06-84 95
Fax: 06-884 1104
Modern hotel, with all amenities, including conference rooms. Air-conditioned and sound-proofed. Near the Villa Borghese. The chain is known for quality service. €€€€

La Residenza
Via Emilia 22
Tel: 06-488 0789
Fax: 06-485 721
A small hotel with only 27 rooms in a relatively quiet street near the Via Veneto. The rooms are a good size, and there is a pleasant roof garden. €€€

Lord Byron
Via G. De Notaris 5
Tel: 06-322 0404
Fax: 06-322 0405
Built into a former monastery, this first-class hotel has the feel of a private club. Only 47 rooms, elegant decor and an excellent restaurant (Le Jardin). It is a little out of the centre beyond the Villa Borghese. €€€€

Margutta
Via Laurina 34
Tel: 06-322 3674
Fax: 06-320 0395
Near Piazza del Popolo. The rooms, especially on the top floor, are pleasant although the outside appearance is slightly run-down. The price is reasonable for the area. €€

Nazionale
Piazza Montecitorio 131
Tel: 06-695 001
Fax: 06-678 6677
This hotel, near the House of Representatives and just off the Corso, is known for its famous past guests, such as Simone de Beauvoir and Sartre. These days, its 78 rooms more often hold politicians, who appreciate its comfort and service, as well as its location. €€€€

Parco dei Principi
Via G. Frescobaldi 5
Tel: 06-854 421
Fax: 06-884 5104
The advantage of this modern luxury hotel near the Villa Borghese is its pool, a much-appreciated rarity in central Rome. €€€€

Pomezia
Via dei Chiavari 32
Tel/fax: 06-686 1371
The rooms in this small hotel just off the Corso Vittorio Emanuele have been recently renovated, and are very comfortable. €€

Raphael
Largo Febo 2
Tel: 06-682 831
Fax: 06-687 8993
The ivy-covered exterior gives this hotel a distinctive look. It is popular with Italian politicians because of its nearness to Piazza Navona, the Senate and the House of Representatives, so much so that Bettino Craxi, a former Prime Minister, once had a private apartment here. Its antique furnishings, extensive art collection and the view from the upper floors make it unique in the Roman hotel scene. €€€€

St Regis Grand
Via Vittorio Emanuele Orlando 3
Tel: 06-47 091
Fax: 06-474 7307
Situated between the station and the quarter around the Via Veneto, this hotel provides 19th-century *belle époque* grandeur. Its restaurant is excellent and the hotel retains considerable individuality and style. €€€€

Sant'Anselmo
Piazza Sant'Anselmo 2
Tel: 06-578 3214
Fax: 06-578 3604
A lovely villa on the Aventine with a peaceful garden. The public rooms have inlaid marble floors and some bedrooms are fitted with antique furniture. €€–€€€

Scalinata di Spagna
Piazza Trinità dei Monti 17
Tel: 06-679 3006
Fax: 06-6994 0598

A small hotel located at the top of the Spanish Steps. Some of the rooms open directly onto a large terrace. Book early. €€€€

Smeraldo
Via dei Chiodaroli 11
Tel: 06-687 5929
Fax: 06-6880 5495
This good-value hotel in a narrow street between Largo Argentina and Campo de' Fiori has clean, comfortable if rather small rooms. The front lobby resembles a trendy ice-cream parlour, but some rooms on upper floors have charming views of Roman roofs. Be aware, however, that other rooms overlook a gloomy courtyard and receive little light. €€

Sole
Via del Biscione 76
Tel: 06-6880 6873
Fax: 06-689 3787
Set close to Campo de' Fiori, this hotel has well-furnished, quiet rooms and a charming inner garden. Book early. €€

Sole al Pantheon
Via del Pantheon 63
Tel: 06-678 0441
Fax: 06-6994 0689
This 500-year-old hotel has been renovated without damage to its charm. It's very conveniently located, just a stone's throw from the Pantheon. €€€€

Bed & Breakfasts

In anticipation of the Holy Year 2000, local authorities strongly encouraged the growth of bed and breakfasts in the city as an economical alternative to hotel lodging. Guests now typically pay from €40–80 or even €100 per night for a double room. Be warned, however, that the accommodation varies considerably in terms of quality, although the B&Bs are required by law to meet certain minimum standards of cleanliness and amenities. Many are nothing more than a private room in someone's home. The APT office on Via Parigi *(see page 249)* has a full listing of all registered bed and breakfasts.

Youth Hostels

Ostello del Foro Italico
Viale delle Olimpiadi 61
Tel: 06-323 6279
Fax: 06-324 2613
Reservations are advised, as this 350-bed hostel is the only true hostel in Rome. It is located some way out of the centre.

YWCA (for women only)
Via C. Balbo 4
Tel: 06-488 0460 or 488 3917
Fax: 06-487 1028
Offers two-, three- and four-bed rooms, located near Via Nazionale and the station. Curfew.

Camping

All the campgrounds are outside the centre of Rome, but can be reached by bus and/or train.

Castelfusano Country Club
Piazza di Castelfusano 1
Tel: 06-5618 5490

Flaminio
Via Flaminia Nuova Km 821
Tel: 06-333 2604
About 9 km (6 miles) from centre.

Nomentano
Via della Cesarina 11 (corner Via Nomentana.)
Tel: 06-4146 9175
About 12 km (8 miles) from Rome's centre.

Roma Camping
Via Aurelia 831 Km 8,200
Tel: 06-662 3018
About 9 km (6 miles) from the city centre.

Where to Eat

Although most hotels offer continental breakfast or buffets, Italians have no tradition of breakfast food. An espresso and a croissant *(un caffè e un cornetto)* takes most people through to midday. Lunch is usually served from 12–2.30pm, dinner from 8–10.30pm, and though menus are organised into *antipasti* (appetisers), *primi* (pastas and soups), *secondi* (meat and fish dishes), *contorni* (vegetables) and *dolci* (desserts), you should never feel obliged to select a dish from each category. Few Italians eat full sit-down meals more than once a day.

Service is included in the bill unless otherwise noted on the menu. It is customary to leave a modest amount of change as a tip, but nothing like the 10–15 percent common in other countries.

By order of the city government, the old cover charge, called *pane e coperto* (bread and table linen), has been abolished, but still appears on many menus. Keep an eye out. In many cases it has turned into a charge for bread. (If you wish, you may refuse the bread, and the fee as well; otherwise consider it a part of eating out.)

Restaurants

The following recommendations are by no means exhaustive – we merely cite some of the best. Some famous places are included because they are pilgrimage sites for tourists, and not to mention them would be an oversight.

The restaurants are classified as very expensive (€€€€), expensive

(€€€), moderate (€€) or inexpensive (€). *See table below for further details* and note that these price ranges are given as guides to charges only, as prices and quality are subject to change. Not all restaurants will accept bookings, but for some they are essential.

Most restaurants close one day a week and many join Rome's great exodus in the summer and close entirely for part or all of August. Call ahead before setting out. Check also on credit card acceptance: the signs in the window may be misleading.

Restaurants are listed according to area.

PIAZZA DEL POPOLO, SPANISH STEPS, VIA VENETO

Andrea
Via Sardegna 28
Tel: 06-482 1891
Rich ingredients and traditional menus. Many excellent pasta dishes. *Antipasti* deserve a special mention. Near Via Veneto. Reservations are recommended. Closed Sat lunch and Sun. €€–€€€

Colline Emiliane
Via degli Avignonesi 22
Tel: 06-481 7538
Friendly family-run *trattoria* offering specialities from the Emilia-Romagna region, famed throughout Italy for the richness of its cooking. The wines are the full-bodied reds of Emilia and the pasta is home-made. Near the Quirinale. Closed Fri. €€

Margutta-Vegetariano
Via Margutta 118
Tel: 06-3265 0577
Imaginative vegetarian cuisine. Open daily 10am–midnight. €€

Porto di Ripetta
Via di Ripetta 250
Tel: 06-361 2376
The proprietor (unusually for Rome, a woman) prepares original versions of dishes from the Marche region. Specialities include seafood dishes and *capretto* (kid). It is worth bearing in mind that the

lunch menu is considerably cheaper than the evening one. Between Via del Corso and the Tevere close to Ponte Cavour. Closed Sat lunch and Sun. €€

PIAZZA NAVONA, CAMPO DE' FIORI, GHETTO

Al Pompiere
Via Santa Maria de'Calderari 38
Tel: 06-686 8377
Refined Roman cooking in an old palazzo near Largo Argentina in the old ghetto. Reserve if possible. Closed Sun. €€

Cul de Sac
Piazza Pasquino 73
Tel: 06-6880 1094
Originally started as a wine bar, the Cul de Sac now serves a wide range of delicious cheese and fish dishes, wonderful soups and salads to go with almost a thousand different types of wine. Just off Piazza Navona. €–€€

Da Gino
Vicolo Rosini 4
Tel: 06-687 3434
Family *trattoria* serving traditional home cooking. Unfortunately, there is limited space. There's a restricted but excellent menu, which varies daily. Just around the corner from Palazzo di Montecitorio, the Parliament building, so you will be competing for a table with politicians. Closed Sun. No credit cards. €–€€

Fortunato al Pantheon
Via del Pantheon 55
Tel: 06-679 2788
Refined Roman cuisine, fresh fish. Favourite haunt of many of Rome's politicians. Closed Sun. €€€

Giggetto
Via del Portico d'Ottavia 21A
Tel: 06-686 1105
Well-known *trattoria* in the ghetto
offers good traditional Jewish and
Roman dishes: *carciofi* and *baccalà*
are specialities. In summer, try to
get a table outside. Near the Teatro
di Marcello. Closed Mon. €€

Il Drappo
Vicolo del Malpasso 9
Tel: 06-687 7365
Serves Sardinian specialities and
Sardinian wines in a charming
setting. Off Via Giulia, not far from
Piazza della Chiesa Nuova.
Reservations are recommended.
Closed Sun and at lunchtime.
€€–€€€

Osteria dell'Antiquario
Piazzetta San Simeone 26
Tel: 06-687 9694
Dishes put together in an interesting
way, for example lasagne with
aubergines and duck sauce.
Closed Sun. €€–€€€

Papà Giovanni
Via dei Sediari 4
Tel: 06-686 5308
Papà's bottles line the brick walls,
and his son is in charge. The accent
is on the use of seasonal foods,
especially vegetables from Rome's
markets: try the artichoke in April
and May. Desserts are delicious.
Between Piazza Navona and the
Pantheon. Reservations essential.
Closed Sun. €€–€€€

TRASTEVERE

Alberto Ciarla
Piazza S. Cosimato 40
Tel: 06-581 8668
Justly famous for its fish dishes
(and fish tank), this is one of the
most prestigious restaurants in
Rome, located in the heart of
Trastevere. The cuisine ranges from
simple traditional dishes through
Japanese recipes to totally new
creations, all excellent.
Reservations recommended. Closed
Sun and lunchtimes. €€€

La Tana de Noantri
Via della Paglia 1–3
Tel: 06-580 6404

Popular venue that has kept up a
very high standard of solid Roman
cuisine using only the very freshest
vegetables, fish, meat and other
ingredients. Their specialty is
Tagliolini alla Tana (thin egg
tagliatelle made with tomatoes,
mushrooms and fresh oregano).
Closed Tues. €€

STAZIONE TERMINI, VIA NAZIONALE, COLOSSEO

Taverna dei 40
Via Claudia 24
Tel: 06-700 5533
Genuine old-fashioned Roman
osteria. The taverna has a friendly
atmosphere and good traditional
cooking. Southeast of the
Colosseum on the corner of Via
Annia. Closed Sun. €€

TESTACCIO

Checchino dal 1887
Via Monte Testaccio 30
Tel: 06-574 3816
Typical and excellently prepared
Roman cuisine: *rigatoni con pajata*,
coda alla vaccinara and other
traditional offal-based dishes. This
was once a cheap *trattoria* which
used ingredients from the local
Testaccio slaughterhouse. It has
become a legend. Reservations are
recommended. Closed Sun and
Mon. €€€–€€€€

Ketumbar
Via Galvani 24
Tel: 06-5730 5338
'Ketumbar' (Malay for coriander) is
one of those very un-Roman places
that has nevertheless become a

Price Guide

The approximate prices you can
expect to pay for an average
three-course meal including wine
and service charge are:
€€€€ = over €65
€€€ = €40–65
€€ = €20–40
€ = under €20

huge hit with the local populace.
Indonesian in inspiration, the fusion
menu lives up to expectations.
Offerings such as *sushi* and *nasi
goreng* (rice, egg and greens
prepared in a wok), or lightly braised
tuna fillets with fried parmesan
wafers, fit the bill perfectly. In one
room pot shards (pieces of broken
Roman amphorae that make up the
Monte Testaccio hill) are
atmospherically lit behind a glass
wall. Closed Sun and at lunch. €€

OUTSIDE THE CENTRE

**Relais Le Jardin dell' Hotel
Lord Byron**
Via Giuseppe de Notaris 5
Tel: 06-322 0404
In the delightful surroundings of a
former monastery, this refined
restaurant serves up Italian *nuova
cucina* at its imaginative best. Many
seafood specialities are included on
the menu, as well as a full range of
meat dishes and vegetables. You
will pay highly for the experience, but
are not likely to forget it. Beyond the
Villa Borghese in the Parioli district.
Reservations essential. Closed Sun.
€€€€

Pizzerias

Italians often eat pizza in the
evenings, usually accompanied with
beer, as a light and sociable meal.
The price is low: usually well under
€11 including the beer and a salad
or dessert.

Da Baffetto
Via del Governo Vecchio 114
Tel: 06-686 1617
Probably the best-known pizzeria in
Rome and a favourite with many
Romans. Fast food and long queues.
Near Piazza Navona. Closed
lunchtime. No credit cards. €

Formula 1
Via degli Equi 13
Tel: 06-445 3866
The student quarter of San Lorenzo
is famous for its cheap and
cheerful *pizzerie*. And the very
casual Formula 1 serves up some
of the best in Rome, using real

mozzarella (not the pizzeria kind so common these days). The fried *baccalà* (salted cod) is excellent, too. Closed Sun and at lunch. No credit cards. €

Ivo in Trastevere
Via S. Francesco a Ripa 158
Tel: 06-581 7082
Loud, crowded and smoky, but the pizzas are good and the prices are low. Closed lunchtime and Tues. €

Bars, Cafés, Tea Rooms & Ice-Cream Parlours

Rome seems to have a bar on every corner, all of which serve coffee, drinks and snacks, including *supplì*. *Supplì* are made of rice, egg and tomatoes deep fried in batter and are eaten luke-warm.

You will pay more in a bar or café if you choose to sit down than if you remain standing at the bar. Drinking or eating ice-cream on the terrace usually warrants a further premium.

The following list singles out cafés with a difference and includes some of the best known ice-cream parlours *(gelaterie)*.

Antico Caffè Greco
Via Condotti 86
Tel: 06-679 1700
Elegantly faded; on the walls hang portraits of famous visitors of the past. Since the Caffè opened in the 18th century, it has had a lot of famous visitors: Keats, Goethe, Gogol among them. Rumour has it that redecoration is scheduled once every 100 years, but price rises clearly take place much more often. Very popular with tourists.

Babington's Tea Rooms
Piazza di Spagna 23
Tel: 06-678 6027
Hopelessly famous and always full, Babington's serves possibly the best and almost certainly the most expensive tea in Rome. Set at the foot of the Spanish Steps, the Tea Rooms have received illustrious tourists ever since they were founded by an Englishwoman in 1893. Fills up with English and Japanese tourists. Closed Tues; and Sun in summer.

Drinking Roman Style

Roman drinking habits tend towards moderation. Despite the occasional breakfast *grappa*, drinking as an occupation is not the done thing here. Wine is habitually drunk with meals, and *digestivi* often follow. But in an evening spent in a bar, many people will have just one drink, often non-alcoholic.

Canova
Piazza del Popolo 16
Tel: 06-361 2231
One of the two well-known cafés on Piazza del Popolo: Canova vies for pride of place with Rosati. Both claim to be the intellectuals' favourite.

Doney
Via Veneto 145
Tel: 06-4708 2805
Former meeting place of literati. A famous name from the 1950s *Dolce Vita* scene. Still elegant.

Giolitti
Via degli Uffici del Vicario 40
Tel: 06-699 1243
Excellent ice-creams, conveniently located for politicians from Montecitorio. Worth a detour from the Corso.

Ombre Rosse
Piazza Sant'Egidio 12
Tel: 06-588 4155
A pleasant and relaxed spot on one of Trastevere's most atmospheric and car-less piazzas. Inside, the choice of music, in keeping with the atmosphere, is chilled out and breezy. There's also an excellent choice of sandwiches, light meals and American sweets.

Rosati
Piazza del Popolo 4
Tel: 06-322 5859
Known as an intellectuals' meeting place. Rivalry with Canova (above) continues.

San Crispino
Via della Panetteria 42
Tel: 06-679 3924
Close to Trevi fountain you will find the best *gelato* in Rome. Additive- and colouring-free, it is made using seasonal ingredients only and

served in paper cups (cones would contaminate its purity). The cinnamon-and-ginger flavour is out of this world. Very little seating. Closed Tues.

Sant'Eustachio
Piazza Sant'Eustachio 82
Tel: 06-6880 2048
This is probably the most famous coffee shop in Rome. The coffee is well worth the price and the wait (at night it gets very crowded), but comes heavily sugared unless you ask for it *senza zucchero* (without sugar). Closed Sun am.

Tazza d'Oro
Via degli Orfani 84
Tel: 06-678 9792
Nowhere to sit but some of the best coffee in Rome. Closed Sun.

Tre Scalini
Piazza Navona 28
Tel: 06-6880 1996
Possibly Rome's most famous *gelateria*. The *tartufo* deserves its reputation, but is better eaten from a cone whilst strolling around the piazza than at one of the cramped tables. Closed Wed.

Culture

Entertainment Listings

For the most comprehensive listings of what's on in Rome, pick up *Roma C'è*, the weekly booklet that comes out on Wednesday and is available from news stands. Listings are in Italian with an abbreviated section in English. The tourist information office and booths *(see page 249)* provide a multitude of leaflets and programmes (and even a monthly magazine called *WHERE*) with all the latest information on cultural events.

Opera & Ballet

The opera and ballet season runs from October to June at the **Teatro dell'Opera**, Piazza Beniamino Gigli 1. Tel: 06-4816 0255, freephone: 800-016 665, www.opera.roma.it. The ticket office is open Tues–Sat 9am–5pm and Sun 9am–1.30pm. Ticket prices run from reasonable to exorbitant. The outdoor summer opera series (same numbers as above) has been held in a number of different venues in past years, including the Baths of Caracalla.

Classical Music

It's wonderful to hear classical music in Rome, not only for the wide range of concerts, but also because of the great variety of venues. The concert season runs from October through to June, but with special summer concerts, there's something going on just about all year round; chances are good that there are several concerts on any given night of the year.

The **Accademia di Santa Cecilia**, Via della Conciliazione, tel: 06-6880 1044, is Rome's most high-profile and important classical music academy, replete with its own orchestra. In December 2002, the academy is scheduled to move from its exclusive home on Via della Conciliazione to Rome's brand new, state-of-the-art music venue, which features three concert halls and was designed by Genoese architect Renzo Piano. A 10-minute tram-ride from Piazzale Flaminio (just above Piazza del Popolo), the complex, or *Parco della Musica* (Music Park), as it has been christened, features a large inner courtyard with perfect acoustics, which will be used for outdoor concerts and events.

For more information on the Accademia visit www.santacecilia.it. Ask at the APT or read the local press for more information on classical music events in Rome.

Summer concert venues

Open-air summer concerts of music ranging from classical through jazz to rock and world music are staged all over Rome in the summer, many of them part of the *Estate Romana* series of events *(see page 259)*. Some of the most atmospheric venues are Villa Ada, the Terme di Caracalla and the Terrazza del Pincio. Apart from *Roma C'è*, a good source of information is the *Repubblica* newspaper's Thursday supplement, *Trovaroma*.

The following agencies can be contacted for information and reservations for music events:
Hello Ticket, tel: 06-808 8352, freephone: 800-907 080.
Orbis, Piazza dell'Esquilino 37. Tel: 06-474 4776.
Ricordi Mediastore, Via Giulio Cesare 88. Tel: 06-3750 0375.

Music Venues

Alexanderplatz, Via Ostia 9 (Vatican). Tel: 06-3974 2171. When the big names come to town, they often come to Rome's most noteworthy jazz club and sushi bar, which runs the summer jazz series at the Villa Celimontana. Closed Sun.

Big Mama, Via San Francesco a Ripa 18 (Trastevere). Tel: 06-581 2551. Mainly a blues venue.
Fonclea, Via Crescenzio 82A, (Vatican). Tel: 06-689 6302. Mostly jazz at this restaurant/pub. The only non-smoking performance space in Rome.
La Palma, Via Giuseppe Mirri 35 (near the Tiburtina metro stop). Tel: 06-4359 9029. A place that is deservedly on Rome's cool radar and features live bands playing new jazz and ethnic music followed by a DJ set. The managers here are also involved in the excellent Villa Celimontana summer jazz festival.
Villaggio Globale, Ex-Mattatoio, Lungotevere Testaccio. Tel: 06-5730 0329. A live-music and cultural venue that is very attentive to Rome's immigrant community and does a nice line in alternative and world music offerings.

Latin Venues

There is a burgeoning Latin music and World Music scene, encouraged by the influx of immigrants to Rome. Most places don't start to get going until after 10pm.
Caffè Caruso, Via di Monte Testaccio 36 (Testaccio). Tel: 06-574 5019. Latin American music and salsa. Mostly live, with DJ on Sun. Closed Mon.
No Stress Brasil, Via degli Stradivari 35 (Trastevere). Tel: 06-5833 5015. Restaurant and nightclub, this lively place lives up to its name. Live music every night (except Sunday), with Brazilian bands and dancers, followed by more of the same music spun by DJs.

Theatre

Since plays are nearly always performed in Italian, an evening at the theatre is only recommended for fluent Italian speakers. However, in some cases it is worth attending a classical drama or play in translation, if the venue itself provides the drama. This is particularly the case for summer events held outdoors, whether in amphitheatres, such as the one at Ostia Antica, or at other classical sites *(see Summer Spectacle, below)*.

Puppet theatre and raucous Roman cabaret can also offer an entertaining evening, even if you're unable to understand much Italian.

Roman theatre embraces mainstream and contemporary theatre but the emphasis is on the tried and trusted Italian dramatists, such as Carlo Goldoni and Luigi Pirandello. However, the university theatres and smaller venues do stage experimental or fringe productions (known as "Teatro off"). The theatre season runs from October to early June, but there are numerous summer events linked to specific Roman festivals *(see Estate Romana, right)*.

Mainstream theatre venues
Teatro Argentina, Largo Argentina 56. Tel: 06-6880 4601.
Teatro Eliseo, Via Nazionale 183E. Tel: 06-488 2114.
Teatro Piccolo Eliseo, Via Nazionale 183. Tel: 06-488 5095.
Teatro Sistina, Via Sistina 129. Tel: 06-420 0711.

Contemporary or experimental theatre
Teatro Ateneo, Piazzale Aldo Moro 5. Tel: 06-445 6784. Rome University theatre.
Teatro Colosseo, Via Capo d'Africa 7. Tel: 06-700 4932. Experimental or fringe theatre.

Summer Spectacle

Anfiteatro Quercia del Tasso, Passeggiata del Gianicolo (Janiculum Hill), Viale Aldo Fabrizi. Tel: 06-575 0827. Summer open-air performances of theatre and dance in the amphitheatre.
Teatro Romano di Ostia Antica, Viale dei Romagnoli 717, Ostia Antica. Tel: 06-5635 8099. Outdoor theatrical performances in the Roman theatre, 25 km (16 miles) southwest of Rome.

Teatro Tor di Nona, Via degli Acquasparta 16. Tel: 06-6880 5890. Rome University theatre.

Puppet theatre & cabaret
Ciceruacchio, Via del Porto 1. Tel: 06-588 2429. Traditional Roman cabaret restaurant in Trastevere.
Teatro Mongiovino degli Accettella, Via G. Genocchi 15. Tel: 06-513 9405. Traditional puppet theatre in Italian.
Teatro Verde, Circonvallazione Gianicolense 10. Tel: 06-588 2034. Well-loved theatre offering puppet shows and plays for children in Italian. Closed May–Oct.

Cinema
Virtually all films on general release are dubbed into Italian, often to interesting effect. Italian dubbers are renowned for their skill but it is still quite amusing to hear American movie stars dubbed into inappropriately elegant or rather ponderous Italian. Again, it is best to check the daily newspapers for what's on, and *Roma C'è*, which has the best listings, including the number of seats in each cinema.

For English-speaking cinema, try the following:
Alcazar, Via Cardinale Merry del Val 14. Tel: 06-588 0099. Current film playing is shown in its original version on Monday.
Metropolitan, Via del Corso 7. Tel: 06-3260 0500. Air-conditioned multi-screen cinema with one screen devoted to original-version films.
Nuovo Olimpia, Via in Lucina 16G. Tel: 06-686 1068. Occasional original-language films.
Il Nuovo Pasquino, Piazza Sant'Egidio 10. Tel: 06-580 3622. Rome's biggest all original-language cinema, with three screens.
Quirinetta, Via Marco Minghetti 4. Tel: 06-679 0012. One-screen cinema showing only original-version films.
Warner Village Moderno, Piazza della Repubblica 45–46. Tel: 06-477 791. Frequent original-version films on one of its screens.

Estate Romana
From June to September the *Estate Romana* (Roman Summer) offers everything from rock, world music and jazz concerts, through theatre and outdoor cinema to dance lessons and other cultural events. Every night various Roman *piazze* and venues all over town host something to suit all tastes, and some of the locations are truly spectacular. For more information see local press (particularly *Roma C'è*), visit the APT information booths or log on to www.estateromana.it.

The Gay Scene
Rome has an active and vibrant gay community. The national magazine, *Babilonia*, is published monthly and is available from most news stands. For more information, contact:
Circolo di Cultura Mario Mieli, Via Ostiense 202. Tel: 06-541 3985. Advice and details on gay events in the capital.
Arci-Lesbica Roma, Via dei Monti di Pietralata 16. Tel: 06-418 0211. A lesbian group that runs a helpline and organises social get-togethers.
Babele, Via dei Banchi Vecchi 116. Tel: 06-687 6628. Gay bookshop. A good source of information. Closed Sun and Mon am.

Nightlife
Alibi, Via di Monte Testaccio 44. Tel: 06-574 3448. Predominantly gay disco.
Hangar, Via in Selci 69A (near Via Cavour). Tel: 06-488 1397. Well-established gay club. Closed Tues.
Max's Bar, Via Achille Grandi 7A (near Porta Maggiore). Tel: 06-7030 1599. Closed Wed.
Side, Via Labicana 50 (near the Colosseum). A recent addition to the Roman gay scene that has become so popular it is often as crowded on the pavement outside as inside. Part of a burgeoning gay area – a nearby street (Via Pietro Verri) is now home to a gay bar, disco, bookshop and restaurant.

Nightlife

Roman nightlife tends to be fun rather than frenzied, sleepy rather than sophisticated. Apart from a few privileged or exclusive clubs, the nightclub scene is far less elegant than in Paris, less assured than in Munich, and far less adventurous than in Berlin, London or New York.

As a general rule, nightclubs attract a wealthy middle-class clientele whereas clubs and discos are predominantly for the young.

Yet within this distinction there is considerable variety. Romans, like all Italians, are fashion-conscious though culturally fairly conservative. As a result, places fall in and out of fashion for little apparent reason. However, once out, the club is forever abandoned. In common with nightlife in other capital cities, door policy determines whether you even get to cross the threshold of a club. If your look is not right (whether designer bejewelled, designer casual or preppy), you will either not get in or not fit in. As a general rule, however, in Rome it is safer to dress up rather than dress down, even if a rejection by the doorman makes your efforts all the more humiliating.

You may be required to obtain temporary membership (a *tessera*, or membership card, should be available at the door). The entry price may include a free drink but nightclub drinks are normally quite expensive. Groups of young men together are usually not welcome and, in some clubs, a male may be turned away unless accompanied by a female companion.

Geographically, it is difficult to label areas as nightlife quarters. The big exception to this is Trastevere, which has long been the destination for Romans in search of a good time. However, Testaccio is fast taking its place as a slightly more "alternative" location. The historic quarters around Piazza Navona, the Pantheon and the Spanish Steps also contain a number of popular bars and clubs.

The Via Veneto, the scene of Fellini's mythical *Dolce Vita*, is now somewhat clinical and staid. However, the quarter is still home to certain elegant nightclubs and piano bars, which tend to be more popular with American visitors than with Romans.

In summer, much young Roman nightlife moves to the beach resorts south of the city. However, the glut of summer city festivals ensures that Rome remains lively.

The best and most typical forms of Roman nightlife tend to be centred on a leisurely meal, a musical event or a summer festival (so consult the relevant sections of *Travel Tips*). That said, Roman nightlife can be so low-key that residents are happy to wander through the beautiful historic centre, pausing to chat, greet friends, glance in shop windows, eat the occasional ice-cream, nonchalantly stop for a drink, *digestivo* or a restorative *tisane* (herbal or fruit tea). That might be the sum total of their activities for one evening.

Wine Bars

Many wine shops (*enoteche*) are also wine bars, or have them adjacent. There are always a few bottles open and served by the glass. Or you can choose wine by the bottle from an extensive list.
Antica Enoteca, Via della Croce 76B. Tel: 06-679 7544. Beautifully restored wine bar just off Piazza di Spagna. Open daily 11.30am–1am.
Bevitoria Navona, Piazza Navona 72. Tel: 06-6880 1022. A wide selection of wines by the glass, which can be enjoyed outside on one of Rome's most beautiful piazzas. Open 4pm–midnight; closed Sun.
La Bottega del Vino da Bleve, Via di Santa Maria del Pianto 9–11. Tel: 06-686 5970. Wine bar open for lunch only Mon–Sat, *enoteca* open Mon–Sat.

Enoteca 313, Via Cavour 313. Tel: 06-678 5496. Casual wine bar at the bottom of the Via Cavour, across from the entrance to the Roman Forum. Good selection of salads, cured meats and wines.
Il Simposio di Piero Costantini, Piazza Cavour 16 (behind Castel Sant'Angelo). Tel: 06-321 3210. A gorgeous Art Nouveau wine bar with especially fine food (over 85 kinds of cheese). Open for lunch and dinner until 1am. Closed Saturday lunch in August, and all day Sunday. The huge *enoteca* in the basement is closed all day Sunday and Monday morning.
Trimani Wine Bar, Via Cernaia 37B (near Stazione Termini). Tel: 06-446 9630. Open for lunch and dinner until midnight, with ample offerings from the kitchen to go with your wine. Their wine shop around the corner is one of Rome's finest. Closed Sun and August.

Nightspots

The following bars possess an indefinable Roman ambience.
Bar della Pace, Via della Pace 3–7. Tel: 06-686 1216. Situated close to Piazza Navona, this Roman institution is redolent of Victorian times. It was traditionally a haunt of writers and artists in search of inspiration. Today it is better known for its superb desserts and, in the evening, for its clientele of posing Romans. Open 9am–2am.
Bar del Fico, Piazza del Fico 26. Tel: 06-686 5205. Lots of outdoor seating at this nightspot popular with locals. Open 8am–2am.
Ciampini al Café du Jardin, Viale Trinità dei Monti. Tel: 06-678 5678. The ideal place to watch the sun go down over the city while sipping an *aperitivo*. Very close to the Spanish Steps and Villa Borghese. A great place to pass a quiet night. Open June–Sept, 8am–1am; closed Wed.
Jonathan's Angels, Via della Fossa 16. Tel: 06-689 3426. Quirky decoration and a loyal crowd of regulars. The toilets alone are worth the visit. Good cocktails. Open Mon–Sat 2pm–2am, Sun 5pm–2am.

Pubs

Pubs have really taken off in the last few years in Italy, and in Rome you can choose from several dozen, all serving the major brands in English/Irish-style wood-panelled premises.
Abbey Theatre, Via del Governo Vecchio 51. Tel: 06-686 1341.
Birreria Marconi, Via di S. Prassede 9C. Tel: 06-486 636.
The Druid's Den, Via di S. Martino ai Monti 28. Tel: 06-4890 4781.
The Drunken Ship, Campo de' Fiori 20–21. Tel: 06-6830 0535. Popular with foreign students.
The Fiddler's Elbow, Via dell' Olmata 43. Tel: 06-487 2110. Good Irish pub.
Finnegan's, Via Leonina 66. Tel: 06-474 7026.
Trinity College, Via del Collegio Romano 6. Tel: 06-678 6472. A classic on the Roman pub scene.
Victoria House, Via di Gesù e Maria 18. Tel: 06-320 1698.

Clubs

There are dozens of places to dance the night away in Rome, though most don't get going until midnight. Several of the better clubs are found around Via di Monte Testaccio. In summer, most clubs relocate to the seaside, but the gap is filled with night-time activities that are part of the Estate Romana (see page 259).
Akab, Via di Monte Testaccio 68–9. Tel: 06-575 7494.
Alibi (for details, see The Gay Scene, page 259).
Alpheus, Via del Commercio 36. Tel: 06-574 7826.
Ex-Magazzini, Via Magazzini Generali 8 bis. Tel: 06-575 8040.
Radio Londra, Via di Monte Testaccio 65b. Tel: 06-575 0044.
Villaggio Globale, Ex-Mattatoio, Lungotevere Testaccio. Tel: 06-5730 0329.

Festivals

Many of the festivals and special events celebrated in Rome through the year are linked to the Catholic church. There are also commercial fairs and cultural activities.

Many towns in the Castelli Romani celebrate religious festivals and harvest festivals (sagre) during the year. Roma C'è has the most complete listings (in Italian), though the tourist office usually has some information on what's happening.

Diary of Events

JANUARY

Christmas fair in Piazza Navona, culminating in the celebration of **Epiphany (befana)** on 6 January, the traditional witch festival in which good children receive presents and naughty children are given sweets shaped like coal.
La Festa di Sant'Antonio Abate. Blessings for animals in Rome in the church of Sant'Eusebio all'Esquillino on 17 January.

FEBRUARY–MARCH

Carnevale is not celebrated in Rome as in other cities, but the towns in Castelli Romani (see pages 229–35) host street processions and other celebrations.
La Festa di San Giuseppe. St Joseph's day is celebrated on 19 March, especially near the church of the same name (north of the Vatican).
Easter week is really the festive time of the year, from the big Mass on Palm Sunday and the distribution of palm fronds, the mass pilgrimages for **Holy Week (Settimana Santa)** and concerts all over the city. The Pope also leads an outdoor Mass at the Colosseum on **Good Friday**, followed by a procession passing the stations of the cross. The week culminates on **Easter morning** with the Pope's Urbi et Orbi speech to the world.
La Festa della Primavera. The arrival of spring is marked by the decoration of the Spanish Steps with a sea of azaleas.
Settimana dei Beni Culturali. Museum Week in all of Italy (usually held in late March or early April), during which entrance is free to all state-run museums and historical sites.

APRIL

Il Natale di Roma. On 21 April Rome celebrates the anniversary of its legendary founding with fireworks and songs.
La Festa della Liberazione. A public holiday on 25 April to commemorate the liberation of Italy by allied forces at the end of World War II.

MAY

May Day is widely celebrated in Rome – it's the one day of the year when no buses run. A huge free concert is held in front of San Giovanni in Laterano.
Sporting Events – the **Italian Open Tennis Championship** is usually held in the first half of May, and the **International Horse Show** is at the end of the month in the Villa Borghese.
La Fiera d'Arte di Via Margutta and **La Mostra dell' Antiquariato**. Twice-yearly (late May and late October) arts and crafts fairs along two charming streets. Via Margutta, just off Piazza di Spagna, is full of galleries. Via dei Coronari, which begins near Piazza Navona, is packed with antiques shops.

JUNE

San Pietro e San Paolo. The founders of the Catholic church are honoured on 29 June with a public holiday. Special Masses are held in their basilicas, and most shops close for the day.
Estate Romana starts in June – a tremendous summer-long series of concerts, plays, opera, outdoor films and performances *(see page 259).*

JULY

Summer Opera Series. Opera in the open air at the Baths of Caracalla.
Festa de'Noantri. A street festival in Trastevere that runs for two weeks from mid-July.
Roma Alta Moda. A series of fashion shows featuring the new lines from the major design houses.

AUGUST

La Festa della Madonna della Neve. Simulated snow falls on 5 August to commemorate the miraculous founding of the Basilica of Santa Maria Maggiore.

DECEMBER

Immacolata Concezione. The Immaculate Conception of the Virgin is celebrated on 8 December at the statue of the Madonna in Piazza di Spagna.
Christmas. A beautiful time of year in Rome, with major shopping streets decorated and *presepi* (nativity scenes) set up in many churches around town.

Shopping

Rome may not be renowned as a shopping mecca par excellence in the way that Milan, or even Florence, are, yet it has enough haute couture, chic clothing and leather goods stores to satisfy the hungriest of *fashionista* appetites, as well as a strong dose of variety and flair that make it an alluring shopping destination. Moreover, there are very few places in the world where you can shop against such a beautiful backdrop.

What the city is renowned for, however, is its rude or insufferable shopping assistants, particularly in clothing shops. Though the phenomenon is on the wane, you may still find yourself given the cold shoulder by an assistant. The trick is to take no nonsense; give as good as you get and they will soon come round.

As a general rule, it is not possible to return merchandise for a refund, though you may be able to exchange items if you state your case convincingly.

Where to Shop

Via del Corso, Piazza di Spagna and Via del Babuino mark the boundaries of the classic window-shopping area. Here you can find everything from designer jeans to hand-crafted jewellery and antique furniture. Nearby Via della Croce and Via del Corso offer fashion at more accessible prices.

Streets around Piazza Navona, the Pantheon and Campo de' Fiori offer unusual hand-crafted artisanal goods and a range of smaller boutiques. The Campo de' Fiori quarter is still home to craftsmen, art restorers and market traders, a traditional working-class mix that is fast dying out in trendy Trastevere.

Via del Babuino, Via Margutta, Via Giulia, Via dei Coronari and Via del Pellegrino are the main streets for antiques, *objets d'art* and paintings.

Via Nazionale is an undistinguished but relatively inexpensive shopping street, with a wide range of basic clothes.

Via Cola di Rienzo, the thoroughfare linking the Vatican with the Tiber (and Piazza del Popolo on the other bank) is lined with small boutiques and elegant shops selling a wide range of goods.

Via della Conciliazione, the street linking the Vatican with Castel Sant'Angelo, offers a wide range of religious artefacts including Vatican coins, statues, stamps, religious books and souvenirs. Similar objects are on sale on the streets around the Vatican itself and on Via dei Cestari, which runs between the Pantheon and Largo Argentina.

Via del Governo Vecchio is one of the best streets for stylish second-hand clothes, as are the markets at Porta Portese and Via Sannio.

Shopping Hours

Shops are usually open Mon–Sat 9.30am–1pm and 3.30–7.30pm (4–8pm in summer). However, there are many exceptions to this rule. Smaller or independent (especially clothing) boutiques do not open until 10am and are closed on Monday morning. Food stores, or *alimentari*, close on Thursday afternoon.

In highly commercial and touristy areas (such as the Tridente, Via del Corso, Fontana di Trevi and Via Nazionale), most shops, especially chain stores or department stores, now open through lunch, operating the so-called *orario continuato* (continuous opening hours). Many are also open on Sunday. Most supermarkets are also open at lunchtime and on Sunday. A high percentage of shops close (for at least two weeks) in August.

Designer Fashion

The art of looking good is almost a religion in Italy. Although Milan, rather than Rome, is the centre of Italian fashion and design, Rome is still an important focus for the fashion-conscious. The city specialises in *alta moda* (high fashion), from sharp suits and separates to sexy lingerie, designer knitwear and must-have accessories.

Battistoni, Via Condotti 61A. Tel: 06-697 6111. Top men's tailor. Elegant classics.
Emporio Armani, Via del Babuino 140. Tel: 06-322 1581. Armani's

prêt-à-porter range, less expensive than his classic range.
Ermenegildo Zegna, Via Borgognona 7E. Tel: 06-678 9143.
Fendi, Via Borgognona 36–40. Tel: 06-696 661. Exclusive Roman furriers produce fun fake furs and the real thing.
Gianfranco Ferrè, Via Borgognona 6. Tel: 06-679 7445. Chic designs.
Gianni Versace, Via Bocca di Leone 26. Tel: 06-678 0521. Designer to the stars.
Versus by Versace (menswear range) is just a short distance

away at Via Borgognona 25. Tel: 06-679 5037.
Giorgio Armani, Via Condotti 77. Tel: 06-699 1460. Exclusive designer rags.
Laura Biagiotti, Via Borgognona 43–4. Tel: 06-679 1205. Roman designer producing classic women's styles in cashmere and fine fabrics.
Valentino, Via Condotti 13. Tel: 06-679 5862. Extravagant designs.
Valentino Uomo is his menswear line, located at Via Bocca di Leone 15. Tel: 06-678 3656.

SHOPPING CENTRES & DEPARTMENT STORES

There are several purpose-built shopping centres – a new development for Rome, and a fairly un-Italian practice. *Grandi magazzini*, department stores, are few and far between in Rome. Goods are mostly sold in specialist shops.
La Rinascente, Piazza Fiume, tel: 06-884 1231; and Largo Chigi 20 (level with Piazza Colonna), tel: 06-679 7691. Up-market department store with very wide range of goods.
Oviesse-Standa, Viale Trastevere 62, tel: 06-5833 3633. Basic department store for household goods, clothes and food.
Upim, Via del Tritone 172, tel: 06-678 3336; and Piazza Santa Maria Maggiore, tel: 06-446 5579. Economical department store for household goods and children's clothes.

MARKETS

Markets are an enticing invitation to the nitty gritty of Roman life. There are lively food markets in most quarters, which are worth visiting for their atmosphere alone.
Campo de' Fiori. Rome's liveliest fruit and vegetable market. Also several flower stalls, good delicatessens and bars around the

square. This is a good place to pick up the ingredients for a picnic. Open Mon–Sat 7am–1.30pm.
Mercato dei Fiori, Via Trionfale (Prati). Situated north of Via Andrea Doria, the covered wholesale flower market sells the whole range of Mediterranean plants and flowers. Open to the public Tues 10am–noon.
Mercato delle Stampe (or Mercato di Fontanelle Borghese), Largo della Fontanelle Borghese. Near the Corso; sells prints and second-hand or antiquarian books. Open Mon–Sat 8am–sunset.
Mercato di San Cosimato, Piazza di San Cosimato, Trastevere. This small, popular, fruit and vegetable market is set in an attractive square. It has wonderful salad produce, such as *rughetta* (rocket). Open Mon–Sat 7am–1.30pm.
Mercato di Via Sannio, Piazza San Giovanni in Laterano quarter (San Giovanni Metro stop). A new and second-hand clothes market in stalls abutting the Aurelian Walls. Open Mon–Fri 8am–2pm, Sat 8am–5pm.
Porta Portese, Via Portuense and Via Ippolito Nievo, Trastevere. The best flea market in Rome. Awaiting your delectation are reproduction (or fake) antiques, Mussolini memorabilia, Russian military insignia and uniforms, cast-off clothes and jewellery, pirated cassettes, kitchen equipment, icons, plants and cute

pets. Skill is required to get a real bargain. (Look out for pickpockets.) Open Sun 6.30am–2pm.

What to Buy

Rome has plenty to offer the shopper, with all the major designers and national chains represented in a range of shopping areas. Particularly attractive buys include upmarket books on art and architecture, striking kitchenware, herbalists' concoctions, marbled notepaper from a *cartoleria*, a stylish modern lamp, or an old print. Regional wines, cheeses and olive oil are also good value.

However, the city really comes into its own with leather and designer goods. Attractive buys include leatherware, designer luggage, eclectic ceramics, glassware, lighting, inlaid marble tables, gold jewellery and *objets d'art*. For those with the time and excess baggage allowance to spare, browsing for textiles, antiques and hand-crafted furniture can also be a pleasant occupation in Rome.

BOOKSHOPS

The Anglo-American Bookstore, Via della Vite 102. Tel: 06-679 5222.
Bibli, Via dei Fienaroli 28. Tel: 06-588 4097. Large bookshop and café that also hosts cultural events.

Feltrinelli International, Via V.E. Orlando 84. Tel: 06-482 7878. Books in many languages.
Franco Maria Ricci, Via del Babuino 49. Tel: 06-320 7126. Luxurious but costly art books.
Libreria del Viaggiatore, Via del Pellegrino 78. Tel: 06-6880 1048. Travel books in Italian and English.
The Lion Bookshop, Via dei Greci 33. Tel: 06-3265 4007. The best selection of books in English.
Rizzoli, Largo Chigi 15. Tel: 06-679 6641. Italy's largest bookshop.

GIFTS

Cartoleria Artistica, Piazza della Rotonda 69A. Tel: 06-679 0483. Old and new postcards of practically every sight in Rome.
Costantini, Piazza Cavour 16. Tel: 06-321 1502. Over 2,000 Italian wines to choose from.
Leone Limentani, Via del Portico d'Ottavia 47–8. Tel: 06-688 06949. A wide variety of ceramics, crystal, china and cutlery.
Messaggerie Musicali, Via del Corso 472. Tel: 06-684 401. Large music shop with latest trends and good video and classical music selection. Also sells concert tickets and magazines. Open late.
Trimani, Via Goito 20. Tel: 06-446 9661. Good selection of wines and delicacies.
Vertecchi, Via della Croce 70. Tel: 06-679 0155. Stationery and fine art shop.
Volpetti, Via Marmorata 47. Tel: 06-574 2352. Probably the best delicatessen in Rome.

INTERIOR DESIGN

c.u.c.i.n.a., Via del Babuino 118A. Tel: 06-679 1275. Trendy but good quality kitchenware.
Spazio Sette, Via dei Barbieri 7. Tel: 06-6880 4261. One of Rome's premier furniture and home furnishings stores.
TAD, Via di San Giacomo 5. Tel: 06-3600 1679. Unusual, avant-garde furniture, some imported.

JEWELLERY

Buccellati, Via Condotti 31. Tel: 06-679 0329. Famous jeweller's.
Bulgari, Via Condotti 10. Tel: 06-696 261. The supreme jeweller to royalty and the stars.
Ivano Langella, Via di Ponte Sisto 73A. Tel: 333-420 9100. Not your run-of-the-mill jeweller, Langella moulds chunks of silver, gold and bronze into unique and stunning pendants, rings and necklaces.
Massimo Maria Melis, Via dell'Orso 57. Tel: 06-686 9188. Custom-made jewellery, inspired by Roman and Etruscan artefacts.

LEATHERWARE & SHOES

Bruno Magli, Via del Gambero 1. Tel: 06-679 3802. Prestigious shoemaker.
Calzature Fausto Santini, Via Santa Maria Maggiore 165. Tel: 06-488 0934. His main store is on Via Frattina, but this is where you get Italian shoemeister Santini's gems from past collections at half-price.
Di Cori, Piazza di Spagna 53. Tel: 06-678 4439. All sorts of gloves.
Diomedi, Piazza San Bernardo 99. Tel: 06-488 4822. An old-fashioned shop selling exquisite beauty cases, suitcases, briefcases and some jewellery.
Pollini, Via Frattina 22–24. Tel: 06-679 8360. Classic shoes and handbags.

Sport

Sporting life in Rome, as elsewhere in Italy, revolves around football *(calcio)*. The local teams, A.S. Roma and S.S. Lazio, play on alternating schedules at Rome's Olympic Stadium between September and May. The city is also a major European venue for other sporting tournaments and competitions, notably the International Tennis Tournament (Italian Open) and the International Horse Show, both in May. Check listings during your stay.

Participant Sports

JOGGING

Popular jogging places are the parks in town, notably Villa Borghese and Villa Pamphili, and along the Circus Maximus/Via delle Terme di Caracalla.

SWIMMING

For a hot city, Rome is definitely underprovided with swimming pools. There are at least 60 (the tourist office, *see page 249*, can supply a list), but for many of them membership is required; however, some do give temporary membership fairly cheaply.
Cavalieri Hilton, Via Cadiolo 101 (Monte Mario). Tel: 06-35 091.
CSI Roma Nuoto, Lungotevere Flaminio 55 (Flaminio). Tel: 06-323 4732.
Hotel Parco dei Principi, Via G. Frescobaldi 5. Tel: 06-884 5104.
Piscina delle Rose, Viale America 20. Tel: 06-592 6717. Take the Metro to EUR Palasport. Large outdoor pool with rose gardens nearby. June–September only.

Other possibilities for swimming are the beaches and the lakes. The lakes are more pleasant than the beaches nearest to Rome. Swimming is possible in the Lago di Bracciano, the lakes of the Castelli Romani and several other smaller lakes.

TENNIS

Most tennis courts belong to private clubs and are open to members and their guests only. Check with your hotel or tourist office for any clubs that allow non-members to play.

Spectator Sports

You can find information on sporting events in two national papers devoted solely to sport: *Corriere dello Sport* and *Gazetta dello Sport*. Many local sporting events are also listed in the Rome editions of the daily papers.

The football stadium is home to both of the local clubs: Lazio and Roma. For schedules, ticket information and official team paraphernalia, stop by the Lazio Point on Via Farina (near Termini) or the Roma Point (Piazza Colonna.)

MAJOR EVENTS

The following are a few of the major sporting events that take place regularly in Rome during the year and which attract both international stars and international audiences.

The Concorso Ippico Internazionale (International Horse Show) takes place at Piazza Siena in the gardens of the Villa Borghese during May.

Racing takes place all year round at the following:

Le Capannelle, Via Appia Nuova. Tel: 06-718 3143.

Ippodromo di Tor di Valle, Via del Mare. Tel: 06-592 4205.

Also in May is the **International Tennis Championship** at the Foro Italico: this is part of the professional tennis circuit and many top tennis stars attend.

Language

The language of Italy is Italian, supplemented by regional dialects. In large cities and tourist centres you will find many people who speak English, French or German. In fact, due to the massive emigration over the last 100 years, you may encounter fluent speakers of foreign languages: do not be surprised if you are addressed in a New York, Melbourne, London, Brussels or Bavarian accent – the speaker may have spent time working abroad.

It is well worth buying a good phrase book or dictionary, but the following will help you get started. Since this glossary is aimed at non-linguists, we have opted for the simplest options rather than the most elegant Italian.

Basic Phrases

Yes *Si*
No *No*
Thank you *Grazie*
Many thanks *Mille grazie/ tante grazie/molte grazie*
You're welcome *Prego*
All right/That's fine *Va bene*
Please *Per favore/per cortesia*
Excuse me (to get attention) *Scusi* (singular), *Scusate* (plural)
Excuse me (in a crowd) *Permesso*
Excuse me (sorry) *Mi scusi*
Excuse me (to attract attention, e.g. from a waiter) *Senta!*
Could you help me? (formal) *Potrebbe aiutarmi?*
Certainly *Ma, certo*
Can I help you? (formal) *Posso aiutarla?*
Can you show me…? *Può indicarmi…?*
Can you help me? *Può aiutarmi, per cortesia?*
I need… *Ho bisogno di…*

Pronunciation Tips

Italians claim that pronunciation is straightforward: you pronounce it as it is written. This is approximately true but there are a couple of important rules for English speakers to bear in mind: **c** before **e** or **i** is pronounced ch, e.g. *ciao, mi dispiace, la coincidenza*. **Ch** before **i** or **e** is pronounced as k, e.g. *la chiesa*. Likewise, **sci** and **sce** are pronounced as in sheep and shed respectively. **Gn** in Italian is rather like the sound in onion while **gl** is softened to resemble the sound in bullion.

Nouns are either masculine (**il**, plural **i**) or feminine (**la**, plural **le**). Plurals of nouns are most often formed by changing an **o** to an **i** and an **a** to an **e**, e.g. *il panino: i panini; la chiesa: le chiese*.

Words are stressed on the penultimate syllable unless an accent indicates otherwise.

Like many languages, Italian has formal and informal words for "you". In the singular, "**Tu**" is informal while "**Lei**" is more polite. Confusingly, in some parts of Italy or in some circumstances, you will also hear "**Voi**" used as a singular polite form. (In general, "Voi" is reserved for you plural, however.) For visitors, it is simplest to use the formal form unless invited to do otherwise.

There is, of course, rather more to the language than that, but you can get a surprisingly long way in making friends by mastering a few basic phrases.

Wait a minute! *Aspetti!*
I'm lost *Mi sono perso/a*
I'm sorry *Mi dispiace*
I don't know *Non lo so*
I don't understand *Non capisco*
Do you speak English/French? *Parla inglese/francese?*
Could you speak more slowly? *Può parlare piu lentamente, per favore?*
Could you repeat that please? *Può ripetere, per piacere?*

here/there *qui/là*
yesterday/today/tomorrow
ieri/oggi/domani
now/early/late *adesso/*
presto/tardi
What? *Quale/Come...?*
When/Why/Where? *Quando/*
Perché/Dove?
Where is the lavatory? *Dov'è*
il bagno?

GREETINGS

Hello (Good day) *Buon giorno*
Good afternoon/evening
Buona sera
Good night *Buona notte*
Goodbye *Arrivederci*
Hello/Hi/Goodbye (familiar) *Ciao*
Mr/Mrs/Miss *Signor/Signora/*
Signorina
Pleased to meet you (formal)
Piacere di conoscerla
I am English/American/
Irish/Scottish/Canadian/
Australian *Sono inglese/*
americano/a/ irlandese/ scozzese/
canadese/ australiano/a
Do you speak English?
Parla inglese?
I'm here on holiday *Sono qui*
in vacanze
Is it your first trip to Rome? *É il*
Suo/la Sua primo viaggio a Roma?
Do you like it here? (formal)
Si trova bene qui?
How are you (formal/informal)?
Come sta (come stai)?
Fine, thanks *Bene, grazie*
See you later *A più tardi*
See you soon *A presto*
Take care (formal/informal)
Stia bene/Sta bene
Do you like Italy/Florence/
Rome/Venice/my city? *Le piace*
Italia/Firenze/Roma/Venezia/
la mia città?
I like it a lot *Mi piace moltissimo*
It's wonderful *È meravigliosa*

TELEPHONE CALLS

the area code *il prefisso telefonico*
I'd like to make a reverse charges
call *Vorrei fare una telefonata a*
carico del destinatario

May I use your telephone, please?
Posso usare il telefono?
Hello (on the telephone) *Pronto*
My name's *Mi chiamo/Sono*
Could I speak to...? *Posso parlare*
con...?
Sorry, he/she isn't in *Mi dispiace,*
è fuori
Can he call you back? *Può*
richiamarLa?
I'll try again later *Riproverò piu*
tardi
Can I leave a message? *Posso*
lasciare un messagio?
Please tell him I called *Gli dica, per*
favore, che ho telefonato
Hold on *Un attimo, per favore*
a local call *una telefonata urbana*
Can you speak up please? *Può*
parlare più forte, per favore?

In the Hotel

Do you have any vacant rooms?
Avete delle camere libere?
I have a reservation *Ho fatto una*
prenotazione
I'd like... *Vorrei*
a single/double room *una camera*
singola/doppia
a room with twin beds *una camera*
a due letti
a room with a bath/shower *una*
camera con bagno/doccia
for one night *per una notte*
for two nights *per due notti*
How much is it? *Quanto costa?*
On the first floor *Al primo piano*
Is breakfast included? *E compresa*
la prima colazione?
Is everything included? *E tutto*
compreso?
half/full board *mezza pensione/*
pensione completa
It's expensive *E caro*
Do you have a room with a
balcony/view of the sea? *C'è una*
camera con balcone/con una vista
del mare?
a room overlooking the park/the
street/the back *una camera con*
vista sul parco/che da sulla
strada/sul retro
Is it a quiet room? *E una stanza*
tranquilla?
The room is too hot/cold/
noisy/small *La camera è troppo*
calda/fredda/rumorosa/piccola

We have one with a double bed *Ne*
abbiamo una doppia/matrimoniale
Could you show me another room
please? *Potrebbe mostrarmi un*
altra camera, per favore?
Can I see the room? *Posso vedere*
la camera?
What time does the hotel close?
A che ora chiude l'albergo?
I'll take it *La prendo*
big/small *grande/piccola*
What time is breakfast? *A che ora*
è la prima colazione?
Please give me a call at... *Mi può*
chiamare alle...
Come in! *Avanti!*
Can I have the bill, please? *Posso*
avere il conto, per favore?
Can you call me a taxi, please?
Può chiamarmi un taxi, per favore?
dining room *la sala da pranzo*
key *la chiave*
lift *l'ascensore*
towel *un asciugamano*
toilet paper *la carta igienica*

At a Bar

I'd like... *Vorrei...*
coffee:
(small, strong and black) *un caffè*
espresso
(with hot, frothy milk) *un cappuccino*
(like café au lait in France) *un caffè*
latte
(weak, served in tall glass)
un caffè lungo
(with alcohol, probably brandy)
un caffè corretto
tea *un tè*

Bar Notices

Prezzo al tavolino **Table price**
(often double what you pay
standing at the bar)
Si paga alla cassa **Pay at the**
cash desk
Si prende lo scontrino alla cassa
Pay at the cash desk, then take
the receipt (lo scontrino) **to the**
bar to be served (this is common
procedure)
Signori/Uomini **Gentlemen**
(lavatories)
Signore/Donne **Ladies**
(lavatories)

lemon tea *un tè al limone*
herbal tea *una tisana*
hot chocolate *una cioccolata calda*
(bottled) orange/lemon juice *un succo d'arancia/di limone*
orange squash *aranciata*
freshly squeezed orange/lemon juice *una spremuta di arancia/di limone*
(mineral) water *acqua (minerale)*
fizzy/still mineral water *acqua minerale gassata/naturale*
a glass of mineral water *un bicchiere di acqua minerale*
with/without ice *con/senza ghiaccio*
red/white wine *vino rosso/ bianco*
(draught) beer *una birra (alla spina)*
a gin and tonic *un gin tonic*
a bitter (Vermouth, etc) *un amaro*
milk *latte*
(half) a litre *un (mezzo) litro*
bottle *una bottiglia*
ice-cream *un gelato*
cone *un cono*
pastry/brioche *una pasta*
sandwich *un tramezzino*
roll *un panino*
Anything else? *Desidera qualcos'altro?*
Cheers *Salute*
Let me pay *Offro io*
That's very kind of you *Grazie, molto gentile*

In a Restaurant

I'd like to book a table *Vorrei prenotare una tavola*
Have you got a table for... *Avete una tavola per...*
I have a reservation *Ho fatto una prenotazione*
lunch/supper *pranzo/cena*
we do not want a full meal *Non desideriamo un pasto completo*
Could we have another table? *Potremmo spostarci?*
I'm a vegetarian *Sono vegetariono/a*
Is there a vegetarian dish? *C'è un piatto vegetariano?*
May we have the menu? *Ci dia la carta?*
wine list *la lista dei vini*
What would you like? *Che cosa prende?*
What would you recommend? *Che cosa ci consiglia?*

What would you like as a main course/dessert? *Che cosa prende di secondo/di dolce?*
What would you like to drink? *Che cosa desidera da bere?*
a carafe of red/white wine *una caraffa di vino rosso/bianco*
fixed price menu *il menù a prezzo fisso*
the dish of the day *il piatto del giorno*
home-made *fatto in casa*
VAT (sales tax) *IVA*
cover charge *il coperto/ pane e coperto*
that's enough/no more/thanks *Basta così*
the bill, please *il conto per favore*
Is service included? *Il servizio è incluso?*
Where is the lavatory? *Dov'è il bagno?*
Keep the change *Va bene così*
I've enjoyed the meal *Mi è piaciuto molto*

Menu Decoder

Antipasti – Starters
antipasto misto **mixed hors d'oeuvres: cold cuts, cheeses, roast vegetables (ask for details)**
buffet freddo **cold buffet**
caponata **aubergine, olives, tomatoes**
insalata caprese **tomato and mozzarella salad**
insalata di mare **seafood salad**
insalata mista/verde **mixed/green salad**
melanzane alla parmigiana **fried or baked aubergine with parmesan and tomato**
mortadella/salame **similar to salami**
pancetta **bacon**
proscuitto **ham**
peperonata **grilled peppers drenched in olive oil**

Primi – First Courses
Typical first courses include soup, risotto, gnocchi or myriad pastas in a wide range of sauces.
gli asparagi **asparagus (in season)**
brodetto **fish soup**
brodo **broth**
crespolini **savoury pancakes**
gnocchi **potato and dough dumplings**

Pasta

cannelloni stuffed tubes of pasta
farfalle bow or butterfly-shaped pasta
penne pasta quills, smaller than rigatoni
ravioli and *tortellini* different types of stuffed pasta
tagliatelle similar to *fettucine*

Typical pasta sauces include:
aglio e olio garlic and olive oil
arrabbiata spicy tomato
burro e salvia butter and sage
matriciana ham and tomato
panna cream
pesto with basil and pine nuts
ragù meat sauce

la minestra **soup**
il minestrone **thick vegetable soup**
pasta e fagioli **pasta and bean soup**
il prosciutto (cotto/crudo) **(cooked/cured) ham**
i supplì **rice croquettes**
i tartufi **truffles (fresh in season, otherwise bottled or vacuum-packed)**
la zuppa **soup**

Secondi – Main Courses
Typical main courses are fish, seafood or meat-based, with accompaniments *(contorni)*, including vegetables, that vary greatly from season to season.

La Carne – Meat
allo spiedo **on the spit**
arrosto **roast meat**
ai ferri **grilled without oil**
al forno **baked**
al girarrosto **spit-roasted**
alla griglia **grilled**
involtini **skewered veal, ham, etc**
stagionato **hung, well-aged**
ben cotto **well-done (steak, etc)**
media cottura **medium (steak, etc)**
al sangue **rare (steak, etc)**
l'agnello **lamb**
la bresaola **dried salted beef**
la bistecca **steak**
il capriolo/cervo **venison**
il carpaccio **wafer-thin beef**
il cinghiale **wild boar**
il controfiletto **sirloin steak**

le cotolette **cutlets**
il fagiano **pheasant**
il fegato **liver**
il filetto **fillet**
la lepre **hare**
il maiale **pork**
il manzo **beef**
l'ossobuco **shin of veal**
la porchetta **roast suckling pig**
il pollo **chicken**
le polpette **meatballs**
il polpettone **meat loaf**
la salsiccia **sausage**
il saltimbocca (alla Romana) **veal escalopes with ham**
le scaloppine **escalopes**
lo stufato **braised, stewed**
il sugo **sauce**
la trippa **tripe**
il vitello **veal**

Eating Out

For restaurant listings, see *pages 255–7.*

Frutti di Mare – Seafood
Beware the word *"surgelati"*, meaning frozen rather than fresh.

affumicato **smoked**
alle brace **charcoal grilled**
al ferro **grilled without oil**
fritto **fried**
alla griglia **grilled**
ripieno **stuffed**
al vapore **steamed**
acciughe **anchovies**
l'anguilla **eel**
l'aragosta **lobster**
il baccalà **dried salted cod**
i bianchetti **whitebait**
il branzino **sea bass**
i calamari **squid**
i calamaretti **baby squid**
la carpa **carp**
le cozze **mussels**
i crostacei **shellfish**
il fritto misto **mixed fried fish**
i gamberi **prawns**
i gamberetti **shrimps**
il granchio **crab**
il merluzzo **cod**
molecche **soft-shelled crabs**
le ostriche **oysters**
il pesce **fish**
il pescespada **swordfish**

il polipo **octopus**
il risotto di mare **seafood risotto**
le sarde **sardines**
le seppie **cuttlefish**
la sogliola **sole**
il tonno **tuna**
la triglia **red mullet**
la trota **trout**
le vongole **clams**

I Legumi/La Verdura – Vegetables
a scelta **of your choice**
gli asparagi **asparagus**
la bietola **(similar to spinach)**
il carciofo **artichoke**
i carciofini **artichoke hearts**
le carote **carrots**
il cavolo **cabbage**
la cicoria **chicory**
la cipolla **onion**
i contorni **side dishes**
i fagioli **beans**
i fagiolini **French beans**
fave **broad beans**
il finocchio **fennel**
i funghi **mushrooms**
l'indivia **endive/chicory**
l'insalata mista **mixed salad**
l'insalata verde **green salad**
la melanzana **aubergine**
le patate **potatoes**
le patatine fritte **chips/French fries**
i peperoni **peppers**
i piselli **peas**
i pomodori **tomatoes**
le primizie **spring vegetables**
il radicchio **red, slightly bitter lettuce**
i ravanelli **radishes**
ripieno **stuffed**
rughetta **rocket**
spinaci **spinach**
la verdura **green vegetables**
la zucca **pumpkin/squash**
zucchini **courgettes**

La Frutta – Fruit
le albicocche **apricots**
le arance **oranges**
le banane **bananas**
le ciliege **cherries**
il cocomero **watermelon**
i fichi **figs**
le fragole **strawberries**
frutti di bosco **fruits of the forest**
i lamponi **raspberries**
la mela **apple**
la pera **pear**

la pesca **peach**
le uve **grapes**

I Dolci – Desserts
al carrello **desserts from the trolley**
la cassata **Sicilian ice cream with candied peel**
il dolce **dessert/sweet**
le fritelle **fritters**
un gelato (di lampone/limone) **(raspberry/lemon) ice cream**
una granita **water ice**
una macedonia di frutta **fruit salad**
un semifreddo **semi-frozen dessert (many types)**
il tartufo (nero) **(chocolate) ice-cream dessert**
il tiramisù **cold, creamy rum and coffee dessert**
la torta **cake/tart**
zabaglione **sweet dessert made with eggs and Marsala**
zuccotto **ice-cream liqueur**
la zuppa inglese **trifle**

Basic Foods
aceto **vinegar**
aglio **garlic**
burro **butter**
formaggio **cheese**
frittata **omelette**
grana **parmesan cheese**
grissini **bread sticks**
marmellata **jam**
olio **oil**
pane **bread**
pane integrale **wholemeal bread**
parmigiano **parmesan cheese**
pepe **pepper**
riso **rice**
sale **salt**
senape **mustard**
uova **eggs**
yogurt **yoghurt**
zucchero **sugar**

Sightseeing

abbazia (badia) **abbey**
basilica **church**
belvedere **viewpoint**
biblioteca **library**
castello **castle**
centro storico **old town/ historic centre**
chiesa **church**
duomo/cattedrale **cathedral**
fiume **river**

Visiting a Sight

Can one visit? *Si può visitare?*
Is it possible to see the church?
È possibile visitare la chiesa?
Entrance/Exit *Entrata/Uscita*
Where can I find the custodian/sacristan/key? *Dove posso trovare il custode/il sacristano/la chiave?*
We have come a long way just to see X *Siamo venuti da lontano solo per visitare X*
It is really a pity it is closed *È veramente peccato che sia chiuso.*
(The last two should be tried if entry seems a problem!)

giardino **garden**
lago **lake**
mercato **market**
monastero **monastery**
monumenti **monuments**
museo **museum**
parco **park**
pinacoteca **art gallery**
ponte **bridge**
ruderi **ruins**
scavi **excavations/archaeological site**
spiaggia **beach**
torre **tower**
ufficio turistico **tourist office**
il custode **custodian**
il sacristano **sacristan**
Suonare il campanello **Ring the bell**
Aperto/a **Open**
Chiuso/a **Closed**
Chiuso per la festa/per ferie/per restauro **Closed for the festival/holidays/restoration**

At the Shops

What time do you open/close?
A che ora apre/chiude?
Pull/Push (sign on doors)
Tirare/Spingere
Entrance/Exit *Entrata/Uscita*
Can I help you? (formal) *Posso aiutarla?*
What would you like? *Che cosa desidera?*
I'm just looking *Sto soltanto guardando*
How much does it cost? *Quant'è, per favore?*

How much is this? *Quanto viene?*
Do you take credit cards?
Accettate le carte di credito?
I'd like... *Vorrei...*
This one/that one *questo/quello*
I'd like that one, please *Vorrei quello lì per cortesia*
Have you got...? *Avete...?*
We haven't got (any) *Non (ne) abbiamo*
Can I try it on? *Posso provare?*
the size (for clothes) *la taglia*
What size do you take? *Qual'è la Sua taglia?*
the size (for shoes) *il numero*
Is there/do you have X? *C'è (un/una)...?*
Yes, of course *Si, certo*
No, we don't (there isn't)
No, non c'è
That's too expensive *È troppo caro*
Please write it down for me *Me lo scriva, per favore*
cheap *economico/a buon prezzo*
Don't you have anything cheaper?
Ha niente che costa di meno?
It's too small/big *È troppo piccolo/grande*
brown/blue/black *marrone/blu/nero*
green/red/white/yellow
verde/rosso/bianco/giallo
pink/grey/gold/silver
rosa/grigio/oro/argento
No thank you, I don't like it *Grazie, ma non è di mio gusto*
I (don't) like it *(Non) mi piace*
I'll take it/I'll leave it *Lo prendo/lo lascio*
It's a rip-off (impolite) *Sono prezzi da strozzini*
This is faulty. Can I have a replacement/refund? *C'è un difetto. Me lo potrebbe cambiare/rimborsare?*
Anything else? *Altro?*
The cash desk is over there
Si accomodi alla cassa
Give me some of those *Mi dia alcuni di quelli lì*
(half) a kilo *un (mezzo) kilo*
100 grams *un etto*
200 grams *due etti*
more/less *piu/meno*
with/without *con/senza*
a little *un pochino*
That's enough/no more *Basta così*

Types of Shops

antique dealer *l'antiquario*
bakery/cake shop *la panetteria/pasticceria*
bank *la banca*
bookshop *la libreria*
boutique/clothes shop *il negozio di moda*
bureau de change *il cambio*
butcher's *la macelleria*
chemist's *la farmacia*
delicatessen *la salumeria*
department store *il grande magazzino*
dry cleaner's *la tintoria*
fishmonger's *la pescheria*
florist *il fioraio*
food shop *l'alimentari*
greengrocer's *l'ortolano/il fruttivendolo*
grocer's *l'alimentari*
hairdresser's (women) *il parucchiere*
ice-cream parlour *la gelateria*
jeweller's *il gioielliere*
leather shop *la pelletteria*
market *il mercato*
news stand *l'edicola*
post office *l'ufficio postale*
shoe shop *il negozio di scarpe*
stationer's *la cartoleria*
supermarket *il supermercato*
tobacconist *il tabaccaio* (also usually sells travel tickets, stamps, phone cards)
travel agency *l'agenzia di viaggi* (also usually books domestic and international train tickets)

Travelling

aeroplane *l'aereo*
airport *l'areoporto*
arrivals/departures *arrivi/partenze*
boarding card *un biglietto di bordo*
boat *la barca*
bus *l'autobus/il pullman*
bus station *l'autostazione*
coach *il pullman*
couchette *la cucetta*
connection *la coincidenza*
ferry *il traghetto*
ferry terminal *la stazione marittima*
first/second class *la prima/seconda classe*
flight *il volo*
left luggage (office) *il deposito bagagli*

At the Airport

Where's the office of BA/Alitalia?
Dov'è l'ufficio dell'Alitalia/ della British Airways?
I'd like to book a flight to Venice
Vorrei prenotare un volo per Venezia
When is the next flight to...?
Quando parte il prossimo aereo per...?
Are there any seats available? *Ci sono ancora posti liberi?*
Have you got any hand luggage?
Ha bagagli a mano?

I'll take this hand luggage with me
Questo lo tengo come bagaglio a mano
My suitcase has got lost *La mia valigia è andata persa*
My suitcase has been damaged
La mia valigia è rovinata
The flight has been delayed *Il volo è rimandato*
The flight has been cancelled *Il volo è stato cancellato*
I can put you on the waiting list
Posso metterLa sulla lista d'attesa

first left/second right *la prima a sinistra/la seconda a destra*
Turn to the right/left *Gira a destra/sinistra*
Go straight on *Va sempre diritto*
Go straight on until the traffic lights *Va sempre diritto fino al semaforo*
Is it far away/nearby?
È lontano/vicino?
It's 5 minutes' walk *Cinque minuti a piedi*
It's 10 minutes by car *Dieci minuti con la macchina*
You can't miss it *Non può non vederlo*
opposite/next to *di fronte/ accanto a*
up/down *su/giù*
traffic lights *il semaforo*
junction *l'incrocio, il bivio*
building *il palazzo (could be a palace or a block of flats)*
Where is...? *Dov'è...?*
Where are...? *Dove sono...?*
Where is the nearest bank/petrol station/bus stop/hotel/garage?
Dov'è la banca/il benzinaio/la fermata di autobus/l'albergo/ l'officina più vicino?
How do I get there? *Come si può andare? (or: Come faccio per arrivare a...?)*
How long does it take to get to...?
Quanto tempo ci vuole per andare a...?
Can you show me where I am on the map? *Può indicarmi sulla cartina dove mi trovo*
You're on the wrong road *Lei è sulla strada sbagliata*

motorway *l'autostrada*
no smoking *vietato fumare*
platform *il binario*
port *il porto*
porter *il facchino*
railway station *ferrovia (la stazione ferroviaria)*
return ticket *un biglietto andata e ritorno*
single ticket *un biglietto solo andata*
sleeping car *la carrozza letti/ il vagone letto*
smokers/non-smokers *fumatori/non-fumatori*
station *la stazione*
stop *la fermata*
taxi *il taxi*
ticket office *la biglietteria*
train *il treno*
WC *gabinetto*

libero/occupato questo posto?
I'm afraid this is my seat *E il mio posto, mi dispiace*
You'll have to pay a supplement
Deve pagare un supplemento
Do I have to change? *Devo cambiare?*
Where does it stop? *Dove si ferma?*
You need to change in Rome
Bisogna cambiare a Roma
Which platform does the train leave from? *Da quale binario parte il treno?*
The train leaves from platform one
Il treno parte dal binario uno
When is the next train/bus/ferry for Naples? *Quando parte il prossimo treno/ pullman/ traghetto per Napoli?*
How long does the crossing take?
Quanto dura la traversata?
What time does the bus leave for Siena? *Quando parte l'autobus per Siena?*
How long will it take to get there?
Quanto tempo ci vuole per arrivare?
Will we arrive on time? *Arriveremo puntuali?*
Next stop, please *La prossima fermata per favore*
Is this the right stop? *È la fermata giusta?*
The train is late *Il treno è in ritardo*
Can you tell me where to get off?
Mi può dire dove devo scendere?

AT THE STATION

(trains, buses and ferries)
Can you help me please? *Mi può aiutare, per favore?*
Where can I buy tickets? *Dove posso fare i biglietti?*
at the ticket office/at the counter
alla biglietteria/allo sportello
What time does the train leave?
A che ora parte il treno?
What time does the train arrive?
A che ora arriva (il treno)?
Can I book a seat? *Posso prenotare un posto?*
Are there any seats available?
Ci sono ancora posti liberi?
Is this seat free/taken? *E*

DIRECTIONS

right/left *a destra/a sinistra*

ON THE ROAD

Where can I rent a car? *Dove posso noleggiare una macchina?*
Is comprehensive insurance included? *È completamente assicurata?*
Is it insured for another driver?
È assicurata per un altro guidatore?
By what time must I return it?
A che ora devo consegnarla?
underground car park *garage sotterraneo*
driving licence *la patente (di guida)*
registration number *la targa*

petrol *la benzina*
petrol station/garage *la stazione
servizio*
oil *l'olio*
Fill it up please *Faccia il pieno,
per favore*
lead free/unleaded diesel *senza
piombo/benzina verde diesel*
My car won't start *La mia
macchina non s'accende*
My car has broken down
La macchina è guasta
I've had an accident *Ho avuto
un incidente*
How long will it take to repair?
*Quanto tempo ci vorrà per
la riparazione?*
The engine is overheating *Il motore
si scalda*
Can you check the...? *Può
controllare...?*
There's something wrong (with/
in the)... *C'è un difetto
(nel/nella/nei/nelle)...*
– *l'acceleratore* accelerator
– *le candele* spark plugs
– *la cinghia del ventilatore* the
fanbelt
– *i freni* the brakes
– *la gomma (le gomme)* tyre (tyres)
– *i luci* headlights
– *il motore* engine
– *il parabrezza* windscreen
– *lo scarico/scappamento* exhaust
– *la scattola del cambio* gear box

ROAD SIGNS

Accendere le luci in galleria Lights
on in tunnel
Alt Stop

Attenzione Caution
Autostrada Motorway
Avanti Go/Walk
Caduta massi falling rocks
Casello Toll gate
Dare la precedenza Give Way
Deviazione Deviation
Divieto di campeggio No camping
allowed
Divieto di passaggio/Senso Vietato
No entry
Divieto di sosta/Sosta vietata
No parking
Dogana Customs
Entrata Entrance
Galleria Tunnel
Guasto Out of order (eg. phone box)
Incrocio Crossroads
Limite di velocito Speed limit
Non toccare Don't touch
Passaggio a livello Railway crossing
Parcheggio Parking
Pedaggio Toll road
Pericolo Danger
Pericolo di incendio Danger of fire
Pronto Soccorso First Aid
Rallentare Slow down
Rimozione forzata Parked cars will
be towed away
Semaforo Traffic lights
Senso unico One way street
Sentiero Footpath
Solo Uscita No Entry
Sosta Vietato No Parking
Strada chiusa Road closed
Strada interrotta Road blocked
Strada senza uscita/Vicolo cieco
Dead end
Tangenziale Ring road/Bypass
Tenersi in corsa Keep in lane
Traffico di transito Through traffic
Uscita Exit

Emergencies

Help! *Aiuto!*
Stop! *Fermate!*
I've had an accident *Ho avuto
un incidente*
Watch out *Attenzione*
Call a doctor *Per favore, chiama
un medico*
Call an ambulance *Chiama
un'ambulanza*
Call the police *Chiama la Polizia/
i Carabinieri*
Call the fire brigade *Chiama i
pompieri*
Where is the telephone? *Dov'è
il telefono?*
Where is the nearest hospital?
Dov'è l'ospedale piu vicino?
I would like to report a theft
Voglio denunciare un furto
Thank you very much for your
help *Grazie dell'aiuto*

Uscita (autocarri) Exit for lorries
Vietato il sorpasso No overtaking
Vietato il transito No transit

Health

Is there a chemist's nearby? *C'è
una farmacia qui vicino?*
Which chemist is open at night?
Quale farmacia fa il turno di notte?
I feel ill *Sto male/Mi sento male*
Where does it hurt? *Dove Le fa
male?*
It hurts here *Ho dolore qui*
I suffer from... *Soffro di...*
I have a headache *Ho mal di testa*
I have a sore throat *Ho mal di gola*

Numbers

1	Uno	13	Tredici	70	Settanta
2	Due	14	Quattordici	80	Ottanta
3	Tre	15	Quindici	90	Novanta
4	Quattro	16	Sedici	100	Cento
5	Cinque	17	Diciasette	200	Duecento
6	Sei	18	Diciotto	500	Cinquecento
7	Sette	19	Dicianove	1,000	Mille
8	Otto	20	Venti	2,000	Duemila
9	Nove	30	Trenta	5,000	Cinquemila
10	Dieci	40	Quaranta	10,000	Diecimila
11	Undici	50	Cinquanta	50,000	Cinquantamila
12	Dodici	60	Sessanta	Million	Un Milione

I have a stomach ache *Ho mal di pancia*
Have you got something for air sickness? *Ha/Avete qualcosa contro il mal d'aria?*
Have you got something for sea sickness? *Ha/Avete qualcosa contro il mal di mare?*
It's nothing serious *Non è niente di male*
Do I need a prescription? *Ci vuole la ricetta?*
antiseptic cream *la crema antisettica*
insect repellent *l'insettifugo*
mosquitos *le zanzare*
sticking plaster *il cerotto*
sunburn *scottato del sole*
sunburn cream *la crema antisolare*
tissues *i fazzoletti di carta*
toothpaste *il dentifricio*
upset stomach pills *le pillole anti-coliche*
wasps *le vespe*

Times and Dates

morning/afternoon/evening *la mattina, il pomeriggio, la sera*
yesterday/today/tomorrow *ieri/oggi/domani*
the day after tomorrow *dopodomani*
now/early/late *adesso/presto/in ritardo*
a minute *un minuto*
an hour *un'ora*
half an hour *un mezz'ora*
a day *un giorno*
a week *una settimana*
Monday *Lunedì*
Tuesday *Martedì*
Wednesday *Mercoledì*
Thursday *Giovedì*
Friday *Venerdì*
Saturday *Sabato*
Sunday *Domenica*
first *il primo/la prima*
second *il secondo/la seconda*
third *il terzo/la terza*

Further Reading

General

Italian Wines, by Maureen Ashley (Sainsbury's/Websters International).
Italian Wines, by Phillip Dallas (Faber & Faber).
Italian Food, by Elizabeth David (Penguin Cookery Library).
Teach Yourself Italian, and *Let's Talk Italian*, by Lydia Vellaccio and Maurice Elston, Teach Yourself Books (Hodder & Stoughton).
Italia dal Vivo (BBC language course with cassettes).

History & Society

The Early History of Rome, by Livy (Penguin).
Daily Life in Ancient Rome, by Jerome Carcopino (Peregrine).
The Roman Emperors, by Michael Grant (Weidenfeld and Nicolson).
The Caesars, by Allan Massie (Secker & Warburg).
The Twelve Caesars, by Suetonius (Penguin Classics).
The History of the Decline and Fall of the Roman Empire, by Edward Gibbon (Dent and Penguin).
The Last Years of the Roman Empire (Croom Helm).
History of the City of Rome in the Middle Ages, by Ferdinand Gregorovius (London).
The Roman Way, by Edith Hamilton (Norton).
A History of Rome, by Michael Grant (Faber).
Rome: Biography of a City, by Christopher Hibbert (Penguin).
The Vicar of Christ, by Walter F. Murphy (Cassell).
The Pope from Poland: An Assessment, edited by John Whale (Collins).
The Church, by Hans Kung (Burns & Oates).
In God's Name, by David Yallop (Jonathan Cape).

Italy, by Russell King (Harper and Row).
The Italians, by Luigi Barzini (Hamish Hamilton).

Art & Literature

Roman Italy, by T.W. Potter (British Museum Publications).
The Aeneid, by Virgil (Penguin).
Meditations, by Marcus Aurelius (Penguin).
Memoirs of Hadrian, by Marguerite Yourcenar Gallimard (in French). Translated into English by Grace Frick (New York).
Lives of the Artists, by Giorgio Vasari (Penguin).
The Life of Benvenuto Cellini, by Benvenuto Cellini, translator John Addington Symonds (Macmillan).
The Cambridge History of Classical Literature, Vol. II – Latin Literature.
Metamorphoses and Other Poems, by Ovid (Penguin).
Selected Works, by Cicero (Penguin).
Rome, by Emile Zola (Paris and New York).
Portrait of a Lady, by Henry James.
The Woman of Rome and *Roman Tales*, by Alberto Moravia (Oxford University Press).
History, by Elsa Morante (Penguin in English; Gallimard in French).
A Violent Life, by Pier Paolo Pasolini (Carcanet).
Fellini on Fellini, by Federico Fellini (New York).

Famous Travellers

Pictures from Italy, by Charles Dickens (Granville).
Italian Journey, by Johann Wolfgang von Goethe, translated by W.H. Auden & Elizabeth Mayer (Pantheon Books and Penguin).
Italian Hours, by Henry James (Century).
The Roman Journals of Ferdinand Gregorovius, edited by Friedrich Althous, translated by Gustavus W. Hamilton (G. Bell & Son).
The Fountains of Rome, *A Traveller in Southern Italy* and *A Traveller in Rome*, by Henry V. Morton (Methuen).

Byron in Italy, by Peter Quenell (Viking Press, New York).
The Grand Tour, by Christopher Hibbert (G.P. Putnam & Sons, New York).

Travel Companions

Rome: A Literary Companion, by John Varriano (John Murray).
The Rome Address Book (Berlitz Cityscope).
Le Promeneur Amoreux, by D. Fernandez (Gallimard).

Other Insight Guides

Europe is covered by the over 400 books in Apa Publication's three series of guidebooks, which embrace the world.

Insight Guides

Other *Insight Guides* to Italian destinations include: Italy, Northern Italy, Southern Italy, Venice, Florence, Umbria, Tuscany, Sicily and Sardinia.

Pocket Guides

Insight Pocket Guides, including a pull-out map, feature tailor-made itineraries and are ideal for short breaks. Guides in the Italian series include: Venice, Rome, Milan, Florence, Sicily, Sardinia and Tuscany.

Compact Guides

Insight Compact Guides are handy, information-packed books, which are ideal for on-the-spot reference. There are *Compact Guides* to: Florence, Milan, Rome, Tuscany, Venice, the Italian Riviera and the Italian Lakes.

Fleximaps

Insight Fleximaps combine clear, detailed cartography with essential travel information. The laminated finish makes the maps durable, weatherproof and easy to fold. Italian maps include *Florence, the Italian Lakes, Milan, Rome, Sicily, Tuscany* and *Venice*.

Feedback

We do our best to ensure the information in our books is as accurate and up-to-date as possible. The books are updated on a regular basis, using local contacts, who painstakingly add, amend and correct as required. However, some mistakes and omissions are inevitable and we are ultimately reliant on our readers to put us in the picture.

We would welcome your feedback on any details related to your experiences using the book "on the road". Maybe we recommended a hotel that you liked (or another that you didn't), as well as interesting new attractions, or facts and figures you have found about the country itself. The more details you can give us (particularly with regard to addresses, e-mails and telephone numbers), the better.

We will acknowledge all contributions, and we'll offer an Insight Guide for the best letters received.

Please write to us at:
Insight Guides
APA Publications
PO Box 7910
London SE1 1WE
Or send e-mail to:
insight@apaguide.demon.co.uk

ART & PHOTO CREDITS

AKG 16/17, 33, 36, 60/61
American Numismatic Society
230T
Ping Amranand 20, 22, 23, 24, 27, 29, 113, 119, 123B, 190, 193B, 202
Adina Tovy Amsel/Eye Ubiquitous
110
AP/Wide World Photos 39
Archiv Gumpel 35
Associated Press/Topham 19
British Film Institute 59
Heather Brown/The Anthony Blake Photo Library 84
Giuliano Colliva/The Image Bank 141, 178/179
Cooperativa Culturale Blond 240
Patrizia Giancotti 8/9, 10/11, 12/13, 42/43, 46, 50, 51, 52L, 53, 55, 74, 77, 90/91, 92/93, 98, 105B, 107B, 108B, 109, 111B, 116/117, 118, 121L, 122B, 125, 127, 129B, 131, 132B, 133, 135B, 136, 138/139, 147, 150/151, 152, 158, 166, 171, 176, 180, 183, 194/195, 196, 200/201, 205B, 206/207, 211, 213, 215, 216/217, 218/219, 222, 226B, 227B, 228, 229, 230B, 232, 233B, 234, 235, 236, 237B, 238, 239
Frances Gransden/APA 1, 6/7, 41, 49, 100, 102T, 103T, 105T, 106T, 107T, 108T, 111T, 112T, 112B, 120, 122T, 123T, 124T, 126, 128, 129T, 130BR, 132T, 134, 135T, 143T, 144T, 145T, 153, 154T, 160,

163T, 169T, 170T, 175T, 177T, 182, 187, 188, 193T, 197, 198, 203T, 205T, 223, 224, 225T, 225B, 226T, 227T, all small cover pictures except back cover left and right and spine
Blaine Harrington III 79, 169B
John Heseltine 101, 143B, 156, 159, 177B, 189
Jim Holmes 14, 48L, 48R, 54, 62, 63, 64, 65, 69, 71, 73, 75, 76L, 76R, 78, 81, 88/89, 94, 99, 102B, 103BL, 103BR, 104, 121R, 130BL, 137, 140, 144B, 145B, 154B, 162, 163BL, 163BR, 165, 167, 173, 174, 175B, 184/185, 191, 199, 203B, 209, 212
Jim Holmes/Axiom 18, 25, 170B, 208, 210
James Davis Travel Photography 106B
Graham Kirk/The Anthony Blake Photo Library 85
Lyle Lawson 44/45, 157
Marka/Kay Reese & Associates 237T
Mary Evans Picture Library 26, 28, 30, 32, 34
The Museum of Modern Art/Film Stills Archive 56, 58
Gerd Pfeifer 70, 231
Catherine Randall 52R, 80, 161
Rosenfeld Images/The Anthony Blake Photo Library 86
John Sims/The Anthony Blake Photo Library 87

Spectrum Colour Library 68
Paul Thompson/Eye Ubiquitous 124B, 186
Topham Picturepoint 37, 38, 40L, 40R, 57
Bill Wassman/APA back cover left, back cover right, spine
Max Whittaker 47

Picture Spreads

Pages 66/67, from bottom left-hand corner: Scala, John Heseltine, Scala, John Heseltine, Scala, Scala, Scala, Scala.
Pages 82/83, from top left-hand corner: Corbis, Corbis, Scala, Scala, Scala, Scala, Corbis, A. Tessore/Aisa, Aisa
Pages 114/115, from top left-hand corner: Blaine Harrington, AKG London, AKG London, Blaine Harrington, AKG London/Erich Lessing, AKG London, Scala, AKG London/Erich Lessing.
Pages 148/149, from bottom left-hand corner: Scala, Frances Gransden/APA, Scala, Scala, John Heseltine, Scala, Scala

Map Production
Polyglott Kartographie, Berndtson & Berndtson Publications
© 2003 Apa Publications GmbH & Co.
Verlag KG (Singapore branch)

Cartographic Editor **Zoë Goodwin**
Production **Linton Donaldson**
Design Consultant
Graham Mitchener
Picture Research **Hilary Genin**

Index

*Numbers in italics refer
to photographs*

☀ INSIGHT GUIDES

The world's largest collection of visual travel guides

A range of guides and maps to meet every travel need

Insight Guides

This classic series gives you the complete picture of a destination through expert, well written and informative text and stunning photography. Each book is an ideal background information and travel planner, serves as an on-the-spot companion – and is a superb visual souvenir of a trip. Nearly 200 titles.

Insight Pocket Guides

focus on the best choices for places to see and things to do, picked by our local correspondents. They are ideal for visitors new to a destination. To help readers follow the routes easily, the books contain full-size pull-out maps. 120 titles.

Insight Maps

are designed to complement the guides. They provide full mapping of major cities, regions and countries, and their laminated finish makes them easy to fold and gives them durability. 60 titles.

Insight Compact Guides

are convenient, comprehensive reference books, modestly priced. The text, photographs and maps are all carefully cross-referenced, making the books ideal for on-the-spot use when in a destination. 120 titles.

Different travellers have different needs. Since 1970, Insight Guides has been meeting these needs with a range of practical and stimulating guidebooks and maps

INSIGHT GUIDES

The classic series that puts you in the picture

Alaska	Dominican Rep. & Haiti	London	Rio de Janeiro
Amazon Wildlife	Dublin	Los Angeles	Rome
American Southwest	East African Wildlife	Madeira	Russia
Amsterdam	Eastern Europe	Madrid	St Petersburg
Argentina	Ecuador	Malaysia	San Francisco
Arizona & Grand Canyon	Edinburgh	Mallorca & Ibiza	Sardinia
Asia, East	Egypt	Malta	Scandinavia
Asia, Southeast	England	Mauritius Réunion	Scotland
Australia	Finland	& Seychelles	Seattle
Austria	Florence	Melbourne	Sicily
Bahamas	Florida	Mexico	Singapore
Bali	France	Miami	South Africa
Baltic States	France, Southwest	Montreal	South America
Bangkok	French Riviera	Morocco	Spain
Barbados	Gambia & Senegal	Moscow	Spain, Northern
Barcelona	Germany	Namibia	Spain, Southern
Beijing	Glasgow	Nepal	Sri Lanka
Belgium	Gran Canaria	Netherlands	Sweden
Belize	Great Britain	New England	Switzerland
Berlin	Great Railway Journeys	New Orleans	Sydney
Bermuda	of Europe	New York City	Syria & Lebanon
Boston	Greece	New York State	Taiwan
Brazil	Greek Islands	New Zealand	Tenerife
Brittany	Guatemala, Belize	Nile	Texas
Brussels	& Yucatán	Normandy	Thailand
Buenos Aires	Hawaii	Norway	Tokyo
Burgundy	Hong Kong	Oman & The UAE	Trinidad & Tobago
Burma (Myanmar)	Hungary	Oxford	Tunisia
Cairo	Iceland	Pacific Northwest	Turkey
California	India	Pakistan	Tuscany
California, Southern	India, South	Paris	Umbria
Canada	Indonesia	Peru	USA: On The Road
Caribbean	Ireland	Philadelphia	USA: Western States
Caribbean Cruises	Israel	Philippines	US National Parks: West
Channel Islands	Istanbul	Poland	Venezuela
Chicago	Italy	Portugal	Venice
Chile	Italy, Northern	Prague	Vienna
China	Italy, Southern	Provence	Vietnam
Continental Europe	Jamaica	Puerto Rico	Wales
Corsica	Japan	Rajasthan	Walt Disney World/Orlando
Costa Rica	Jerusalem		
Crete	Jordan		
Cuba	Kenya		
Cyprus	Korea		
Czech & Slovak Republic	Laos & Cambodia		
Delhi, Jaipur & Agra	Las Vegas		
Denmark	Lisbon		

INSIGHT GUIDES

The world's largest collection of visual travel guides & maps